INSIGHT
DIALOGUE

INSIGHT DIALOGUE

The Interpersonal
Path to Freedom

GREGORY KRAMER

SHAMBHALA
BOSTON & LONDON
2007

SHAMBHALA PUBLICATIONS, INC.
Horticultural Hall
300 Massachusetts Avenue
Boston, Massachusetts 02115
www.shambhala.com

9 8 7 6 5 4 3 2 1

First Edition
Printed in the United States of America

∞ This edition is printed on acid-free paper that meets the
American National Standards Institute z39.48 Standard.

Distributed in the United States by Random House, Inc.,
and in Canada by Random House of Canada Ltd

Designed by Dede Cummings Design

Library of Congress Cataloging-in-Publication Data

Kramer, Gregory
Insight dialogue: the interpersonal path to freedom /
Gregory Kramer.—1st ed.
    p. cm.
Includes bibliographical references.
ISBN 978-1-59030-485-3 (pbk.: alk. paper)
1. Religious life—Buddhism. 2. Interpersonal relations—
Religious aspects. 3. Buddhism—Doctrines. I. Title.
BQ5395.K73 2007
294.3'444—dc22
2007015358

In memoriam
Irving Kramer

———

I dedicate this book to my generous teachers.
The more I mature along the Path, the more
grateful I become for their gifts:
Anagarika Dhammadina
Ananda Maitreya Mahanayaka Thero
Achan Sobin Namto (Bhikkhu Sopako Bodhi)
Punnaji Maha Thero

Contents

Part One

THIS COMES FROM THE WORLD

~ 1 ~
ON THE PATH
TOGETHER

T HE WHOLE of our path of awakening, including the profound contributions of meditation, can be fully integrated with our lives with
others. A great deal of our suffering in life is in relationship to other
people. We cannot reasonably expect individualistic philosophies and solitary practices to directly address the pain and confusion that arise between
two people or in society at large. Nor can we expect solo endeavors to yield
a direct path to the rewards of relational ease and insight. What is required
is a fundamentally interpersonal understanding of the path and a meditation practice explicitly evolved to take place in relationship with others.
This book is about such an understanding and such a path.

We meditate alone but live our lives with other people; a gap is
inevitable. If our path is to lead to less suffering, and much of our suffering is with other people, then perhaps we need to reexamine our sole commitment to these individual practices. Meditating alone reinforces an
unreflected assumption: that the deep work of awakening is a private
affair. From this assumption we build a sense of the path—its overall direction and its particulars—that favors solitary and internal endeavor. Meditating individually, we lack any practice that explicitly addresses the
interpersonal realm. We may sense vaguely that something is awry but
cannot see what is missing. We are not clear that the personal and interpersonal paths are profoundly connected, nor do we know how easily and
even elegantly they can be interwoven. A wider vision is available to us. It
is so simple.

All meditation helps us calm down, become more aware of what is
going on within us, and meet difficulties with honesty and acceptance.
Meditation involves both an explicit practice of tranquillity and reflection
and a lifestyle of mindfulness and care.

When we meditate alone, we might be quiet for a few minutes or a few days, possibly attending to the breath or to some quality of the heart. We calm down; the mind clears and becomes still. In the stillness of individual meditation we perceive the suffering associated with our relationship to ourselves. We notice how easily we become lost in automatic thoughts and emotions. We notice bodily suffering, personal grasping and fear, and confusion. Against the backdrop of simple awareness, our longings and fears—our struggles to attain pleasure and to avoid pain—become starkly visible. Seeing the stress involved in satisfying our desires, we glimpse how we habitually fabricate many of our problems, and begin to release these habits. As individual practice deepens, it may yield true ease. We get a taste of freedom. But whether we practice meditation in seclusion or independently alongside other meditators at a meditation group or retreat, individual meditation approaches the confusion and pain of our relational lives only indirectly.

When we meditate together, as in Insight Dialogue, the same process unfolds—with two significant differences. Interpersonal meditation reveals the suffering associated with our relational lives, and in society as a whole, much more directly. It is exceptionally effective at revealing desires and fears about being seen, the dynamics of loneliness, and the powerful but hidden processes by which we construct a self-image. Interpersonal meditation also provides us with a more direct way to unbind the knots behind this relational suffering and confusion. Its dynamics are similar to those of traditional, personal meditation: we gradually cultivate mindfulness and tranquillity; these qualities allow us to apprehend the moment-to-moment nature of experience; what we then realize, frees us. But because interpersonal meditation works with the moment-to-moment experience of interacting with another, it brings the liberating dynamic of meditation into our interpersonal lives. From there it migrates to society as a whole.

In Insight Dialogue—whether on retreat or in a weekly group—a simple practice unfolds: after a period of silent sitting meditation, people are invited into pairs or larger groups to reflect together on a topic such as change, death, or doubt. Some basic instructions are offered about pausing to be mindful and relaxing in the face of reactivity. In Insight Dialogue, meditators encounter more stimulation to react or cling to than they would in silent practice. Along with this challenge, they discover the unique gift of mutual support for seeing things as they actually are. Because the guidelines, the practice, and the insights all address the dynamics of relating with other human beings, they follow us into our everyday lives easily and naturally. We spontaneously remember to relax in interaction with a coworker or notice how we are positioning ourselves in a conversation or see our own clinging with clarity and compassion. We also learn to recognize the spark of clear awareness present behind the clamor of human encounter. Each moment of human interaction becomes part of the path to awakening.

The group practice of Insight Dialogue is portable and accessible: a practice group may be formed anywhere. Insight Dialogue groups might meet once a week; typically, they begin with a review of the goals and methods of the practice. We meditate silently and individually for a time, releasing the whirling of our everyday lives. Then we are invited to find a partner and are given new instructions. We are offered a topic to reflect upon, usually a real-life issue considered in the light of wisdom drawn from an established spiritual tradition. We are invited to pause periodically during that reflection and release habitual stories and routine reactions, meeting the present moment of interpersonal contact with mindfulness. A bell is rung, and we step into interpersonal practice as mindfully as we are able.

Immediately, stories well up. We find our own stories, and those of our co-meditators, to be absorbing, sometimes touching. We form judgments about the stories, about the actors in them, about the way they are told. We are carried away by habits of speech; we find ourselves grasping at the emotions aroused by this encounter. A bell is rung, and everyone drops into silence. Stopped in our habitual spinning, we come home to mindfulness. We notice how our thoughts and emotions have proliferated. Mindfulness stabilizes a bit and we calm down, letting the mind settle on simple bodily awareness or the breath. When the bell is rung again, we reengage with our partner. Excitement and identification still arise easily, but soon we begin to pause on our own, without the bell's reminder. We also have the support of each other's practice: our partners also begin to pause on their own, bringing us back to the moment when our own mind wanders.

By the end of a single evening of practice we have paused many dozens of times. We carry back to our everyday lives an awareness of the possibility of pausing, of not identifying with the proliferations of our hearts. As we enter our everyday relationships, we sometimes find ourselves pausing spontaneously, meeting experience with acceptance and including others in our field of mindfulness. At work and at home, as well as in our weekly practice group, we find opportunities to cultivate flexibility of mind; we begin to move easily from internal mindfulness to mindfulness of others.

The retreat form of Insight Dialogue is a more concentrated form of interpersonal practice. During the first few days of the retreat, we settle in and calm down, setting aside our concerns with the outer world. As in many traditional meditation retreats, most of our time is structured in support of meditation and most of our needs are taken care of, giving us the opportunity to relax and attend to meditation.

After we have calmed down a bit and established some measure of mindfulness, we are invited into dialogue. As in a weekly group, we are offered a topic. As we begin, a story might arise about some tension at work. We notice tightness somewhere in our body and relax. The story remains present—the truth of the moment—so we share it. We pause from time to time in the telling to unhook from habitual emotions. As we finish, our partner looks at us, and we see compassion in his or her eyes. We wonder if we have said too much; we observe the mind racing as it tries to contrive some happiness in these circumstances, or at least avoid the pain of embarrassment. We sit; mindfulness grows clearer. We see these thoughts as they come; after a moment they vanish. Our partner speaks of longing to be free from this stress; he or she understands our experience, and we know we have been heard. Then there is silence. The heart is less hungry now. The sense of self we fought to protect softens; thoughts and sensations rise and fall in a wide awareness. This sense of the unfolding moment is shared with our partner, but awareness is still autonomous. We recognize how we had identified with the noises of our mind. We rest in awareness. There is joy in letting go like this, and peace. For a moment mental fabrications cease. We taste freedom.

As the retreat continues for another few days, our tranquillity continues to be deepened by silent meditation sessions, silent meals, and the nurturing environment of the meditation retreat. Mindfulness becomes more consistent, sharper, lighter, and more precise. Tranquillity begins to ripen and our minds are steadier, even amid the complex dynamics of interpersonal relationship. We become increasingly comfortable. Our awareness widens to encompass both our internal experiences and those of others. We discover for ourselves that the meditative mind can be cultivated during interpersonal contact and can become strongly established in that contact.

As the retreat unfolds, the contemplations—such as impermanence or the constructing mind—become increasingly profound and astonishingly real in each moment of experience. A naturally kind, clear awareness dwells behind every moment. Even though the struggles of retreat may continue—the sore body, occasional boredom—we notice hints of wisdom and compassion bloom, revealing the tenderness and contingency of life in the instant of interpersonal contact.

Because this practice is interpersonal, we cultivate mindfulness and acceptance of others, continually challenging those qualities to expand. We see, over and over again, with different meditation partners and in groups, that everyone has similar stresses, doubts, joys, and insights. We are all tender, we are all brilliant, we all hunger for kindness. Compassion grows in the most natural way possible: through simple, honest contact. The meditation practice reveals the pain and isolation that come from judgment and selfishness. We are inspired by the joy of lovingkindness and by our capacity to face our fear of emptiness. When we cannot meet our own confusion with awareness, often our meditation partners can. In the field of loving awareness, clinging diminishes, unbinding happens. Unhelpful habits are seen clearly and drop away, like a skin outgrown.

In the light of this kindness and wisdom, limiting and stressful personality formations begin to soften. Delusions about ourselves, such as our unworthiness, importance, or fragility, begin to dissolve. The most sticky and painful knots in our being—those associated with our relations to other people—unbind. We notice in ourselves a deep calm and realize, by contrast, how tense we have been. The fabricating tendency of the mind is observed for what it is. Transformation of the structures we use to form our lives, our self-concepts, is happening at a very deep level. Mindfulness and concentration shine into the moment of interpersonal contact, and we find these forms of awareness to be compassionate. We have apprehended the nature of our imprisonment and our exquisite potential for freedom.

2

THE EMERGENCE
OF A PRACTICE

INTERPERSONAL MEDITATION emerged naturally from my personal life and from my life in relationship to the teachings of the Buddha. It emerged from the social and philosophical milieu of Buddhism newly arrived in the West and from the peculiar needs and gifts of our present era, including science, modern alienation, and changing patterns of wealth. From these conditions the practice of Insight Dialogue developed—and alongside it, step-by-step, developed an interpersonal vision of the Dhamma (*Dharma* in Sanskrit). The interpersonal practices and teachings I now share emerged in phases from a plethora of possibilities. Each stage felt like an arrival; I never anticipated the next vista that would open.

The seeds of this path were planted when I entered the path of Buddhist meditation. My first teacher, Anagarika Dhammadina, was kind, ferocious, and resilient in the face of my selfishness. She taught me to meditate; when meditation showed me the pain inherent in my self-centeredness, she helped orient me toward selflessness and clarity. Anagarika revealed to me that the Buddha's teaching was a path of human formation, a path joining decency with wisdom.

She also introduced me to other teachers, teachers from whom she herself wanted to learn. Ananda Maitreya Mahanayaka Thero seemed to me, at first, just a kindly old monk; slowly I became aware of the depth of his wisdom. I had been told he was the oldest and most respected monk in Sri Lanka. I gradually learned that he was also a mystic and a scholar of the highest order. Working with him, I deepened my formal knowledge of the Dhamma and studied Buddhist psychology, the Abhidhamma. Through our time together in retreat, and while I hosted him in my home or accompanied him on visits to retreat centers and universities, Ananda Maitreya also gave me a powerful transmission of lovingkindness—a wordless teaching that later unfolded as central to my path and understanding of the Buddha's teachings.

Anagarika also introduced me to Achan Sobin Namto, a Thai monk who became my primary meditation teacher for more than fifteen years. His precise teachings were combined with an equally precise understanding of the dynamics of the mind. The rigor of his retreats, together with the deep and sincere teaching of Anagarika and Ananda Maitreya, fostered in me a profound respect for formal, in-depth meditation practice. This emphasis was instrumental in the eventual formation of Insight Dialogue as a retreat practice.

Anagarika's invitation to a retreat with Punnaji Maha Thero turned out to be her parting gift to me—she died a week before the retreat, before I could see her again. Our gathering became both memorial and retreat. She had eagerly recommended this teacher to me, saying "Gregory, we've been working much too hard. Venerable Punnaji's teachings are fresh. I have heard the first new insights on the Dhamma in many years." She was right: Bhante Punnaji influenced me profoundly. His emphasis on relaxing was revelatory, and mindfulness emerged easily as I learned to calm down. His multistep method of teaching meditation began with contemplations drawn from the Buddha's teachings; I was astonished at how my mind became concentrated when I directed thought toward traditional themes such as the truth of impermanence in my life. After days of immersion in these contemplations, and then in lovingkindness meditation, the mind was relaxed and focused, and it was easy to remain present when I turned my attention toward the breath. His teaching that relaxation was fundamental, and his use of traditional contemplations, have influenced the development of Insight Dialogue.

Punnaji's greatest influence on me, and on the emergence of interpersonal Dhamma, was his approach to the Buddha's teachings. Based on deep insights experienced in meditation practice, he observed that the ways the Dhamma was being taught obscured essential truths. He had immersed himself in early Buddhist teachings and found that he had to retranslate key words and reconstrue substantial portions of the Dhamma. On the scaffolding of these teachings, Punnaji integrated Western psychology and philosophy, his own background as a medical practitioner in Sri Lanka, and the continued fruits of his life and practice. From him I learned a deep respect for the earliest sources, together with fierce integrity regarding life and meditation as I experienced it. I also learned that integrity sometimes requires new expressions in practice, and that this is acceptable and appropriate.

A second phase in the development of Insight Dialogue began during my doctoral studies. Partway through the first year, my colleague Terri O'Fallon and I decided to study the approach to dialogue offered by David Bohm, a physicist who worked closely with Krishnamurti.[1] As a class project, we presented this type of dialogue as an online practice. At first our work was animated by an interest in shared meaning and in the ways people learn collectively how to think and act. It soon became clear that something else was emerging—something that inspired us to move on from the style and intentions of Bohmian dialogue.

Terri had begun to study *vipassana* (Insight) meditation with me, and both of us noticed that when we brought our meditation practice to the dialogue sessions, something shifted. The power of mindfulness came into play and a new clarity emerged; the dialogue itself became meditative. When she and some of my meditation students joined me at a retreat, I condensed the twelve or so guidelines for meditation in conjunction with dialogue that Terri and I had developed down to about six and gave this practice the name Insight Dialogue, inspired by its basis in insight meditation. At that first retreat, our afternoon dialogues were awkward interludes during long days of silent vipassana meditation; out of respect for people's traditional practice, I stopped the dialogue practice after a few days. But by bringing meditation into the sphere of interpersonal interaction, Insight Dialogue had been launched between Terri and me; it would continue to inspire me for years.

Four of us from that retreat engaged in regular online dialogue via private chats for the next year and met twice to explore the practice in person. The guidelines expanded to nine, but the basic idea remained constant: mindfulness can grow when people practice together. Online meditation was emerging as a powerful practice in its own right. Terri and I developed a meditative research methodology, Insight Dialogic Inquiry, and used it to produce a fully joint PhD dissertation, with the online meditation practice as our topic. After we completed the dissertation, Terri began to teach in higher education and continued to share a version of the practice we developed with her students and with her spiritual community.

When I started offering Insight Dialogue to weekly meditation groups in Portland, Oregon, another phase began. An ongoing, committed group allowed me to develop and refine the guidelines, which I made the basis of weekly talks and practice.

In 1998 I offered a retreat that was virtually all Insight Dialogue practice at the Barre Center for Buddhist Studies in Massachusetts. It was an awkward affair. Thirty-six people sat in a large circle without any theme other than mindfulness, and as the teacher, I talked too much, wanting to be heard. I didn't know what else to do! Despite my awkwardness, the retreat yielded beautiful moments and, for many, helpful experiences—owing to the power of mindfulness, the emerging practice itself, and our basically wholesome intentions.

Over the next six or seven years, the practice evolved considerably. It became obvious that this interpersonal meditation had a life of its own. My primary discipline was to trust whatever emerged and to pay careful attention to where the truth vibrated, and also to where confusion, self-making, cultural habits, and tension were dominant. The practice, and my understanding of the Dhamma, were maturing. One by one, breakthroughs and quiet evolutions formed the practice.

The first real freeing of its form began with an explosion of creativity while I was teaching a retreat in India at Auroville, the spiritual community gathered around the teachings of the Hindu sage Sri Aurobindo and his spiritual collaborator, the Mother. At home in Portland I had been undergoing the deepest challenges to my spiritual path that I had ever experienced; this seemed to set the stage for exploration and risk. Working with this community of people deeply dedicated to their spiritual path, I introduced many elements for the first time: breaking the group into subgroups, changing group sizes throughout the retreat, introducing explicit topics to the dialogue groups, and presenting the meditation instructions in language that encompassed a spiritual tradition other than Buddhism.

Freed from my self-made prison of what this practice should look like, I made other changes when I brought the practice back to America. Attending to my intuition and to the needs of the moment, I began to integrate practices such as yoga to bring bodily ease, meditating in nature to encourage a gentle opening of awareness, and occasionally combining walking meditation with dialogue.

Another major breakthrough arose out of quiet desperation while teaching a retreat at the Bhavana Society, a monastery in West Virginia. Following my commitment to trust emergence—that is, not to let planning interfere with riding the moment—I had just introduced a roomful of meditators to the meditation instruction "Pause," but I had no topic, no contemplation theme for the dialogue. While the group of monks, nuns, and laypeople sat in pairs, the room grew silent as I paused midsentence, not knowing what to say next. As I stood in front of the huge Buddha statue, hoping for some inspiration, the story of the Buddha's entrance into spiritual search came to me. I had contemplated this on retreats with Bhante Punnaji, and now it was bearing fruit. The son of a tribal leader, Gautama, wishing to experience things beyond his protected and privileged life, asked his horseman to take him through the city. Along the way he saw an old person, a sick person, and a corpse. In each instance he asked if this happens to all people; in each instance he was told, yes: all people grow old, grow ill, and die. These three messengers appalled the sheltered twenty-nine-year-old but also shocked him into integrity and truthfulness. He renounced his worldly life, beginning the path that would lead him to profound awakening. In the moment I recalled this story, I turned and offered the group the first of three contemplations: "As you enter into dialogue, I invite you to contemplate aging."

These contemplations opened the doorway between the Buddha's entire teaching and interpersonal practice and began the next phase in the development of Insight Dialogue. Though I did not yet fully recognize it, the gate opened for me between the content of all wisdom traditions and Insight Dialogue. The basic meditative qualities of this practice could be developed while contemplating any essential truths. The power of this content—the contemplations—clarified for me the relationship between contemplation and meditation and led me to condense the meditation instructions to three simple elements: Pause-Relax-Open, Trust Emergence, and Listen Deeply–Speak the Truth. Mindfulness and tranquillity were the foundation of the meditative process, while the contemplations enabled the practice to reach deeply into our mental and emotional constructions and to transform them with a power that I had never even imagined. This is now the foundation of Insight Dialogue.

The current phase of development of Insight Dialogue began with the training of others to teach the practice. With their input, retreats have become more spacious, with more time for silent meditation. Most significantly, the new teachers have brought to Insight Dialogue their personal understanding of the Dhamma and their unique approaches to teaching. As these gifts become integrated into the core practice, this is a time of flowering and growth.

A new understanding of the Dhamma has unfolded from my search to apply the Buddha's teachings as honestly as possible to both meditation and human relationships. This vision encompasses personal and mutual meditation and is guided by an understanding of human vulnerability and a vision of the human potential for freedom. A path toward interpersonal ease and awakening has emerged. This path includes group practice in both retreat and other settings as well as the use of Insight Dialogue guidelines to transform our daily lives into a process of awakening and release. My path toward this has involved many debts to the wisdom, discernment, and guidance of others. Above all, the development of Insight Dialogue has glided on the rails of the Dhamma; I am simply trying to remain true to this remarkable emergence.

~ 3 ~

AN AWAKE
HUMAN BEING

THE TEACHINGS of the Buddha are about human life. Rituals and philosophies have gathered around the Buddha's teachings—different forms in different places—but the heartwood of the teachings is not about these things. It is about coping with our all too human lives of suffering and joy. We can take heart in the fact that the Buddha was a man, not a god. The Buddha taught what he learned from his own human experience. He offered his teaching to other human beings, who were able to benefit from them because they were human. This humanity does not deny the subtle or mysterious aspects of our being, those attributes only realizable by a still, keenly alert mind. Being born into a human's sensitive body and heart-mind is both exquisite and challenging. The Buddha's insights have astonishing depth and right-now relevance because they were based upon his direct, embodied experience. He rose to the challenges of his human life and taught others how to do the same. It makes little difference that the earth touches my bare feet thousands of years later or that the thoughts crowding my mind were influenced by the Internet or that my emotions have a modern Western flavor. The facts of our shared physiology, and of the heart-mind's tender responses, ensure the continued relevance of those human teachings.

The Buddha recognized that we spend most of our lives in stress and confusion. Our pain is sustained by hunger and grasping and often near-total ignorance of cause and effect. He saw that we have a capacity for clarity and compassion that remains largely untapped and that we are capable of freedom from misguided selfish desires and ignorance. To realize these capacities, the Buddha prescribed a virtuous lifestyle together with an array of what I call extraordinary personal practices. These are the meditation practices most of us are familiar with. These practices call for our individual, personal effort (whether in solitude or in a group); they differ from our ordinary activities and are engaged in at times and places set aside for fostering qualities such as mindfulness, tranquillity, concentration, and spaciousness. These teachings unfold in our everyday lives as well as during times of set-aside practice. Like the teachings of other wisdom traditions, they are grounded in millennia of empirical research into what results in ethical behavior and personal happiness. When we engage the path, these clear results inspire confidence and also form the basis for further development of the path.

People in incredibly diverse cultures have tried the teachings of the Buddha and found them helpful. As they applied these teachings to their lives and made them their own, the teachings took on the flavors and textures of different cultural forms and indigenous wisdom. Practices, philosophies, deities, rituals, and discoveries blossomed. There were sixth-century Chinese hermits, twelfth-century Zen warriors, and indigenous people on the Tibetan plateau engaged in a mélange of sorcery and meditation. From Zen emptiness to the twentieth-century human potential movement, these inquiries have focused primarily on individual and personal growth and employed a huge range of individual and personal meditation methods to foster that growth—even though the meditation was usually taught in supportive communities and monasteries. In some traditions community life was a central transformative practice, but even in these traditions, meditation itself was entirely internal and personal. This individual focus continues now, in scientific research into the neurophysiological basis of emotions and meditative states. Throughout these developments, interpersonal manifestations of individual practices, and interpersonal forms of practice, have been largely ignored.

Many of our stresses in life arise in relation to other people; much of our imprisonment, fear, and longing has to do with relationships. Our relational lives are often quagmires where ignorance is fostered and sustained. Someone attacks my honor, for example, and anger begins to boil. I grasp at my imagined injury and become blinded to things as they actually are. Proliferating thoughts and emotions resulting from such interpersonal contact become the basis for arguments, disputes, and war. When we engage with others from behind a thin veneer of cheerfulness, or a brick wall of hatred, we are not clear minded. We quickly become trapped in habitual cycles of sameness. Unaware of our potential for greater ease, joy, and compassion, we leave the fruits of interpersonal freedom untouched—unaware even of their existence. What might life be like free from interpersonal longings and fears? How would we treat other people if we recognized their kinship with us, seeing the sad sameness of the hurts in our hearts? Can we truly release our socially constructed self-concepts? And if we can, what might our lives be like? What might the world look like if we could meet each other undistorted by stress, grasping, and wanting? What if, together, we tasted the love inherent in receptive stillness?

Neglecting the interpersonal dimension of our spiritual unfolding seems unwise. Interpersonal practices can help us to be happier and more caring people. They can also open the way to extraordinary interpersonal development, development paralleling the personal realizations described by sages of old and appreciated anew by Western psychology. This development includes the rarified states, remarkable insights, and movements toward freedom that may arise in deep practice. It also includes the realization of our capacity to care deeply about others, and to live with them in a kind and generous way. On the path to awakening, there is no separation between emotional and spiritual bondage. To be free and to be a mensch—a decent human being—both lie on the same path of extraordinary interpersonal development, a path to greater happiness, wisdom, and compassion.

This deeply human sense of the path is central to the Buddha's teachings, but as Stephen Batchelor and others have pointed out,[1] the concrete sense of Gautama as a person, and of the ways his teachings address the everyday problems of our existence, have repeatedly mutated into something more mythological than human. In early Buddhism the Buddha came to be imagined as absorbed only in quietude. His sore back, his devilishly clever wordplay, and his ironic humor were ignored; for most he became a nonhuman ideal rather than a highly developed human being. The person was lost who, in his last year, said, "Ananda, I am now old, worn out, venerable, one who has traversed life's path, I have reached the term of life, which is eighty. Just as an old cart is made to go held together with straps, so the Tathagata's body is kept going by being strapped up."[2]

In reaction to this dehumanization, the Buddha was rehumanized by Mahayana Buddhism as the Bodhisattva—someone who cared deeply about people. The example of his life was then seen as more compelling than his formal teachings. In Chinese Ch'an Buddhism and Japanese Zen Buddhism, it was emphasized that he was one among many buddhas— and since these traditions focused on multiple lineages of great teachers, both the humanity of Gautama and the kernel of his early teachings diminished in prominence. The Buddha and his teachings were again revitalized and made concrete in Tibet, enfleshed in the rich practices of Vajrayana Buddhism. Over time, ritual and formality ascended in importance, distancing the person and the teachings. In each of these cases, from early Buddhism and the Theravada tradition through Mahayana, Zen, and Vajrayana, in one society after another, appreciation of the Buddha as fully human faded. And whenever, wherever, a sense of the Buddha's humanity was lost, a priceless understanding was lost with it: that liberation might blossom from this fleshy, fecund human experience.

Humans are a social species. The path is presented here as encompassing our innately, inescapably social nature. The Dhamma is offered in very direct human terms and so must include our relational lives. The particular practice offered here as a part of that path, Insight Dialogue, is both a lifestyle practice and a practice for deep retreat. It fills out that part of the path that has been most neglected—the interpersonal—enabling profound serenity and insight, along with fully engaged compassion. The wisdom that arose from the issues of the Buddha's human experience addresses the issues we face daily. After all, the elevated and mundane are intertwined in this shared human experience.

Part Two

FOUR
INTERPERSONAL
TRUTHS

~ 4 ~
THE FIRST
NOBLE TRUTH
Interpersonal Suffering

THE BUDDHA was a practical teacher. The rules for monastics, his analysis of the mind, and a wide variety of meditation practices all grew out of an inquiry into the nature of human experience. At every turn he taught others not to take his word for things but to see for themselves how life is. The Buddha's most basic teaching, the Four Noble Truths, was also his first teaching after his enlightenment. It is fundamental. This teaching is offered here in interpersonal terms.

In the spirit of "see for yourself," the reader will find in this part of the book a series of reflections or small exercises in observing the truths discussed. These are offered as examples of ways this wisdom can be verified in experience and taken directly into our lives. They provide a few starting points for those seeking to internalize and benefit from these teachings.

The Fact of Suffering

When we look honestly at the human condition, we see stress.

Interspersed with moments of pleasure, we see stress in the little discomforts—a neighbor's grating voice, the urge to urinate—as well as in the huge pains of disease, divorce, and natural disaster. Whole industries have evolved to help distract us from our miseries, to help deaden our dissatisfactions and pains: stylish clothing, luxurious homes, enticing films and music, and alcohol and the bars that proffer it. Human suffering is not news.

We can look directly at these tensions; they are always there if we bother to notice. Often we don't want to look straight at suffering. It can feel safer to deny or ignore it. Maybe we fear that looking steadily at our suffering would make it more intense, even overwhelming. These fears are unfounded, however. Looking clearly at the fact of suffering is one of a small number of things we can actually do that, together, bring real relief. This was found empirically in the Buddha's time and can be proven again now by experiment.

Stress is sometimes hidden because it is mingled with happiness. For example, when my sons were home one holiday season, our house was filled with life, boisterous activity, and the control issues of newly minted young adults. Dishes of food were everywhere, and the noise level was high. The days were rich with jokes, wrestling, and tender moments. But when the boys left, my wife said she felt "picked clean," as if by vultures. It was a time of much joy—but also a lot of work, agitation, and the give-and-take that constitute the sweet and prickly character of family life.

Some experiences of stress are unmistakably miserable. One meditator described her experience living with a painful and debilitating disease. As we sat together on an astonishingly clear autumn day, the trees surrounding the meditation hall luminous with color, she spoke through her tears. Her fear that her disease would never go away was more enervating even than the physical pain. "There's no cure, no escape, not even any pre-dictability," she said. "I can't know from one day to the next how much I'll be able to do—not even whether I'll be able to get out of bed tomorrow." And beneath this painful state of constant apprehension lay a still deeper pain of loneliness: she was facing the disease without an intimate partner and without an adequate support system. Her last few years had felt like a desert. "People don't understand about chronic pain," she said. "After a while they just don't want to talk about it, don't want to talk to *me*. I feel so terribly alone."

Many experiences of everyday stress are less obvious. A gray sense of dissatisfaction or alienation might follow us through the day, clouding our natural potential for ease and understanding. We don't want to sit behind a desk today; we just don't feel like taking out the garbage. Our relation-ships are full of such small discomforts: we don't feel like talking to the cashier; we put off returning that phone call. I recall a time when my teenage son closed me right out of his moment with a dismissive grunt. No great drama: but right then, I was sucked away from the world around me into a little cage of dissatisfaction.

Even our joys set us up for pain. Sometimes the mind is clear enough to see this setup. One participant in an Insight Dialogue retreat delicately described a series of stresses that followed each other rapidly: a pleasant feeling of love for the other retreatants; followed by joy and relief to be in their supportive company; then anxiety about losing this community; then a sense of sadness, colored by the memory of earlier losses; then a different feeling of love, less pleasant and tempered now by guardedness. She added, "All of this happened within the space of a minute or two." Such kaleidoscopic shifting of emotion is not unusual; joy may be transformed quickly into sadness, sadness into something else. The interpersonal losses we have all experienced—death, divorce, trauma, moving homes, changing jobs, or the slow drifting apart of friends—have conditioned us, have become almost part of us, and profoundly affect the ways we meet experience. Like shadows, the residue of experiences lurk just beyond our conscious awareness, ready for action at a moment's notice, when conditions are right. We are always tender and sometimes raw; we may as well admit it. Even those with tough exteriors began life with sensitive nervous systems and in complete vulnerability. We only become armored as the natural sensitivity of childhood is abraded into the relative callousness we call adulthood.

Because of our complex conditioning, even joy can be stressful because we reach out to grasp the source of happiness—tense and unbalanced, even when there is no immediate prospect of separation or loss. Little gains and losses are happening nearly all the time. Comfort, discomfort; gain, loss; praise, blame: these show the conditioned character of life. There is no escape from the basic fact that as long as we have a body, there will be some pain or discomfort. There is no escape from the fact that the world around us is constantly changing; pleasurable or comfortable circumstances inevitably alter or vanish. We ourselves change; who we are now is not who we once were. Denial of these things sends us into exile from reality, pushing us deeper and deeper into disconnection and anxiety.

But by looking clearly at how things actually are, we can escape from the jungle of unnecessary anguish. In a physical jungle, orienteering teaches us to look for signs of where we are and where we have been. Just so, we would do well to look for signs in this jungle of distress. An automotive engineer cannot afford to be ignorant about friction; an architect must understand gravity. In the same way, a person looking to understand peace must not be ignorant of the physics of stress. A person seeking joy cannot afford to be ignorant about the causality that governs suffering.

A Bare Assessment of Suffering

The Buddha saw clearly that suffering is a key fact of human life and sought to understand how it functions. In his very first teaching after his enlightenment, he said, "Suffering, as a Noble Truth, is this: birth is suffering, aging is suffering, sickness is suffering, death is suffering, sorrow and lamentation, pain, grief, and despair are suffering."[1] Inherent in this basic teaching we can discern two large subgroups of suffering: physical, or biological, suffering and psychological suffering.

Birth, aging, sickness, and death involve body-based, biological suffering. They arise inevitably from being born into a body that comes into contact with a world full of abrasive, sweet, loud, malodorous, and colorful objects. Right out of the birth canal we are assaulted by cold air touching our skin and entering our lungs, bright lights, and our first unmuffled noises. Mother offers comfort, but it's never the same as it was, never enough. For the next however many years, this body must be fed, kept within a certain temperature range, protected from microbes and injury, helped to heal when it cannot be protected. This sensitive body generates changes of its own, weathering hormonal and neurochemical storms from the dawn of life until its confusing dusk. Having physical form, feelings, and perceptions means being touched continually by the pleasant and unpleasant things of this physical world.

But we also experience suffering that does not derive directly from physical or biological situations. Sorrow, lamentation, pain, grief, and distress derive from our reactions to the situations we experience, not the situations themselves. For example, if I break my hand, I experience more than just the physical pain of damaged tissue and nerves clamoring for attention—I am also upset that I won't be able to work this month. Perhaps I am also angry at myself for being careless. These emotions are themselves painful. They are mind-based, or psychological, suffering. These "uncomfortable feelings born of mental contact"[2]—as the Buddha described them—vastly increase our suffering. Worry, fear, confusion, and anxiety rise out of the ideas, hopes, and memories we fabricate in the course of our lifetime. We have a constructing mind and a consciousness that grasps at what the mind presents to it; this means being touched continually by the pleasant and unpleasant products of our accumulated emotional history.

One summer morning I got a clear view of how the proliferating mind causes suffering. I awoke early. Rather than going downstairs to meditate,

I chose to explore experience as it was here, in my bed. As I looked up at the ceiling beams bathed in the morning light, I contemplated the Buddha's teachings on sensation and perception. I noticed how light was touching the eye, and the eye functioned, and awareness of that function—what we call seeing—arose. At the moment of contact there immediately seemed to be a "me," an experience, "I am seeing." Time and again I released this notion and let go into simple awareness, just seeing. When this was stabilized, I did the same with sounds and bodily sensations, calming down out of the habitual fabrication of self.

In the midst of this my wife, Martha, rolled over and her foot touched my foot. Immediately I experienced a flush of emotion. I was cozy; I was happy. But supported by the stream of practice, I released the mind's clinging and noticed that this was just touching. There was a tangible object (Martha's foot), a functioning sense organ (my skin), and consciousness of the touching.

Along with this simple contact, an "I" arose in relationship to "her." From our long and caring history together, happiness also arose. Then Martha moved her foot away. Instantly I felt sad. The sadness was mildly painful. I had become attached to the pleasant emotion I associated with the bare experience of the sensation of touch. The reaction was automatic, conditioned. The mind held on to that first flush of sadness for about two seconds; then I recognized it as a mind state triggered by circumstances. I relaxed again, settling into the moment-to-moment experience of sensation. But I liked that cozy feeling. I watched that liking build up until I thought: "Meditation or no, I want more touching." So I reached out my leg to touch my wife's. But Martha was mostly asleep, and, seeking comfort, she pulled away. Immediately I felt rejected. This feeling arose automatically, as reflexive suffering.

How did this suffering come up? Its immediate cause was the conditioned emotion of sadness owing to perceived rejection. But what was behind this? The experience was based upon sensory contact (my wife's touch), the sense organ (my skin), and awareness of bodily sensation, which combined with preexisting constructions (love for my wife and our history) to provide the conditions for a mental/emotional experience of happiness (my beloved touches me). Happiness at the initial touch created desire for more touch, which created tension in this form of unsatisfied desire (my longing). This hunger generated tension, which led to action (reaching out to touch her again), resultant sensations (the brief contact), and emotion (fleeting happiness). This was followed by more tension as elaborate formations arose (interpreting her pulling away as rejection, triggering conditioned fears) and more emotion (sadness).

The Buddha continued his analysis of suffering: "Association with the undesirable is suffering, separation from the desirable is suffering, not to get what one wants is suffering." These teachings describe several modes of psychological suffering. Taken as referring to sense-based suffering, this teaching comments on the effects of association with undesirable sensation such as smells or sounds. But the Buddha made it clear that this teaching also comments on human relationships. "Whoever encounters ill-wishers, wishers of harm, of discomfort, of insecurity" is associated with the undesirable. Separation from the desirable refers not only to separation from "what is wanted, liked, pleasant sight objects, sounds, smells," and so forth but also to separation from "well-wishers, wishers of good, of comfort, of security, mother or father or brother or sister or younger kinsmen or friends."[3]

The relational elements of the Buddha's teachings are often overlooked. This is evident in all schools of Buddhism. It is as if some invisible wall has been built, keeping this messy, albeit inescapable, aspect of our humanity out of the pristine beauty of the Buddha's formal teachings. As a result there is much ignorance about the suffering associated with human relationships, its cause, and the nature of freedom. This suffering has been unnamed and overlooked. It is simply a result of being born as a sensitive social being in a complex and changing interpersonal and social environment. This is interpersonal suffering.

> Big suffering is easy to see: it forces itself into awareness. Try to notice some of the smaller discomforts of life—discomfort while sitting too long, boredom, worry—and the nearly incessant things we do to get rid of them: eat, change positions, turn on the television, pick up the phone. Notice the temporary ease that comes with relief; notice when this ease, too, passes.

Interpersonal Suffering

Interpersonal suffering is the suffering that stems from our associations with other people. It is a vast subset of psychological suffering. Stresses with family members, coworkers, and friends are interpersonal suffering. Loneliness and disconnection are also part of interpersonal suffering. Each of us regularly experiences interpersonal suffering. Simply recognizing these dynamics at work, and knowing that they arise as constructions of the sensitive heart-mind, can be helpful.

A huge portion of our emotions, painful and pleasant, arise in relationship to other people. One need only open a book of social psychology, sociology, or history—or any novel—to find countless examples of interpersonal suffering, both intimate and public. Marriage and family problems are interpersonal suffering, as are workplace relationship problems, romantic entanglements, and legal and political disputes. War and its lifeblood of military honor—ranging from the martyrdom of the terrorist to the brittle pride of the sergeant—are infused with interpersonal suffering. The pain of anger and the fear of losing love are interpersonal suffering. Social discomfort, jealousy, and the pain of judging other people, or of being judged, are all interpersonal suffering.

We do not experience these forms of suffering—or any suffering—because we are bad, sick, or unworthy. We experience interpersonal suffering because we are essentially relational beings: our minds seek to grasp and hold, while the social life that touches us is full of uncontrollable changes. Suffering is the natural outcome of this circumstance; any sense of guilt or shame about the fact of suffering is misplaced and can only cloud our vision. And if we're exploring how we can be happier, more compassionate, wiser, and even truly free, we need to look at things as clearly as we are able.

Biological, psychological, and interpersonal suffering are thoroughly interwoven. The kind of suffering we experience depends not directly on circumstances but on our reactions to circumstances. For example, I like washing dishes. I find it satisfying—I can actually see the physical results of my work. But sometimes I resist it. It is personal suffering when I resist because I'd rather be reading. It is interpersonal suffering when I resist angrily, feeling taken advantage of and unappreciated for all I do. As another example, shame about our bodies feels very personal, but it is intimately linked with how we imagine others see us. We may be physically uncomfortable because we are too fat or too skinny, and this is personal suffering. The emotional discomfort that comes with thinking about what other people will think about our body shape is interpersonal suffering. I recall my wife finding a small skin lesion. When she was concerned about possible medical complications, discomfort, or inconvenience, this was personal suffering. When her concern focused on the possibility of a disfiguring scar and her appearance to others, this was interpersonal suffering. Illness is this way, too. The inconvenience and pain of being bedridden cause personal suffering. But it is interpersonal suffering when I'm embarrassed that my spouse must help me to the toilet. Being ill, uncomfortable, and scared to die is personal suffering. Grieving on the deathbed about leaving those we love or feeling remorse about unfulfilled relationships is interpersonal suffering.

Interpersonal suffering is sticky stuff. People are complex, emotions change faster than summer storms, solutions are never certain. If we have to deal with a disease or injury, okay, we do what we have to do. It may be unpleasant, and the right path of action may not always be clear, but it is not usually as complicated and difficult to comprehend as relational pain. When my eldest son, Zed, was diagnosed with cancer, there were many moments when his physical pain and even his fear of death were subservient to his concern for his mother's—my wife's—sadness and grief. At the same time, our pain was due to concern for Zed's suffering and to the possibility of losing him. The three of us were, just then, an intimate system of interlocking anguish.

As human systems get larger, interpersonal suffering becomes social suffering. For example, the pain of a gunshot wound is personal biological suffering; the fear of death is personal psychological suffering. The pain of hatred toward the specific person who shot you is interpersonal suffering. The pain of hatred toward the country or ethnic group of the person who shot you is social suffering. Social suffering is the systemic manifestation of interpersonal suffering, just as interpersonal suffering is the systemic manifestation of personal suffering.

Loneliness is a fundamental form of interpersonal suffering. It is the interpersonal manifestation of our root fear of emptiness and death. It comes in both personal and social forms and is appallingly widespread. In personal loneliness we lack an intimate other; in social loneliness we lack integration into a community. We try to fill the hole of loneliness by consuming food, cars, media, and drugs. We consume enormous telephone and Internet bandwidth, along with large amounts of fuel and other resources, just trying to make meaningful contact with each other. In this mélange, biological, psychological, and interpersonal suffering trigger each other, and each can lead to behavior that exacerbates and prolongs our grief.

People in wealthy nations—driven by loneliness and hunger for pleasure—set in motion a cascade of other forms of suffering. Seeking solace, they suck up the world's resources driving places and importing fancy foods, labor-intensive goods, and irreplaceable resources. In the countries depleted by the consumption of these hungry people of power, biological sufferings such as malnutrition and disease are exacerbated by the massive socioeconomic changes associated with economic domination. When starving people communicate, their affiliation is based on compassion for each other but also—often—on having the shared enemy of the dominant nations. The pain resulting from this hatred can be seen on the faces of both warriors and their victims.

Meanwhile, in the lands where power is centered, the tensions of protecting one's lifestyle and hating those who would attack it are added to the pain of loneliness and daily stress. Perhaps in a small town, some-where, a marriage breaks up because of these added stresses, and the couple experiences the profound interpersonal suffering of divorce. Mean-while, on the national scale, budgets are diverted to pay for military endeavors, and millions of people experience a loss of medical services, adding to biological suffering. Educational and day care services, too, are cut back, adding to psychological suffering. Hatred across constructed political boundaries deepens, and tension becomes each person's private companion. Personal, interpersonal, and social suffering coexist in our personal lives and saturate the heart of society, not because we are bad, but because we are human.

> During a time you are feeling overwhelmed with stress, take a moment to reflect on which stresses are more about things—possessions, jobs, and practical circumstances—and which are more about relationships. Do you notice any differences between the two?

A Realistic First Step

To observe life this directly is not pessimistic; it is realistic. Ignoring the problem doesn't help. Indeed, ignorance keeps the suffering invisible, as-sures its continuity, and establishes it as determining the tenor of our lives. Knowing this, we are invited onto a path of discovery. As the Bud-dha put it, suffering leads either to derangement or investigation.[4] To see how things actually are, we must cultivate mindfulness, which is the ca-pacity to observe our reactions in each moment. We must also calm down enough to remain present with what mindfulness observes and look at the emotional reactions that drive us around these many cycles of stress. What do we notice as we see more clearly into the workings of interpersonal suffering? Can we discern the causes of this suffering? If we can see things clearly, we can begin to reorient our lives toward happiness and freedom. Understanding the causes of suffering is the first step toward freedom.

5

THE SECOND
NOBLE TRUTH
Interpersonal Hunger

Clinging to Hunger Causes Suffering

As the world touches the senses, a self springs into being and longings arise: hungers for pleasure, safety, and life itself. This self grasps for these things and clutches them tightly when it gets them. We cling to our efforts to get what we want, and we also cling to the fear of losing what we have. The tension inherent in such grasping is the root of suffering. As children we learn which interpersonal contacts are pleasant and unpleasant, just as we learn which sensory contacts are pleasant and unpleasant. We form preferences and aversions. We discover that wanting and not wanting are reciprocal: the ending of the pleasant is unpleasant; the ending of the unpleasant is pleasant. The mother's breast is an obvious example—it is warm and sweet, agreeable; when it is taken away, the experience is unpleasant. But that is not the end. Later there is the hunger for its return, not only for sustenance, but as an object of comfort, of pleasure; basic biological hungers transform into psychological hungers. Both place "me" at the center of the universe. We experience pleasure in a smile or in words of praise; we form more nuanced hungers for such attention, which will be given and taken away throughout our lives. We experience pain in words of criticism or rejection; avoiding such contacts becomes urgent. Out of such conditioned hungers grow our most subtle longings for intimacy, acceptance, and community. Longings named and unnamed are active in our lives; we can know only a fraction of them.

Interpersonal pleasure and pain are powerful conditioners. As a child I was praised for eating all of my soup; I learned to perform for praise, even when full, because I hungered for the smiles and words I had enjoyed on previous occasions. All around me kids hungered for praise for hitting the ball far, having the nicest clothing, or doing well in school. But we are all different. My father's longings were not for public recognition but for private love. Long after my mother had died, he still hungered for companionship to bring temporary respite from an ancient loneliness that was re-created throughout his life. The origins of his hunger, however, became buried under nearly a century of accumulated life. My family's hungers, like all of our hungers, took shape as self formed at the confluence of sensory contacts, pleasant and unpleasant feelings, and conditioned emotional habits.

Grasping is the link between hunger and suffering. When we cannot have what we want, the tension of unsatisfied hunger endures. We cling to the images and feelings associated with what we seek. Thirsting for coffee, we hold an image in mind: we see and perhaps hold the coffee cup, breathe in the coffee's aroma, and long for the emotions associated with an idealized satisfaction. As long as we hold that image and its inherent wanting, we remain unsatisfied. Similarly, in the interpersonal realm we may feel an intense longing to be with someone we love: we imagine that person's image and the sound of his or her voice, and we carry the person in our thoughts until we can be together. In both cases the mind clings to—is obsessed by—the desire. When we hold on to the thought of someone we do not like, the fundamental dynamic is the same. The mind grasps the image of the person and is stirred to aversion or even anger. Whether we like or dislike, we are obsessed.

To understand suffering we must take a close look at clinging. When we touch something soft, the mind is pleased and clings to the pleasure, wanting it to last. We experience tension because of the certainty that the pleasant experience will end; when it does, we want it back. If we touch something sharp and are cut, we experience immediate physical pain, and the mind fixates on the desire for this pain to end. A sense of self is also involved in this clinging, as we shall see. Hunger and clinging sustain each other as pleasures and pains come and go.

Interpersonally, the dynamic is the same. We see the form of another person; if we have pleasant associations with this person, conditioned happiness arises. We cling to that happiness. But in interpersonal experiences, the clinging is multilayered and therefore especially challenging. Not only are we enjoying the pleasant sensations of this person, we are also finding in them temporary respite, at many levels, from haunting hungers: you bring me stimulation and pleasure, you make me be seen, you are the one who ameliorates my feeling of unworthiness. As we develop, it is inevitable that we will seek and hold to these pleasures; they tell us we are alive and safe. The hungers take root as we cling internally to the deeply seated notion of self—the one to be pleasured, acknowledged, and protected—and to that self's feelings. At the same time, we are clinging externally to the other person. This clinging is not only the result of the present moment of pleasure or pain; its arising is conditioned by all of our past moments of pleasure and pain.

It is easy to see how we cling to what is pleasant, but it is essential to understand that we also cling to painful thoughts and emotions. All over the world—the Balkans, the Middle East, Africa—there are peoples holding intense hatreds among them. When an individual holds in himself the image of the hated other—Arab, American, foreigner—the mind clings to this image despite the intense pain this hatred causes. Closer to home, irritation with a neighbor, coworker, or relative establishes the clinging mind, and we hold on to hurts big and small. Clinging—whether in hatred or in desire—generates tension, which becomes the basis of dissatisfaction and pain. From such clinging flow actions intended to end the pain and bring satisfaction. We denounce, harm, or even kill the hated other.

Whether the product of karma, DNA, or strong neural patterning, such grasping is rooted in a history subtle beyond imagining. Because mind and body are one whole, not separate, this painful and unsettled state of grasping manifests in both the body and the mind. Encounter with another person is an especially potent form of contact and can result in powerful, subtle, and complex feelings. From these impressions arise the urge to grasp, the stickiness of heart and mind that tinges togetherness with anxiety and makes separation painful.

The next time you notice suffering in one of your relationships, see if you can recognize the grasping in it. Are you holding on to an image, a desire to control, a hope or a fear? Does noticing this cause the clinging or pain to change?

Three Basic Hungers

Probing the mechanism of these cycles of pain and bondage, the Buddha discerned three interrelated hungers as their source. He said:

What, friends, is the noble truth of the origin of suffering? It is hunger, which brings renewal of being, is accompanied by delight and lust, and delights in this and that; that is hunger for sensual pleasures, hunger for being, and hunger for non-being. This is called the noble truth of the origin of suffering.[1]

When I first encountered this teaching, I could readily understand how the hunger for sensory pleasures, and the implied aversion to pain, could lead to all sorts of frustrations and anxieties. The hunger for being made sense to me as the urge for bodily survival, but since my survival was not usually in direct question, I wondered how this teaching could have much moment-to-moment bearing on my life. But the urge for nonbeing seemed downright cryptic to me: abstract and obscure. I trusted that it had some relevance to my life, but I wondered if I'd ever understand it. After a little more study, I understood the hunger for nonbeing as the urge to escape this painful life—the suicide wish; though, again, I did not see how it applied to my own life.

When I came to understand suffering as including interpersonal suffering and saw the origin of this suffering as interpersonal hunger, the Buddha's teaching on the three hungers came alive for me. And once I saw how these three hungers worked in the interpersonal realm, my understanding of them as personal hungers deepened also. I came to understand the craving for interpersonal pleasure as both the urge for pleasant stimulation by other people and the fear of loneliness this pleasure often masks. I saw that the hunger for being[2] was also the hunger to "be" relationally—that is, the hunger to be seen, and its obverse, the fear of invisibility. The hunger for nonbeing, I came to understand, was not only the urge to escape this crazy and painful life but also the urge to escape existing in relationship. Inherent in this urge, I saw, is the fear of being seen, the fear of intimacy.

I came to understand these hungers as almost elemental forces that, sustained by my ignorance of their operation, had kept me locked in confusion and stress. I sensed that beneath their murk, clarity and calm had always existed, even if I didn't know how to access them. It seemed that each of these hungers had somehow prepared a campsite in my heart, even before parental conditioning or cognition meddled with my essentially luminous awareness.

Forming the Relational Self

A key element in our conditioned patterns of reaction—maybe the biggest element—is the sense of self. We are born dependent upon other humans for survival. We emerge into a world of sensations: contacts with objects hard and soft, warm and cold. By reflex we are drawn toward the sensations we find pleasant and pull away from those we find unpleasant. Like all animals, we learn. We learn where the soft places are and learn to nestle there; we learn to turn away from loud noises. We seek the warmth and nurture of the breast and cry for it, tense and screaming for our lives. Comforted by warmth and milk, we relax. It is all part of being born as sensitive creatures in a stimulating and changing environment.

Within three months of life in this body, we begin to distinguish what is I and not-I. We find that what is not-I is responsive. The breast is not only soft, it is offered. Our relational lives have begun. We set about trying to know and be known; we begin social smiling. "Hellooooo," says the new dad. Eyes meet. The father smiles and the child smiles at this recognition, her whole body blowing up like a grinning balloon. Contact! We've made it.

This contact becomes a key experience as our learning floods forward. Our brains are adding nearly two million synapses every hour. Memory is forging links between pure sensation and human interactions. In his writing on interpersonal neurobiology, Daniel Siegel reviews research that explores the ways our brains are configured by contact with others.[3] We learn to feel safe and comfortable with particular people and become attached to them, smiling and cooing and trying to please. We become wary of strangers and tense at the sound of angry voices. These patterns help us get the care we need and avoid danger. With them, a sense of "me" emerges. A tentative "self" forms and re-forms around the tensions produced by sensory and relational contact, in which we desire pleasant feelings and push away unpleasant ones. By the age of two we have developed that most mixed of blessings: the sense of an independent self.

As it was for my mother and father, so it has been for me, and so it is for my sons. We have all formed a self, which is a constructed view that supports an emotional core to our lives. Once this self-sense is spawned, every sensation further feeds the construction. No longer is there just seeing, but there is "I see." My son Jared does not just experience hunger, he experiences "I am hungry." Of vast significance to our future happiness and suffering, there is no longer just the sound and sight of people: there is you independent from me; there is me independent from you. Where there are independent you and me, there is separation and difference, and these become the basis of relationship.

As we get older we relate not only to individuals but also to our peers in general and to the culture at large. During adolescence this forming self constructs our social selves based upon imitation and comparison. At the age of fifteen my son Max was learning the norms of the tribe, the rules of social encounter. "What looks good? How do I measure up? What behaviors are rewarded with friendship and praise? Which lead to condemnation and rejection?" This learning is extended into adult society; at the age of twenty-four, my son Zed was asking questions like "How do I earn my food and lodging?" "How do I attract a mate?" "How do I gain respect?" Our sense of self is reinforced as we grapple with the sense of being a discrete individual embedded in a community, questing for bodily and social survival and happiness. The sense of separation and difference becomes fully reified.

Separation refers to a feeling of a self that is distinct from other beings. Difference refers to the specific distinguishing features of particular individuals, together with identification with those differences. Separation and difference are both constructed views, with separation being the more fundamental.

The feeling of a separate self has its roots in the basic division of experience between the self and what the self experiences. When seeing, we instantaneously create the experience of "I see." This sensation is integrated with the perception, "I see *this object*"; the moment is made up of both the subject and the object, the seer and the seen. Becoming aware of sensations of the hand, there is the feeling of "my hand." When the hand touches something, there is the experience, "I feel." When we identify the object or its texture, we complete the phrase "I feel *something*." That which I feel is separate from me. When I experience another person, I experience this same split: *I see you,* or *I touch you.* As we fully embody this distinction—that is, as we come to live the subject-object split as truth rather than as a way of making sense of simple, sensory experience—separateness becomes real for us. Our culture may or may not engender the feeling that this self is embedded in a greater society; either way, each moment of interpersonal contact generates subtle feelings of private autonomy. This is universal and by no means bad. When we fail to recognize this identification, however, we lay the foundation for loneliness and other forms of anguish.

This sense of separation forms the foundation for notions of difference. Once there is a sense of you and me, comparison and competition begin— and the interpersonal construction crew goes to work in earnest! Once we grasp our separation from others, we focus on differences of gender, age, skin color, and eventually of wealth, nationality, power, and status. An identity forms on the foundation of difference. Feelings of sameness tend to breed safety and identification with a larger community, as we see in expatriate communities all over the globe. On the basis of difference, we seek the social rewards of praise and acceptance. This is manifest as hierarchy and status and the implied difference of "better than." Such rewards refine the sense of "who I am" and strengthen good feelings about the self by identification with members of our group. One might hear, for example, "I feel happy and secure as part of this church community; we are all good people here." The flip side of this is that we also try to avoid social punishments or failures. Blame and rejection come about as we conceive of people outside our group as being even more "other," more different from us, than they actually appear to the senses. Enemies are demonized and made more "other" than they actually are, cementing their status and at the same time firming up the home community.

The self that results from these comparisons and alignments feels inferior, superior, bonded with allies, arrayed against enemies, and swept into a powerful current of likes and dislikes. Judgments, roles, social segmentation, desire, fear, and confusion proliferate. All of these feelings and viewpoints cause bodily tension and emotional dis-ease. Tension increases and locks in place the clinging to identity; after all, it is "I" who must be protected, "I" who must keep "myself" and "my kin" safe, "I" who am right and justified in what I do to maintain this safety. Automatically built up over time from stored ideas about physical characteristics ("I am short") and relational dynamics ("I am vulnerable"), the constructions of separation and difference form the basis of a worldview that affects every aspect of our lives. The self, separate and different, is the one who hungers and hurts.

Notice how you define yourself as similar to or different from other people or groups of people. What elements are involved? Gender? Race? Sexual preference? Political viewpoint? Profession? Income? Age? Fitness? Notice if you habitually attach any sense of superiority or inferiority to each distinction.

How do you define yourself in relation to your parents, children, or siblings?

Spend some time quietly observing strangers. Notice any feeling of separation that arises. Can you catch moments of just seeing, or is there always the felt sense of "me" and "them" and a gap between the two?

The Hunger for Pleasure and the Urge to Avoid Pain

We have already considered the reciprocal relationship between pleasure and pain: we seek pleasure not only for its stimulating effect but also to avoid pain. We find the ending of pleasure painful and therefore fear its ending; we experience the urge to protect and extend our pleasures. We find the ending of pain pleasurable. If we are to understand the hunger for pleasure in interpersonal terms, we must understand what is meant by interpersonal pleasure. It is also essential to identify the dominant interpersonal pain from which we flee. When we understand these simple facts, it becomes easy to see the hunger for pleasure operating in our lives; this insight paves the way to the cessation of these hungers and the dawning of ease and compassion.

Interpersonal pleasure is the pleasant emotions and sensations born of interpersonal contact. I find it helpful to think of two basic classes of this pleasure: altruistic and selfish. Selfish pleasure: I am bored, so I visit you because I know I'll have some good, distracting fun; it's mostly about me. Altruistic pleasure: You are hurt, and I find joy in nursing you; it's mostly about compassion and generosity. In both cases, there is a sense of self and an urge to action. We will explore altruistic pleasure in more depth when we talk about the cessation of these hungers. First we will explore the selfish pleasures.

Selfish pleasure operates just like it sounds: we seek contact to satisfy our hungers for pleasant stimulation. This stimulation serves two purposes. It entertains and excites us, making us feel alive, animated, and not bored. It also distracts us from the pain of unsatisfied longings. Just as the physiological organism seeks stimulation, so does the social organism, and countless interpersonal entertainments attest to this, from parties to online chat rooms, soccer games to office gossip. This is the normal social urge at work.

To understand why selfish interpersonal pleasure is so important in our avoidance of interpersonal pain, we need to understand this pain more clearly. Loneliness is the interpersonal manifestation of the fear of emptiness, which is a manifestation of the fear of death. Out of this pain, and fear of this pain, we experience jealousy, betrayal, and many forms of hatred and anger. Loneliness is based on the perspective of separateness, exacerbated by notions of difference, and rooted in the hunger for pleasure. Aloneness is fundamental to the human experience; loneliness is not. I am alone in this body, you in that one—these are Aldous Huxley's "island universes."[4] We experience myriad emotional and energetic interrelationships, but we feel alone when we cling to the idea of an isolated self that stretches back to infancy and beyond, a self that is actually being reconstructed in each moment. The hunger for pleasure may be fed in contact with others, but when this ends, loneliness returns with sadness. Whenever we hunger for pleasure and the hunger is not satisfied or the satisfaction ends, pain arises.

Nearly everyone is out to satisfy his or her hunger; in response, humans form an interactive system, almost a feeding frenzy, of stimulation and distraction. This mutual tickling undergirds many social norms. People gather at the well or at the water cooler for that relational tickle. Feeling lonely when we walk into the door of an empty house, we might pick up the phone and call a friend: a bid to keep the mind occupied and the fear of emptiness at bay.

We also fill the lonely spaces when we gather in large groups, which offer us even more stimulation. I recall observing this one evening when my wife and I went out to dinner with two other couples. As we ate, the conversation ranged from complaints about our houses to stories about people at work. We touched on the economy and movies, politics and the Internet. Any meeting like this unfolds at many levels. We were expressing our values, venting our frustrations, exchanging practical information, and, in our listening, offering a sort of unselfish kindness to each other. It was also clear, however, that we were entertaining each other for the sheer sake of stimulation and distraction. Clever jokes, interesting anecdotes, and knowing glances all provided one little flush of pleasure after another. This is small talk as a means of distraction, a buffer against the pain of loneliness. There is nothing immoral with this, but it is useful to notice this urge for stimulation with the understanding that relationships based upon greater ease, compassion, and wisdom are also possible.

And then there is sex, the grandparent of the relational tickle, presumed to be the pinnacle of stimulation. For many people sex is a major form of entertainment. It is a singularly powerful meeting point of personal and interpersonal pleasure. The hungers of the body and hungers of the heart meet and can be temporarily slaked in one act. The personal pleasure is driven by the immense power of basic hormonal drives. The interpersonal pleasure is nourished by the unmatched physical intimacy of full-body touching and intercourse. Sex and love are not the same thing, of course, and it is possible to find one's pleasure-hunger fed and an invitation to true caring untouched. This is the nature of sex as distraction, addiction, or satisfaction of a selfish urge. Union, caring, and generosity are often sadly missing.

In seeking to understand these hungers, we are not only concerned with our own pain and happiness. Our kindness and availability to others are also at issue. Why? When we are hungry, we see other people primarily as potential food, not as who they are in and of themselves. Also, when we are experiencing relational pleasure, we may be afraid of losing it, and so we act selfishly to protect what is "ours." When we can't get the pleasure we want, we get hurt and then angry. Aggression is the usual reaction to the frustration of our desires. When someone becomes closer to the person we desire to be with and we are excluded, we feel jealous hatred and may act on that hatred. When a dominant ethnic group prevents us from realizing our dreams, we feel anger toward the members of that ethnic group. We feel hurt and angry when someone we depend on for social entertainment, or for soothing our fear, leaves us.

The hunger that seeks to gain interpersonal pleasure and to avoid interpersonal pain forms the basis of untold sadness, compulsion, and violent crimes. It perpetuates habits of material consumption as we seek to fill the hole of loneliness with food, drugs, consumerism, and work. This hunger for pleasure imbues our lives with a feeling of lack, dissatisfaction, and incompletion. The hunger, by its very nature, will never be lastingly fulfilled, only temporarily satisfied.

The next time you are about to contact some friends, notice the anticipation of pleasure. As you interact with them, notice if you are holding on to the stimulation or perhaps feeling safe from loneliness. These things are natural, so be kind to yourself.

> In a difficult relationship, notice any strategies you may be using to soothe the pain with sensory pleasures such as food or drink, with distracting entertainment, or by seeking solace in another relationship.

The Hunger to Be and the Fear of Nonbeing

The second of the three root hungers in the Buddha's teaching is the hunger to be, to exist. Personally, the urge for bodily survival yields a hunger for safety and a corresponding fear of death. Wanting psychological survival yields a hunger for ego safety, and an existential fear of emptiness. At its root this is a hunger to experience life, to become, in each moment. The interpersonal hunger to be is the hunger to be seen. It is the desire to exist in the eyes of others, and the fear of invisibility. This is relational survival. It is the self's longing to be recognized, acknowledged, appreciated, and loved. It is also the basis of the fear of losing what recognition we currently enjoy. It is everything from "Mommy, look at me," as the child dances across the kitchen, to the dictator's bravado in the limelight of his country's entrapped gaze. This hunger finds strength in fears that we will not be seen, that we are unworthy of being seen, unless we are successful in our performances. If we are unseen, we are not alive.

To properly understand the power of the hunger to be seen, and its accompanying fear of invisibility, it is essential to understand its relationship with our elemental fear of death and of existential emptiness. This primal hunger and fear, along with the psychologically conditioned hungers and fears that accompany them, are profoundly linked. If we understand this, we are better prepared to meet the moment with commitment. We may soften our judgments of social longings—our own and others'—that we might otherwise judge as trivial. We may also glimpse the interrelatedness of psychological and spiritual freedom.

The desire for emotional survival begins, simply, with physical survival. From infancy we have turned to others, especially to the mother, for physical survival. To be abandoned as a helpless baby means death. The fear of death is primal. Not to get what we hunger for—warmth, touch, milk—is also physically painful. In infancy we are dependent upon another person not only for our sensory satisfaction but also for our very existence. Here the hungers for pleasure and for survival are fully enmeshed. Also, personal bodily pain and the interpersonal pain of wanting and needing are thoroughly intertwined. The association between attention from others and survival impresses itself onto our bodies and minds. Driven through our lives by hunger and its shadow, fear, the self turns to others for satisfaction, validation, and relief from its primal fears. Our fear of death has yielded a fear of emptiness, and we fill the emptiness we fear with other people. We begin to fear stillness and silence as harbingers of this emptiness. The thirst to be seen becomes more subtle as we mature. It drives the peer validation of the teenager and the life and work validation of the adult. More delicately, it includes the glances, hugs, handshakes, and words by which we confirm each other's self-concept.

From moment to moment, we create and re-create the sense of a separate self to be seen that is the basis of the hunger to be. If we were taught to perform for love, we keep performing. This is the path of the overachiever and the pleaser, the good boy or girl who must stay good to be liked by others. To have one's accomplishments acknowledged becomes a surrogate for being loved. To be praised is to exist. This is not a small thing; it truly is survival. The emotions are saying, "If you don't recognize and appreciate me (or my work, my appearance, my goodness, and so on), I don't exist." This is a taste of death; it is horrifying, and we will do anything to avoid it.

I am reminded here of my own childhood. Plenty of psychological flesh was laid on the bones of my foundational craving to be. My parents loved me very much, but the combination of their difficulties and preoccupations and the conditioned tendencies I brought to this life resulted in a blossoming of this basic hunger to be. As I grew up, wanting to be seen was a dominant theme in my life. This is why I sought praise for eating all my soup or making my fourth-grade classroom laugh. Later in life I performed music and was always torn between the joy of the music itself and the urge to be seen and liked because I was doing something to entertain or uplift others. In large part I performed so I could be seen. I also performed by appearing smart and by accomplishing things in the world. But there was no end to the hunger; no matter how much I accomplished, it was not enough. When I was active in science or music, I felt I had to make significant contributions to the field. As a meditation teacher, I craved personal respect. But whatever successes came, the hole could never be filled. Recognition is not love. The hunger would not be satisfied. My longings were held in place by the view that feeding them brings happiness. Feeding them, however, brought only a private grandiosity that masked my suffering. What I thought was happiness—for example the flush of pride when I was complimented—was actually tension. Hunger was the root of my suffering.

This hunger to be manifests in myriad ways. In my life the hunger to be took the form of pride, but other forms are common. One meditator described himself as the Resentment Bunny because the resentment that poured from the issues he had around recognition kept on going and going. When he saw those issues as the hunger to be, he was able to relax and experienced some release. Recognizing an urge like this often precedes insight into its insubstantiality. The dynamics of the interpersonal hunger to be seen are easier to spot in the calm and focused setting of a retreat, but they also operate in our mundane interchanges. If we can calmly look within during an everyday conversation, we can see them there, too.

For many it is typical to look for something clever to add to a conversation. When the clever idea arises, we immediately identify with it. We imagine something like, "This thought is clever, I made this thought, people will like the thought, and therefore people will like me." We do not make any distinction between the clever thought and some concept of "me." Looking closely, we can feel the stress, imbalance, and dissatisfaction behind this little flush of longing for visibility. Out of conditioned habit we fixate on any promise that we might be able to put some fat on the starving self's bones. The hunger for positive feedback may be so great that it overrides our sense of decency; for example, we might make a remark at someone else's expense just to get the laugh or to be respected as a clever person.

The same urge to be seen may cause us to fabricate or exaggerate stories so we can be heard. A woman named Della described how this urge surfaced in her childhood: "I remember Mama asking me, 'Haven't you anything to say?' and I learned to make a story for her. I went on doing that the rest of my life and hiding my lying from myself." Even a benign situation—like the child saying "Mommy, listen to my story"—is colored and infused with this hunger to be seen, to be loved. The fashionably dressed woman, saying by her actions "Look at my body, my face, my good taste, my wealth," is acting on her hunger to be. The fashion industry rests on this hunger. Or think about the teenage boy with the fast car. He identifies with it. It is excellent, so he is excellent. The pleasure of driving fast may be a sensual pleasure, but being the center of attention is an interpersonal emotional pleasure. Both the fashionista and the car buff are also moved by the fear of losing what attention they get. "Am I pretty today?" "Will I be pretty when I grow old?" "Is my car safe from damage or theft?"

All of these questions can be boiled down to "Will I continue to be seen, to exist?" Such simple behavior has deep roots.

The hunger to be plagues us with thousands of questions and worries each day. We are forever asking, in one way or another, "Will I exist in the others' eyes?" We have antennae out for praise; we wonder, "Did I say something helpful and insightful?" "Did people value my contribution?" If we don't get the feedback we want and expect, we can be disappointed, even angry. We may become dispirited and stop volunteering down at the soup kitchen or stop trying hard at school or at work because it is not netting us the love we seek. Any task undertaken with attachment to acknowledgment and outcome has a shaky foundation. Given any opportunity, the hunger that drives us will reveal itself. Our questions shift painfully, "Am I looked up to, listened to?" "Am I being slighted, ignored?"

Even in relationships in which we are loved and honored, the hunger to be seen percolates below the surface. The hunger to be seen is a common source of friction in families. We may insist on the form of attention we have learned to expect or prefer; we may resist or reject the love really offered to us because it takes a different form. One meditator described how she rejected her partner's kind attention because he did not remember it was her birthday. She made herself feel miserable and alone despite his loving presence.

The hungers filter our perceptions to an almost unbelievable extent, obscuring what is good. From the subtle tensions of loving relationships to the raging self-absorption of celebrity gone bad, the hunger to be seen pains us. We are trapped in selfish concerns, isolated to the point where our version of reaching out to others for love can't seem to get beyond that old joke: "Enough about me. Let's talk about you. What do you think of me?"

Notice how you decide when to contribute to a conversation. How do you feel if you say something and there is no response? Does the desire to be noticed affect your being present to others?

Inquire into the energy behind your drive to accomplish things in the world and behind the material things you have accumulated. Is hunger part of the motivation? Do you observe stress in relation to accomplishment? Fear of loss or failure?

Notice the ways people draw attention to themselves—clothing, jokes, attainments—and contemplate the hunger to be. Which strategies for gaining attention do you use most? Consider the ancient origins of all of this and allow compassion to manifest in your heart.

The Hunger to Avoid Being, and the Fear of Being Seen

The hunger for what the Buddha called nonbeing is the urge to escape. It is the desire to be out of a certain situation, to reject, or as the Buddhist teacher Ajahn Sumehdo puts it, to get rid of. It is a fundamental recoiling from the hurt of life. Just as desire and aversion are binary, the one and zero of reaction to sensations, the hungers for being and nonbeing are the basic, almost primordial urges of the self. When things are good, we want to "be" in that situation; the self wants to continue its incessant becoming. When they are bad, we want to escape; the self does not want to exist like this. And just as the interpersonal hunger for being is the urge to be seen, the interpersonal hunger for non-being is the urge not to be seen, to be invisible, to escape, to shrink from interpersonal contact and its possible hurt. The hunger for escape also takes the form of fear of losing our current safety.

Just as suicide is the self-murder of the body, social suicide is the destruction of one's being in the social world, the world of interpersonal contacts. In the hunger to escape there is a fear of being exposed, which results in tension and pain. The very common fear of public speaking works in this way. One may experience tension, constriction, almost a paralysis in a way that is personally dramatic and out of proportion to the situation or its risks. The tension comes from thoughts, internal judgments, images, and assumptions: it separates us from the goodwill and energy of others. Perhaps the most common form of the hunger for invisibility is the fear of intimacy. There are parts of us that we simply do not want revealed. We fear exposure, the exposed existence.

A lack of self-acceptance, projected onto others as fear we will be rejected, causes us to shrink from others. While the hunger to be seen is also based upon a feeling of lack, this feeling of inadequacy is the most direct manifestation of what Tara Brach calls the trance of unworthiness.[5]

Being unworthy, I don't want to be seen, to be discovered as worthless, and so to be rejected. Rejection is interpersonal death. So I shrink from you, hide from you, so you won't discover me. At these moments, the self-concept is very strong. Practicing Insight Dialogue, one meditator captured the thoughts and images of this tension when, during a dialogue, she thought to herself: "I can't do this. I'm defective. There is something fundamentally wrong that can't be fixed." She even berated herself for feeling agitated and anxious at a meditation retreat, where she thought everyone was supposed to feel peaceful. When we speak ill of ourselves internally, we are both perpetrator and victim. Each self-criticism is a dart that contracts the heart in pain. Shrinking in submission to this inner voice of inadequacy holds us back from receiving and giving the very love that would free us. The hunger for non-being makes us unavailable to our heart's most needed medicine: full present acceptance. We are in a rainstorm in the desert, dying of thirst as water disappears into the sand. All we need is to open our hands to receive the love we so desperately thirst for.

Too often we choose the known pain over the unknown joy. As another meditator commented, "I'm so afraid of the invisibility, but when people ask me to step out of it, I prefer to stay in its familiarity." The fear of rejection provides architectural plans we use to construct complex personal prisons. We are hurt as children in so many ways. Often we are not loved as who we are. We are abused emotionally, sexually, and physically. Parents who don't have the emotional resources to love us, who are lost in self-concern, may abandon us and betray our trust. As women we are made into objects of lust and compared to idealized and airbrushed models. Perhaps we are raped or otherwise invaded and belittled. As men we are expected to bottle up emotions and perform the strongman act. We are compared to bodybuilders, sages, and corporate chieftains—and we always fall short. We are surrounded by advertisements for makeup, clothing, and cars to improve ourselves. There are countless messages from our employers, parents, and the media that trumpet: "You are not good enough. You should be better." Embarrassment, shame, and self-doubt are some of the thorny plants that grow in this soil.

If we are constantly given the message that we are inadequate, the self's latent and conditioned urge to flee will grow. We feel insecure and anxious, and because the source of our pain is suppressed, we may not know why we feel unsafe and unworthy. We seek to escape this pain and do things to "get my mind off the pain." Thus the inner escape of shrinking from the world leads to the outer escapes of television, sleeping, food, living in fantasy, overwork, drugs, and the fogginess of not being present to experience. These escapes become addictions, enticing us toward the safety of oblivion. We see here the connection between alcoholism or drug addiction and self-hatred and feelings of inadequacy. At Alcoholics Anonymous meetings worldwide, we can hear the varieties of self-hatred and escape. One meditator at an Insight Dialogue retreat who had been in a twelve-step program for more than twenty years became aware of her urge for escape. In the delicate awareness of interpersonal meditation, this woman could clearly perceive the sweetness she had come to attribute to invisibility, her tendency "to romance nothingness" and "to endow oblivion with allure." Our escapes are not always obvious to us; they can assume socially acceptable forms such as retreat into a cocoon of meditation, into the protection of religious rituals or beliefs, or into the secure social routines that consume our daily lives. Interpersonal flight can appear as simple introversion or as full-blown social anxiety. We also escape behind a persona, where even a gregarious mask functions as a hiding place for all we want to conceal. The possibilities are endless.

It is of enormous benefit to understand clearly how these feelings of inadequacy are constructed. First there is sensory contact with the world: we see, hear, touch, or remember another person. The subject-object split happens instantaneously: we experience me and them. Then the deeply conditioned view of separateness and difference arises. We feel fearful, unsafe. Entering this view, we compare ourselves to others; inevitably we either come out on top—and are tense because we seek to be recognized for our superiority, fearful to lose that recognition—or we come out on the bottom and are tense because we fear the social death of rejection. These feelings are being constructed anew in every moment. They are not permanent but continually reconstructed. This is key. Once the thoughts "I am inferior," "I am inadequate," "I am unworthy," are constructed as mental images and as a felt bodily sense, we cling to them and believe in them as if they were stable, permanent. We don't notice that we re-create them all the time. When we realize that we can choose to renew these constructions in each moment, or not to renew them, we may feel momentarily naked—without our accustomed protections—but we are also empowered to be present to ourselves and others in the moment. We are not, just then, running from being.

Watch for the times when you typically make comparisons between yourself and other people, and begin to observe these comparisons with friendly curiosity. Notice any effects this comparing has on your consciousness or on your ability to be present to others.

Think of someone you know who is shy or who withdraws from close interpersonal contact. Considering this ancient hunger, allow compassion to arise.

Notice your feelings when you return to some privacy—when you shut the door to your room or office, get into your car after work, or see the children off to school. Is there a feeling of escape? Listen carefully to these feelings, without judging them, and see if you can catch what you feel you are escaping from.

The Hungers Intermingled

These three hungers do not exist in isolation; like chemical elements, they are nearly always found in compounds. They intermingle, alternate, and feed each other. The hunger for pleasure, along with its inherent fear of pain, is foundational to the other two hungers—for being and non-being. Whether we hunger for pleasure or to be seen or to escape from view, what we crave are pleasant feelings. One fourth grader cracks a joke in front of the class because being seen feels pleasant; another shrinks from speaking up because avoiding the scrutiny of classmates feels safer—because that feels pleasant. Such happiness is relative and full of tension, but often it is the only happiness we know. We are doing the best we can to satisfy our longings.

Just as the three interpersonal hungers do not exist in isolation from each other, neither do they exist in isolation from the personal and physical hungers. The connection between loneliness and eating is well known. One retreatant reported that he had not felt hungry during the retreat, but the experience of hunger reappeared on the drive home. Calmed by interpersonal practice, his physical and relational hungers diminished in tandem—and returned in tandem. The lust for sexual pleasure is intertwined with the hunger for interpersonal pleasure and, usually, with the hunger to be seen.

The hunger for the physical pleasure of alcohol or drugs is often associated, at parties and sports events, with the lust for interpersonal stimulation and pleasure. The pleasure of intoxicants is also closely linked with the hunger to escape personal and interpersonal pain: "I drink to forget my problems." As the urge to escape pain grows, the basic longing to not be increases.

The hungers to be seen and to escape may alternate very quickly. One meditator wrote of her experience at another Insight Dialogue retreat, "I would say: 'Look at me! Look at me!' Then, when people were really looking at me, I would say, 'Okay, that's enough. Stop looking at me!' I wanted the recognition, but then I was scared of it." The hunger to be seen and the hunger to disappear rose and fell in her like the two ends of a seesaw. Similarly, a woman at a retreat in Switzerland experienced something like an existential crisis at each step of walking meditation. "Each step I took alternated between the hunger to be and the hunger to not be." She was a seasoned meditator, and with refined mindfulness and concentration she was able to discern the existential crisis at the base of her existence in society. Fortunately, this same mindfulness helped her remain present with and accept these twin hungers.

The hungers for being and for non-being may also alternate more slowly, sometimes in very mundane ways. Many a drama is concocted from their rise and fall. One retreatant felt misjudged and discounted by another's criticism and sat in the circle feeling worthless and inadequate. One critical remark nearly became the pivot point of his entire retreat. "Earlier in the retreat I had done plenty of inflating," he wrote; "now I was shrinking."

All of these hungers are experienced by everyone; they effectively dominate our conditioned lives. They also diminish our availability to each other. The hunger to be seen reaches outward for recognition. The person motivated by it is obsessed by the craving to be admired and validated as a self and thus is not available to others. The hunger to escape retreats inward. The person motivated by it is obsessed by the need to defend and protect the self and is too busy hiding to be available to others. Both hungers yield conceited self-concern or self-absorption, making people unable to be present to the pain of others and impeded in giving or receiving love. Unworthiness is the basis of both hungers, and isolation is their result. The hungers to be seen and to hide both rest upon the foundational hunger to obtain pleasure and to avoid pain. All of these hungers rest upon self-concept; they are the core around which the self constellates. All obscure our natural capacity for joy and compassion.

The Energy That Drives Greed, Hatred, and Delusion

The hungers drive the heart-mind forward; they condition arising thoughts and the actions that develop from those thoughts. These hungers are like tidal forces, huge and elemental, and thoughts arise on these tides like waves on the sea. In any given moment, a hunger may incline the mind to pull what it wants toward it and to hold on to what it has already grabbed. This is generally stimulated by pleasant contacts. In another moment, the mind may be inclined to push away whatever has touched it. This is generally stimulated by unpleasant contacts. When a contact is neither pleasant nor unpleasant, the mind ignores it in dull indifference. These three tendencies—pulling, pushing, and overlooking—are the blacksmith's shop in which moment-to-moment suffering is forged.

Throughout his teachings, the Buddha referred to these three tendencies, using words in his own language: *lobha, dosa,* and *moha.* These are usually translated as "greed," "hatred," and "delusion."

> What do you think, Kalamas? When greed, hatred, and delusion arise in a person, is it for his welfare or harm?[6]

These are not random qualities. Rather, the pulling, pushing, and foggy disregard are fundamental roots of thought, as fundamental as the plus, minus, and zero of mathematics. Their corresponding opposites—wholesome roots—are nongreed, nonhatred, and nondelusion. Based on their root, thoughts will have specific qualities and predictable results. When the root is unwholesome, the thoughts and actions that flow from it bring suffering.

The pulling mind of *lobha* blossoms in greed and lust. It can arise from the hunger for pleasure. Wanting pleasant tastes, a greedy thought arises and we grab the chocolate bar; wanting the pleasant caress, a lustful thought arises and we reach out for the person who might supply it; longing for social stimulation, thoughts arise to create strategies for satisfying this longing and we call a friend or figure out how to get invited to that party. The monkey mind is working hard. These thoughts are rooted in pulling toward and holding; they are the links in a fence that, collectively, keep us bound.

The hunger for being, and the associated fear of nonbeing, can also give rise to interpersonal greed. The urge to be seen often leads to strategizing how we can be seen. We may become greedy for notoriety and scheme to make that a reality. Each little thought in such a scheming mind has the quality of pulling toward oneself and holding to the desired visibility. Such a mind greedily accumulates social options—friends, acquaintances, memberships, conversation topics, jokes, sports or media trivia—and uses them to bolster prominence. Such a mind can be very subtle, and the pulling forth of validation can be cleverly mixed with genuine intellectual or altruistic interests. But the tension of greed still generates suffering.

The hunger for non-being generates greed when we pull toward us the distractions and addictions in which we hide. The strategies differ, depending on our hiding place. Greed may arise in one moment for alcohol, in another moment for an isolated cabin. In yet another moment, our thoughts may be obsessed with pulling and holding the person with whom we have created a safe, dependent relationship.

Each hunger can just as easily fuel aversive thoughts. The hunger for pleasure carries with it the urge to avoid pain and retain our sources of pleasure; aversion (*dosa* in Pali) arises when someone interferes with that. For example, if someone designs to come between us and our spouse, we may feel anger and spread nasty rumors about the person. The angry words are rooted in aversion in the moment we speak them, even if the moments just preceding this were driven by desire for the pleasure of our spouse. Or perhaps we feel hatred for someone who has caused us pain by striking us or by stealing our belongings. As we feel the anger, we suffer. If we retaliate with violence, we heighten our pain and spread suffering to others. These aversions ride on the underlying hunger for pleasure.

The hunger for being can also drive aversion. If we scheme to be seen and someone interferes with our plans, aversion will probably arise. If I am poised to deliver good news to my boss but a coworker does so first, my hunger for recognition is frustrated and the energy of frustration fuels anger. Or perhaps I am overlooked, or even publicly humiliated, because of my skin color or my religion. A lifelong frustration of my urge to exist is stimulated, and aversion arises. Thoughts rooted in aversion grow and recycle in the mind, and full-blown anger arises. The nature of the aversive reaction will be gross or subtle depending on my conditioning and outer circumstances—but subtle distaste and outright hatred share the same root, and both lead straight to suffering.

The hunger to not be, to escape, is clearly the soil for the arising of aversion. Wanting the apparent safety of invisibility, we feel repelled or even angry at those who see us; anyone who would intrude upon our hiding place is worthy of our aversion. Thoughts rooted in aversion often give rise to angry speech. A young man wants to hide in his anger or shame, while his girlfriend, seeking intimacy, tries to draw him out. He snaps at her. The hunger to escape may itself be rooted in aversion toward people or society in general. We may seek the stupor of drugs; if someone interferes with our toxic strategy, aversion arises. We may have crafted a safe container at school or work—a way to hide, to fit in, to be invisible. If we are forced to speak in class or at a meeting, our world is shattered and aversion arises.

Delusion (*moha*) has a somewhat different quality from pulling and aversion. It is not so directly stimulated or fed by our underlying hungers. Rather, the hungers indirectly sustain the root of delusion and the thoughts that emerge from this root. For example, if we are on the prowl for an attractive partner, we might be oblivious to anyone we do not find appealing or who is not the right age or gender. If we seek to impress the powerful, people of little power do not figure in our drama. Those who do not serve our hungers do not exist for us; we are not present for them. Without someone or something that stimulates a reaction of pulling and pushing, it would seem that peace might arise. But our underlying hungers are still operating. The tidal pressure continues. Rather than dwelling in peace, the mind remains tense but is dull and indifferent in this moment of interpersonal contact. The thoughts that arise from delusion are unclear and automatic, riding on the undulations of ancient desires and fears. The words and deeds that issue from the mind of delusion perpetuate old patterns of stupefaction. Suffering endures.

Whenever we are in contact with people, or even just think about them, greed, hatred, and delusion may be at work in our relational lives. We pull people toward us, push them away, and ignore those who don't stimulate us or serve our needs. It is no different from the pulling, pushing, and disregarding we engage in when we contact inanimate objects. The mind darts from pulling in one moment to pushing in the next, as the underlying hungers maneuver through our hearts.

The mind is disoriented and wounded by all this pulling and pushing; delusion only helps sustain the chaos and abuse. Just as hurricanes and tornadoes are fed by the larger forces of sea and air, these movements of the mind are fed by the weather systems of the basic hungers. Our lives are beset by agitation and dissatisfaction. If we seek relief, short-term benefit can come from addressing the obvious manifestations of greed or lust, hatred, and hazy delusion. We can change our behavior, watch the mind, or alter our environment. Truly fundamental change, however, will come only from addressing the underlying hunger—the energy source driving all these roots, thoughts, and actions.

Like a surgeon preparing to operate on the brain or a peace negotiator interviewing all parties in a conflict, we have carefully examined the nature of the problem. We are prepared to ask, Does it have to be this way? Can these hungers, and the greed, hatred, and delusion they spawn, diminish or even stop? We have already seen some encouraging hints that this is possible: we are not always suffering; the hungers are not all present all the time; we can observe love and compassion, even when hunger is also present. Our careful observations set the stage for some very good news.

What do you do to gain praise, be liked, or garner recognition?

What makes you angry? What connections do you notice between your hungers and the arising of anger?

Have you been in a large group recently? Who captured your attention? Consider who you tended not to notice, and why.

~ 6 ~

THE THIRD NOBLE TRUTH

Cessation

Gradual Cessation

Hungers cause suffering, so it only makes sense that as these hungers diminish, suffering will also diminish. In his very first discourse, the Buddha taught:

> What is the noble truth of the cessation of suffering? The remainderless fading and cessation, renunciation, relinquishment, release, and letting go of that very hunger.[1]

This is a very strong statement. Given the strong biological and psychological basis of the hungers, it is radical to specify remainderless cessation and release as the end point. We notice, however, that the Buddha also speaks about the fading of hunger, its lessening. This is a teaching we can connect immediately to our personal experience.

What would it be like to live with less hunger? What would it be like to see the world, to meet other people, free from the anthill obsessions that occupy our thoughts and congest our emotions? It may be simpler than it first appears. We do not have to try to be happy, cultivate compassion, embrace some religious concept, or withdraw from other people. We can speak simply of the ease at the storm's ending.

We do not usually think of happiness in terms of something ending but rather in terms of good things happening or getting things we want. However, if we observe our lives and think carefully about what we see, it becomes clear that the longings, urges, wishes, and desires we carry are making us pretty tense—and that the lessening of this tension, whenever and however it lessens, feels pretty good.

Our usual benchmark for happiness is set by the temporary satisfaction of our hungers or the abating of our immediate pain, but these satisfactions cannot last. Sensual hungers reveal this quite clearly. If we eat a delicious meal, does this mean our hunger is forever satisfied and we won't seek more delicious meals? Of course not. If anything, our hunger for fine tastes grows. If we crave a large home or elegant clothing, only temporary happiness comes when we obtain these things. Interpersonal hungers are no different; their satisfaction is just as tenuous. Desire and fear work in tandem to keep us off balance. The interpersonal desire for pleasure drives us to seek satisfaction from others; the interpersonal fear of loneliness skulks behind each step. If we crave attention, happiness will come when people fawn over our accomplishments or laugh at our jokes. We will soon seek more attention to fill a hole that cannot be filled. If we crave escape, happiness will take the appearance of successful anonymity, or at least the satisfying sound of our apartment door closing behind us. Yet the mists of fear seep under the doors that would shield us.

Any satisfaction of hunger is temporary and fragile. It does nothing to end the underlying urges, and when the satisfactions pass away, we seek them again, ever hungry. We seek more sensual satisfaction, more attention, more complete safety—in a world where everything is contingent. The sad part is not that these satisfactions are transitory; it is that we are nearly always tense seeking or clinging to them. This state passes for happiness. What would a higher happiness be like? Would it be just another expression of hunger to orient our lives toward such a happiness?

A key dynamic of the ending of suffering, as the Buddha most often taught it, is that it is a *gradual cessation* of hunger. *Gradual* refers to steady change in our heart-mind. Each moment of letting go is a moment of freedom and conditions the next moment; peaceful moments increase in frequency as hungry and tense moments decrease. There may also be sudden changes, moments of release, but these are the ripening fruits of conditioning. Such changes are to be received as gifts, because we do not make them happen—we only establish conditions.

Cessation refers to the lessening of toxic qualities in our lives: specifically, lessening of the hungers for pleasure, being, and nonbeing and diminishment of the unwholesome roots of greed, hatred, and delusion nurtured by the hungers. Ignorance about the nature of identification and impermanence also diminishes in this cessation. As these intoxicants fade, the quality of life improves. Part of the path of their fading involves the cultivation of certain qualities, such as clear awareness, compassion, wise attention, and insight. But fundamentally, the focus is on the fading. What remains is ease, goodness, wisdom, and joy.

The happiness born of peace, when the hungers subside like the last receding wave on a glassy summer sea, is exquisite and stable. In the peaceful moment, there is no clinging and therefore no tension. We do not even cling to the peace. The mind is malleable, the heart receptive. We may experience a lot of energy or be in very dynamic circumstances, but our adaptability and skill can take these conditions in stride.

The peace born of the subsiding of hungers can be personal and internal; it can also include openness to others and to affiliation with them. As we will see, this affiliation is not tainted by the heat of hunger or the chill of indifference. It is compassion rounded with equanimity, and there is great joy in it. Once we have experienced this quality of joy—happiness without tension—it serves as a beacon when we find ourselves again on the seas of desire. We realize that such simple joy is available to us any time clinging is released. We do not deny the human truth of a body and heart with needs, but we also remain open to wakeful being and encounter.

Think about a time when you were peaceful and happy. Perhaps it was during a walk in the park, sitting quietly with a friend, or toward the end of a vacation from work. What was it like to find joy in ease rather than in stimulation? Is that ease available now?

Three Hungers Fading

Each of the three hungers—for pleasure, being, and nonbeing—brings to our lives a particular variety of suffering. Because of this, as each hunger fades, we notice changes in the associated feeling tone as our knots unbind. Pain, however, is the close companion of all the hungers we grasp at, and this binds them into the common experience of suffering. For this reason, the gradual lessening of these hungers shows many common features, regardless of which hunger is involved.

Every hunger creates tension; always, the lessening of hungers means the increase of ease. Each hunger separates us from other people because each hunger leads us to see others as beings who might satisfy us rather than as who they are in and of themselves. The fading of any hunger yields a reduction in feelings of separation and so a greater availability to others. This availability leads to affiliation and connection based on our shared humanity. When any hunger diminishes, compassion grows in its place. This natural emergence of care is the essential dynamic that humanizes and grounds the entire process of awakening.

Each hunger has an associated fear. The desire for pleasure has as its handmaiden the fear of pain, the hunger for being seen is shadowed by the fear of invisibility, and the hunger for escape brings with it the fear of engagement and intimacy. At the root of all these fears is a terror of emptiness, the concern that this self—personal or social—will die in a cold nothingness. This terror is usually kept beneath the surface of consciousness, recognized only by its surface manifestations: an avoidance of being alone, the fear of being criticized, a pulling back from close relationship. In all three cases, the fading of a hunger means the fading of its associated fear, and the fading of a fear brings the fading of its associated hunger. This is because the hunger and the fear are two facets of the same thing. And when the meditative mind sees the root fear and meets it with acceptance, it begins to diminish—and all the hungers dissolve with it. With such fading, relationships cease to be powered by longing and desperation. The anguish of the hungry life softens.

Less tension means greater ease. Less separation means greater affiliation and compassion. Less fear means that we can become fluid, undefended participants in life, more present to our real experience, more available to each other. The body relaxes, the mind calms down, and so we are naturally happy. Less confusing and distracting emotion also means a clearer mind, which can see the world with less distortion. The cessation of hunger sets the stage for the arising of wisdom.

The fading of each hunger manifests these common changes in different ways. The hunger for interpersonal pleasure, like the hunger for any object of pleasure, produces a life fraught with tension. The fading of the manic search for stimulation is like the feeling one has when no longer being tickled. The laughter was tense, the body was tense, and now the body can relax. The mind relaxes, no longer scanning the landscape for social goodies, trifles and truffles of people sweets. No longer blinded by selective filters, we become available to other people's pain and awake to the mundane parts of our and their lives. When not looking to be entertained we can be present for a new kind of social creativity. New ways of relating emerge based on serenity and presence.

The fear that rides along with the hunger for pleasure includes the fear of pain, loneliness, and rejection. These add urgency to an already unpleasant hunger. The stimulations we so desperately seek seem like a thin atmosphere, barely shielding us from a cold, empty universe. Cessation, here, is to let go of this desperate rush away from loneliness. As the tension of clinging subsides and the body-mind becomes more peaceful, relationships are no longer powered by the gnawing fear of loneliness and lack. Our natural grace arises.

Freedom from the hunger to be seen has similar dynamics but its own distinctive qualities. As we release the grasping for acknowledgment born of love starvation, we no longer build our lives around strategies to be seen and admired. We become comfortable with ourselves whether our efforts or personhood are being acknowledged or not. The energy we used to pour into assuring our visibility becomes available for other purposes; the attention we used to lavish on the ego's needs can be offered freely to others as acknowledgment and care. People tend to trust us because they know we are present for them in an uncalculating way. At home and work we are motivated by the joy and beauty of whatever we are doing rather than the ego rewards it might bring. If we excel in sports or dance, it is because they are doorways to a fully present life. Beauty, skill, intelligence, and even niceness are no longer tools to gain attention or admiration, currencies with which to purchase respect. They are the natural gifts of our being, which we can delight in and share. As we release our hunger to be seen—the driving force behind our insecurity—we can be at peace with the gain and loss, the praise and blame inherent in interpersonal life.

The fading of the fear of invisibility—the obverse of the hunger to be seen—is, at the core, a fading of the fear of emptiness. Before, we were always on the alert for dangers to our egos, but now we find ourselves at peace, grounded right where we are. Our fear of invisibility has faded. No longer obsessed with building up the self, we can entertain the possibility of its frailty, even its insubstantiality. We can be humble, now, in a way we could not before. We can meet others without judgments and putting ourselves over and above them. Relationships can now be in true fellowship, grounded in the fearlessness of freedom.

If the hunger to be seen has a manic flavor, the hunger to hide is depressive. Feelings of fear, inadequacy, and unworthiness constrain us and hold us to the safe and narrow path, both socially and professionally. The hunger to disappear sits as a heavy tension in our bodies, a drag on our vigor and our sense of engagement. Emerging from interpersonal and social fear is like taking a heavy wool blanket off our heads. The urge to escape life, escape people, escape ourselves, has fueled a brilliant array of defense strategies and a labyrinth of getaway routes; the fading of this hunger leaves us light and free. Energy is no longer drained by the constant barrage of self-criticism. The world comes alive. The spectrum of each sense expands to its natural capacity. The water over the rocks sings, and the light on the hillsides is no longer gray and dull but crisp and luminous.

The fading of the fear of being seen lands us squarely and fearlessly in the world. Our relationships with people are transformed. When we don't shrink in habitual inadequacy and the urge to flee, we can meet people eye to eye. We are seen, and we can now see others more clearly. We are available to their pain and joy, present and able to offer our sympathy. Since we do not have one foot out the door in preparation for flight, we can participate in the world and meet others with stability and confidence. What we learned from timidity and fear now allows us to be sensitive to others who still tremble. While fear of being seen drove us to escape in television, overwork, drugs, or isolation, the lifting of fear unveils our inherent energy for affiliation. We experience not the urge to be but the willingness to be. We reach out not in hunger but in the full aliveness of the social creatures we are.

The fading of hunger—any hunger—frees us from the narrowness of fear. Social life becomes compassionate encounter rather than an effort to gain pleasurable stimulation, uphold an image, or dodge the gaze of others. There is less fuel for hurtful or erratic behavior. Kindness and care emerge from behind their dark camouflage. Peace settles, clarity emerges, and happiness becomes a more frequent visitor. We see that there are alternatives to the anguish of living in constant tension. No longer obsessed by craving for pleasures, no longer grasping at acknowledgment, and no longer shrinking back from being, the balanced mind of wisdom and compassion emerges quietly.

Recall a time when you were particularly tense with some interpersonal hunger. Do you feel that same tension, longing, or fear right now? If not, take a moment to appreciate the ease of nonhunger.

Spend time with someone with whom you are comfortable. You do not have to reveal anything in particular to the person, but notice how your emotional comfort is linked with the absence of the fear of exposure.

Diminishing Greed, Hatred, and Delusion

While the fading of each of the three hungers unfolds in a unique way but yields a common quality of ease, clarity, and compassion, the fading of greed, hatred, and delusion yields potentials in the heart-mind that are more distinct. A look at the words the Buddha used to talk about these roots, and their opposites, will help us understand their operation, their fading, and the possibility of their complete absence.

The Buddha used the word *lobha* when he spoke of the root we know as greed, and for the corresponding wholesome root he used the word *alobha*. The "*a-*" is a negative prefix. Thus the Buddha did not refer to a positive quality but to the absence of the negative quality—so he referred to nongreed. This negative definition is efficient, easy to comprehend, and less prone to distortions than a positive definition. But it is also important for understanding our practice. It means that in the simple absence of greed—the absence of pulling and holding—wholesome thoughts will manifest in the mind. If one were to try to assess one's mind by, say, generosity, one might wonder, "Am I generous enough?" or "Is my generosity the right kind?" But if one's mind is simply known to be, in that moment, free of greed, this is enough. The rest, the manifestation of the wholesome, will depend upon circumstances.

Nongreed does not refer to a lifelong end of all greedy or lustful thoughts. This only refers to the present moment of mental activity, to presently arising thoughts and emotions. Naturally, the actions that emerge from this mental activity will be wholesome and reflect this quality of nongreed. But the mind is inconceivably quick, and in the very next moment thoughts may again be rooted in greed or aversion.

I have come to understand this moment of nongreed as a potential. The mind is completely free of pulling or holding to any object—any person, possession, information, anything at all. Thoughts will simply be free of selfish wanting. When this potential field is touched by the need of another being, this nongreedy potential manifests as the active force of generosity—*dana* in Pali. Generous thoughts and actions emerge naturally from the heart-mind that is free of the root of greed.

This can be easily illustrated by a thought experiment. We can begin by thinking about some object about which we feel greedy and possessive. It should be something we value but not something we consider indispensable to our happiness. Now perhaps we can imagine a situation in which this thing would be of no use to us, maybe even a burden. Perhaps we imagine we are headed to a monastery, to a tiny house, or to a foreign island to lead a blissfully simple and unadorned life. Now someone appears in our life who has a true need for exactly that object. If we give it to the person, he or she will be happier, safer, more at ease, more able to give to others, or whatever. Do we give it to the person? Remember, our greed has been unlocked by our changing circumstances. Does the gift now flow?

I have asked this question of countless people, and except when something too dear was originally selected, the universal answer is "Yes, I can joyfully give this to the person in need." This is the active principle of generosity arising naturally in the potential created by nongreed. As nongreed becomes more complete, we are able to freely give even that which is dear to us.

The effects of interpersonal nongreed are beautiful. In even the momentary absence of pulling and holding, relationships are steeped in generosity not only between two people but also within families and in communities. People give of themselves more easily. Jealousy and envy do not arise in the mind of nongreed, nor does manipulative behavior. People give each other freedom to be who they are, unconstrained by selfish desires. As moments of nongreed become more common, ease and generosity become the norm.

Nonaversion, *adosa,* is the wholesome root that corresponds with *dosa,* the root of aversion or hatred. The mind that is free from aversion generates, in that moment, thoughts and actions utterly lacking in pushing away, negative judgment, fear, or even a hint of dislike. There is simple and complete nonaversion. As with greed and generosity, the foundation is a definition by absence of the negative quality, not by the presence of a positive quality such as receptivity or kindness; again, this spareness of definition protects our practice from judgments or distortions.

A mind of nonaversion is in a state of great potential. The mind totally free from aversion, when touched by another, blossoms with the active principle of lovingkindness, or *metta*. We can best understand this if we consider the totality of nonaversion: the absolute absence of any pushing away of anything. This is not a permanent state, just a mind moment—a sliver of time from which the current thought blooms. For just this instant, no revulsion is operating. This is the place of the great potential of love, the heart-mind that receives all phenomena with unconditional acceptance. When such a field is touched by another, lovingkindness blossoms naturally. This is not an emotional or syrupy kindness or love. It is the natural and simple response of the receptive heart.

This contemplation may reveal how love arises naturally in the total absence of aversion: Begin by taking time to consider and cultivate pure and profound receptivity. A specific object may be helpful, such as the touch of clothing against your skin, or perhaps a tree or another neutral object. There is no need to focus on kindness, only the absence, in just this moment, of any resistance to receiving this object fully. We let the object touch an undefended awareness. Having established that, perhaps we can now think of someone with whom we have a mildly pleasant relationship. Can we allow this person to fully touch our heart, our awareness, with no recoiling or aversion, just as we did with the tree? If there is a fear of intimacy, we will now see the resistance this fear generates and how it has the quality of aversion. But if any and all pushing away is met with kindness and acceptance, the aversion, too, will dissolve. Now perhaps we can notice that when this field of complete acceptance and receptivity is touched by another, kindness spontaneously arises. This is the nature of the heart-mind without aversion: when it is touched, there is love. Love is the spontaneous response of the nonaversive heart. Put another way, awareness is inherently loving.

When moments of nonaversion arise in any relationship, ease and lovingkindness manifest. Even if the person we encounter in that moment has been an enemy, in the moment of nonaversion, the hatred or revulsion will not manifest. Relationships touched by nonaversion reflect harmony and joy. There is lightness, ease, and authenticity without fear. Moments of nonaversion and thoughts born of lovingkindness weave together into concordant, caring personal characteristics and behavior.

Nondelusion, or *amoha*, is the root that arises when the mind is free from foggy indifference. It will be easier to understand nondelusion if we recall the nature of delusion. Delusion, or *moha*, arises when the mind is not stimulated into a reaction of greed or hatred but is nevertheless locked in obsession and fear by the tidal tension of the hungers. There is also an element of delusion in all moments of greed and aversion, since the object of our pulling or rejecting mind is obscured by confusion and we do not clearly know the thing as it is nor our reactions to it as they are. The result of this cloudy tension is a quagmire of confused nonattention. People are ignored, words and actions are misinterpreted, and things go unnoticed; we ignore entire events, our own emotions, and the finer texture of experience. Thoughts that emerge from the root of delusion reflect this poor information intake, conditioned predictability, and haziness.

In the absence of indifference, dullness, and confusion, the mind is simply present for things as they are. A clear field is established wherein objects are what they are, people are who they are, and thoughts and actions emerge from this clarity. The mind entirely free of delusion is a field for the arising of the active quality of wisdom, or *pañña*. Wisdom is seeing things as they actually are in the present moment. As multiple moments of nondelusion arise, experience takes on the tone of lucidity. One easily discerns the nature of external situations and clearly knows and sees the nature of one's own mind.

To explore this, perhaps we can imagine or remember a moment in which we felt relaxed but alert, finely focused and attuned to our own thoughts and feelings as well as our environment. A time when we felt grounded and free from desire and fear. Perhaps we are in nature, perhaps we are simply awake and present with a friend. This is a moment in which we see and hear exceptionally clearly. Each sensation, each word our friend speaks, is received, fully experienced, and released. In the moment of nondelusion, we clearly perceive the other—person, tree, whatever—and from this readiness, this potential, the wisdom quality is activated in the mind. We clearly perceive the tree and our relation to it and to all of nature. The texture of our friend's humanity is clear to us. The knowing is complete, simple, and direct.

Interpersonal nondelusion, and its active expression as interpersonal wisdom, manifest in relationships as compassion, skillfulness, and perceptivity. The mind is, for the moment, unclouded and able to discern one's own and others' emotions and motivations. One sees oneself, others, and the social situation as they are. One is not lost in concepts and constructions. The actions, expressions, and decisions that issue in such moments tend to be caring but clear, loving and unattached, incisive yet kind, complete and still simple. As more moments of nondelusion arise, they weave together into a life of discernment and give rise to consistently wise speech and action. The heart-mind rests in nondelusion frequently enough that wisdom shifts from a temporary, almost accidental thing to a robust quality in our lives. Shared with others, interpersonal wisdom manifests as prudence, peace, and insight into the matters at hand.

It is not hard to see how fewer moments of greed, aversion, and delusion equate with more moments of nongreed, nonaversion, and nondelusion and how this, in turn, results in more moments of generosity, love, and wisdom. It is also easy to understand that a life with more such moments will be happier; there will be less suffering in ourselves and, as our behavior changes, in those around us. The mind is bright and free. It is also clear that a person who has developed these qualities will exhibit many of the desirable qualities associated with emotional and spiritual maturity: charity, benevolence, consideration, sympathy, humility, respect, good judgment, equanimity, poise, and presence. Such a person is not fashioning herself in the world. She stands in relationship with warmth and integrity, has a light footprint on the natural world, and evidences peace and a concern for all.

> When you encounter an act of generosity, whether your own action or another's, take a moment to reflect on the nonholding, the absence of grasping in it. Notice, too, the ease and joy.

> Reflect on the moments of nonaversion in your close relationships. Notice the times when you are feeling comfortable: not pushing away or holding back. Is kindness naturally present in these times?

> When have you been clear and skillful in relationship? Were you more or less energetic? More or less happy?

Ignorance and Freedom

Ignorance is another quality of the heart-mind we should consider as we seek to understand the third noble truth. Ignorance is the opacity of the mind as it believes and identifies with its own fabrications. The Buddha taught that ignorance gives rise to constructs like memories, ideas, emotions, personal tendencies, and moods and that these constructs in turn give birth to the self. Ignorance is the unknowing with which we inhabit these outpourings and mistake them for reality. This is what the Buddha referred to as "the conceit of *I am*."[2] Ignorance is as foundational as hunger to sustaining suffering. Buddhaghosa, a Buddhist commentator who lived sixteen hundred years ago, said, "Sorrow, pain, grief and despair are inseparable from ignorance, and lamentation is the norm for the deluded being. For that reason, when sorrow is fully manifest, so also is ignorance fully manifest."[3]

Clearly, then, the fading of ignorance brings with it the fading of suffering. Also, it is clear that hunger and ignorance are related. Hunger sustains ignorance. It is a force that keeps us tense, off balance, and unclear; it is the fuel of the construction process. As hunger fades, we relax, gain balance, and see things as they are; constructions diminish. Ignorance is, at base, ignorance of suffering, its cause, and its cessation; ignorance underpins the blindness in which we believe that lasting satisfaction of our yearnings is possible, and our credence in a self who is hurting and yearning. In other words, ignorance sustains hunger.

Identification born of ignorance is a source of grief, and its fading a move toward freedom, as I learned in the days following the death of my only daughter, Ona. She had been congested; her doctor failed to notice her swollen ankles and pale complexion. She was a cherubic child, and we, too, were slow to appreciate the extent of her listlessness. A trip to another physician led to a rush to the hospital; Ona died that night. Her heart had a hole in it and could not keep up with the increased burden of pneumonia.

Days and nights followed in a blur of emotion. Relatives wept with us, visitors came and went, sleep was elusive. The pain made a home in my body and lived there. I had never known such grief. Yet, sometimes, I was able to experience this grief in a nonidentified way, noticing feelings rise and fall, as I did in meditation. And I began to detect a pattern. Whenever a telephone call came—yet another person expressing sympathy—my grief erupted anew. Emotion welled up from my belly through my heart, my head flushed with sensation, my eyes filled with tears.

Watching this time and again, I saw how, at the moment of contact with the caller, an image formed in my mind: the father who lost his child. Instead of experiencing the shifting emotions of the moment—now sadness, now disbelief, now compassion for my wife—I inhabited the image of someone overwhelmed with grief. I identified with that fabricated image, stepped into it as if boarding a train, and became overwhelmed.

The immediate suffering was compounded, distorted, and amplified. Knowing this was freeing. Once I discovered this pattern, I was able to watch the train come into the station but not board it. I still felt grief: Ona was of my heart; her absence was confusing and painful. But when I stopped stepping into the mental-emotional construction of "the grieving father," that pain became less sharp and turbulent because it was not proliferated into a "second arrow" of suffering.

Hunger and ignorance work together, they lean on each other, run circles around each other. Each is involved in the conditions that sustain the other. Together they are powerful supports for suffering. We looked at the fading of hunger and the natural emergence of ease. As ignorance fades, wisdom arises. Personal wisdom is knowing suffering, impermanence, and nonself. Interpersonal wisdom is exactly the same but refers to knowing the manifestations of suffering in relation to other people, the impermanence of our interactions with them, and the insubstantiality of the socially constructed self.

So far we have talked about fading; now it is time to talk about cessation. There are moments when ignorance simply does not manifest. Such moments can be subtle or exceedingly luminous. Sometimes belief systems dissolve; sometimes they just crack open a little. For this reason we are pushed to go beyond the fading of hunger and ignorance to contemplate full cessation, the absence of ignorance. Before we do so, however, we must take a look at why many of us resist any talk of freedom.

The personal and interpersonal paths to peace share a dilemma: both are misunderstood and derided by people ensconced in the life of tension, because both are contrary to the culture of excitement. People lust for sensual pleasure, be it in delicious food or exquisite scenery, and hold their desires in high esteem. Hunger and its occasional satisfaction are seen as the essential value in life. We lust for interpersonal pleasures, pursuing hunger-based relationships, remaining ignorant of the stress inherent in the incessant search for pleasure. Because we are unacquainted with the harmlessness and joy in the heart that is free, the path of cessation is often viewed as life denying, empty, repellant. Occasionally the criticism is made that only people afraid of their bodies, and of sensuality and emotion, would follow the path toward the cessation of hungers.

In this way the ignorant mind protects itself. This mind does, indeed, have something to lose. The Buddha was asked about this fear of cessation; you can almost see him rubbing his chin and grinning as he answered:

"Venerable Sir, can there be agitation about what is nonexistent internally?"

"There can be, bhikkhu [monk]," the Blessed One said. "Here, bhikkhu, someone has the view, 'that which is the self is the world'; . . . [He hears the teaching] for the elimination of all standpoints . . . for the relinquishing of all attachments . . . for cessation [and] thinks thus: 'So I shall be annihilated! So I shall perish! So I shall be no more!' Then he sorrows, grieves and laments."[4]

Just as we cling to a personal self, we cling to a social self. As long as we believe in our social identity and seek to rest in a solid self fabricated by our interpersonal relationships, we will fear the loss of this self. As one meditator put it, "As I had the insights that I am not my stories and I am not my roles, I became confused and anxious; if I am not these things, who *am* I?" We devote all of our resources to feeding and defending the concept called the self, believing we are defending life itself. We may enjoy the idea of freedom from interpersonal and social suffering but recoil from letting go of our hard-won social identities. Who am I if not the parent, child, teacher, friend, American, Christian, Buddhist, Latino, nature lover?

These identities are based on the hungers; they are locked into place by ignorance. In the hunger for interpersonal pleasure, we find self-definition in the ways we are pleased and who pleases us and by how we avoid loneliness by pleasing others. "Do I find that person handsome? Does he find me beautiful?" "I'm a sports fan, and when I'm with others like me, I don't feel lonely." In the hunger to be seen we define ourselves by how we become visible—by whose attention we draw and how we draw it. "I am an artist, a great parent, a dutiful child, a hard worker, a collector of unique glassware, president of the arts council, a good person." In the hunger not to be seen, we find identity in our fear and inadequacy. We merge with our cocoon, identify with our armor; that armor becomes "me." "I am an introvert." "I am a drug addict and twelve-stepper." "I am fragile and easily hurt." Self-concept, unrecognized, can easily lead to pain and to self-centered thoughts and behavior; self-centered behavior spreads our suffering to others.

Our identities are concepts, impermanent by nature. Such concepts are clearly known in the cessation of ignorance. One does not enhance the happiness or compassion of the "I"; instead one sees through the "I" concept entirely. The Buddha said, "The tides of conceiving do not sweep over one who stands upon these foundations [of wisdom, truth, relinquishment, and peace]."[5] In the moment when conceiving stops—especially self-conceiving—we are freed from the selfish hungers, because we are freed from the constructed self-concept that sustains them. In this moment we are freed from what practitioners of Ordinary Mind Zen call "the self-centered dream." This freedom is possible. Indeed, if we are attentive, we will notice that freedom visits us each time the mind relaxes out of self-sustaining tensions.

These specks of liberation multiply and link together as understanding grows. This is the alchemy of nonclinging. Sometimes, too, there is an avalanche of awakening, which may be sustained by the steadiness of mind engendered by meditation. In the moment of liberation, we cease to cling to an imagined stability or security in what is always changing. We cease our quest for pleasure in what is painful and for an enduring identity in the flux of personal and social fabrications. In the absence of clinging, something wonderful is possible.

> Bhikkhus, when ignorance is abandoned and true knowledge has arisen in a bhikkhu, then, with the fading away of ignorance and the arising of true knowledge he no longer clings to sensual pleasures, no longer clings to views, no longer clings to rules and observances, no longer clings to a doctrine of self. When he does not cling, he is not agitated. When he is not agitated, he personally attains Nirvana. He understands: "Birth is destroyed, the holy life has been lived, what had to be done has been done, there is no more coming to any state of being."[6]

Beyond the hungers and ignorance is a very high happiness. The self is no longer birthed, in this life or in others. More simply, we cease to believe in the dream of "me" that the mind continually weaves. In this joy, rapture and equanimity conjoin. Wisdom vanquishes constructed identities, which liberates generosity and love from the anchors of self. There is acceptance without greed, discernment without rejection, and stability without the illusion of permanence. This is an ongoing moment in life's process that the Buddha described as "beyond reasoning" and "sorrowless" and "the stilling of the conditioned—bliss."[7] Nirvana is also called the deathless. It is what my teacher Ananda Maitreya simply referred to as coolness. Thanissaro Bhikkhu, an American Buddhist monk and translator, refers to nirvana as unbinding.

It is tempting, almost unavoidable, to idealize this unbinding. We take it to be unhuman, almost sterile in its purity. But logic and the very earthy stories of the Buddha's later years tell us otherwise. Even when ignorance has vanished as a dominating force in our lives, we still have bodies, and they still defecate, age, and hurt. We still engage in relationships, and it is still complex. The body still hungers, and the mind still constructs. The key difference is that we do not react to the hungers of the body and heart, and we do not believe the constructs of the mind. We remain human— just not ignorant.

Unbinding is a process of transformation. While there may be a state of being unbound, it is the process of unbinding that is most obviously relevant to our lives. Interpersonally, the stilling of the conditioned includes, but is not limited to, the quieting of relational desire and fear. Personal and relational desire and fear naturally diminish in tandem, because the personal and social self are intertwined. When we are no longer concerned with upholding self-identity, there can be no concern for the death of any given social identity. This cooling is why it is sorrowless— but there is more to it than that. When we are with others and not constructing a self, the heart is poised and balanced. Because there is no reaching out or retreating inward, it is not surprising or frightening that conditioned, fabricated boundaries of the self have vanished. The natural wisdom of the heart-mind is realized.

This interpersonal wisdom is compassion. It is sympathetic joy. We dwell in the paradox of selfless intimacy. We are the sea and the sky, sharing blueness and a horizon, partaking of the same empty spaciousness. It does not bother us that this state is impermanent. The next moment, like this one, is met with equanimity.

Spend some time noticing impermanence, suffering, and nonself. Try this anytime—even right now—but also try it sometime when you are with other people. Look at simple things: moving bodies (as impermanence), the coming and going of small discomforts (as suffering), the way conditioned thoughts are triggered and unfold automatically (as indications of nonself). Stay with this contemplation awhile, or work separately with each of the three parts. Do you begin to see these qualities spontaneously, or do habitual responses take over?

Cessation and the Happiness
of the Unintoxicated Life

What are we to make of all this fading and cessation? The fading of the hungers yields benefits we can relate to immediately, such as less pain and more ease, while the cessation of ignorance challenges what we are willing to believe or are even able to understand. As one meditator reflected on releasing the "I" construct: "I'm not here, you're not here—but I'm just not there yet." Does releasing the self sense imply some idealized freedom that we should strive for? Are we feeding grasping and setting ourselves up for almost certain failure by focusing on accomplishment? Or is there a middle way available to us, neither an idealized social nirvana nor a denial of the human capacity for the profound ease of release?

Ease encompasses the relinquishment of selfish wanting, aversion, and delusion. We release the endless search for lasting sensual pleasure, abandon anger and resentment, and drop the inattentive torpor and accumulated conceptual scum that obstruct our seeing things as they are. In his teachings on the Four Noble Truths, the Buddha spoke only of fading, relinquishment, and cessation; he did not say there is anything to get. There is no mention of attainment, accomplishment, or self-improvement. In these most basic teachings, there is no mention of nirvana; there is only the cessation of hunger. The only attainment is that of letting go, of the stillness of the unseeking heart. While each hunger has a different manifestation and feeling tone, the happiness and compassion of freedom have one taste. And whether or not one believes freedom is possible, each step in the direction of less hunger brings goodness in the very moment that step is taken.

Letting go of interpersonal hunger is not a trivial undertaking. We are challenged by its everyday manifestations, like the lack of self-confidence or the tendency to pride. How much more challenging is the complete freedom suggested by the Buddha when he says, "This is peaceful, this is sublime, that is the stilling of all formations, the relinquishment of all attachments, the destruction of craving, dispassion, cessation, Nibbana."[8] As we apply this teaching to our interpersonal lives, we must be careful not to imagine an idealized social nirvana that ignores and denies the inevitable complexities of human relationships. When two or more are gathered, there may be something divine, as Jesus suggested, but it is also true that when two or more are gathered there are also two or more opinions, two or more sets of needs; the opportunities for difficulty increase exponentially.

Relational ease is possible, but there are problems in seeking a state, a heaven, a selfish bliss. We can still contemplate the cessation of interpersonal hunger, however, perhaps also considering the ending, or at least diminishment, of the gnawing pain and confusion in our relational and social lives. And we can recall the simplicity of turning toward wakefulness.

When I was teaching about the three hungers at an Insight Dialogue retreat, one participant asked, "A lot of my work is helping people learn to fill their social needs without getting in their own way. How do these hungers relate to needs that are normal and healthy?" As a therapist, he had worked with many people unable to see themselves as lovable, unable to seek or give emotional gratification. In such a context, hoping for "normal" is quite reasonable, even if normal means a more or less constant state of tension and dependency. One of Freud's best insights was that there is a level of neurosis shared by nearly everyone that can be called normal. This is the mental aspect of suffering the Buddha talked about, at the level most of us experience it. Freud understood his work as helping clients leave behind unusual and disabling levels of neurosis and attain to the "ordinary suffering" shared by most people. Many of the schools of Western psychology, whether Freudian or not, have taken something like this as their goal and have developed helpful strategies to accomplish it. But such ordinary unhappiness is not the whole story. We can aspire to something beyond a more efficient way of managing our cravings, beyond a less conflicted path to filling our hungers. A deeper, steadier happiness is possible. If we acknowledge this and gain some experience of such happiness, our whole view of life changes—and with it, the aspirations behind our interpersonal encounters also change.

This higher happiness is said to come from the cessation of hunger. But doesn't cessation imply nothingness? Experience tells us otherwise. As I was coming to understand the interpersonal manifestations of the three hungers, I looked for them in all types of social encounters. My observations confirmed that the hungers are ubiquitous. But something troubled me. Is the human condition nothing but the greedy, needy interplay of interdependent selfish desires? When I looked around me with this new question, I saw that it was not so: the world was awash in goodness, too. At the same time, I trusted my observation that these hungers were at work. What was going on here? How could there be so much goodness and joy when we are driven so incessantly by these longings?

I began to look for love and compassion in the same situations where I was seeing selfish desire and fear. To my surprise and delight, I saw bits of compassion everywhere. In the small talk of family and friends, I saw that discussing movies and families was both mutual tickling and generous sharing of information and attention. In the exchange of workplace anecdotes between friends, I saw both trivial distraction and genuine compassion. When one sports fan says to another, "Our team won by seven points," he is engaging in the dance of mutual acknowledgment—making a bid to be seen but also offering his buddy the kindness of saying, "I see you." In each response to the same underlying loneliness, selfish and altruistic elements were both present.

This ubiquitous caring is based upon a deep, natural empathy. The same empathy makes us wince when we see a photo of a torture victim. It even crosses species: we feel tension and sadness upon seeing a starving animal. We unconsciously seek relief from another's pain because it will relieve our pain. That is, for our own happiness, we seek the happiness of others. Caring for others not only brings happiness, it aids survival. Early humans needed empathy and cooperation to survive in the face of superior predators. In evolutionary terms, compassion is adaptive: it is as primal as our urge to compete.

It became clear to me that each moment of interpersonal contact is infused with both selfish and altruistic desire—with hunger and with love. When I saw this, I understood an important dynamic of personal transformation. I knew from experience that whenever my hungers diminished, love and compassion appeared. When I realized how love and hunger are intermingled, I understood why this is so. Since both are usually present, whenever one is attenuated, the other becomes more prominent. Imagine a jar of muddy water—if you let it settle and then remove the silt, what remains is clear. It is that simple: when hungers diminish, love remains.

Each of us is, I realized, a casserole of hunger and love, bubbling and complex. I began to see this mixture everywhere in my life. On retreats, where people are working diligently to calm down and release habits of hunger, the dynamic of less hunger yielding more love and compassion shows up reliably, crisp and strong in the clear light of mindfulness. I see it in everyday life. As our latent wholesome tendencies outweigh the unwholesome, our behavior changes. Small talk—chatter to hide our fears, a kind of whistling in the dark—transforms into tiny expressions of kindness and care. Meanwhile, the stronger movements within us of compassion—the caring social worker, dedicated healer, generous teacher—are purified of selfish motives and imbued with ever more powerful purpose. This is exactly what I was hearing about from people at my retreats and from the letters and e-mails of people who were integrating the principles of Insight Dialogue into their lives. They were not only happier but also more caring and kind.

Something very beautiful happens as self-centered longings diminish. Because the happiness of others brings us joy, seeking this joy becomes a way of life. The original selfishness of the sympathetic response—"I just can't stand to witness your pain"—transforms into "For your sake, not for my own, I want you to be happy." Compassion alerts us to suffering, and we resonate with sympathetic joy when another's suffering ends. Compassion and joy create a virtuous cycle that promotes our finest relational qualities: lovingkindness, compassion, sympathetic joy, and equanimity.

When the clear mind witnesses suffering, caring arises. Love, anchored in caring, becomes purified of self. Love purified of self does not constrain. Without hunger, love emerges naturally as availability to experience. Undefended and unshrinking, open to being touched by others, the loving heart is close to the world. This is not the intimacy of selfish need but the intimacy of unfettered awareness.

When this sensitive being is touched by another's pain, compassion arises. Like love, compassion does not bind. We resonate with the pain of others because of our simple availability to experience, an availability formerly hidden beneath a blanket of hungers. Compassion is free of self-reference, and in this lies its accuracy and its power.

This sensitive being is also touched by others' joy. When selfish hungers encounter the good fortune of others, envy and coveting arise. When hungers diminish, appreciation and generosity shine through. When I am free from concern about what I have or lack, I can be happy for what you have, happy for your accomplishments and your joys. Unfettered by fear, I can express this joy to you, and we can be happy together—and awake.

As the hungers fade and these qualities grow, the notion of me and mine also fades. Boundaries are recognized but not clung to; they are simply perceptions. This vision combines with the latent capacity for love, compassion, and joy, to produce affinity, or (to use and extend Thich Nhat Hanh's word) *inter-being*. Inter-being is not experienced as an idea or even as an emotion but as a characteristic of the flux of life. Pain comes and goes, our own and everyone else's. Our own joy, and the joy of all other people, comes and goes. We remain present and open to this, but we rest in equanimity. The heart is poised, balanced, and open; because it is open, commonality, communality, arises. That is all. One meditator was quite surprised at the way her heart opened in Insight Dialogue. She said, "It is not love or compassion as I have previously understood them. It feels like heart opening that has elements of both interpenetration and emptiness— beyond the person, yet distinctly in and of form." Her words capture the exquisite juxtaposition of the personal, embodied experience of love and the impersonal experience of unattached awareness. Fleshiness and emptiness in the same moment.

Can we hold all of our potential in consciousness, not denying the conditioned and constructed, not denying the unbound? We are conditioned beings; while this conditioning is the nexus, the domain of our humanity, untethered awareness is also available to us. Such awareness offers habitmind no landing pad; it is as tangible as the softness of a baby's fontanel or the calloused hardness of aged feet.

We come full circle here. We see that freedom from interpersonal hunger, and from the interpersonal suffering it creates, is interwoven with letting go personally. Interpersonal and personal wisdom are not two. This is the pivot point of personal and interpersonal, individual and social. Personal wisdom knows things as they are in the barest way: all forms are changing and empty. When wisdom encounters others, it manifests as compassion. Interpersonal wisdom is compassion, together with unshakably knowing the empty nature of social self-concept. One who has cultivated these qualities is naturally inclined to generosity, empathy, justice, and community and to seeing things clearly, with balance, curiosity, ease, and joy. Unlike the pleasure that comes from satisfying selfish hungers, the joy based upon letting go lingers, infusing one's life with easy and warm happiness. Just as happy people are more likely to be kind, kind people are more likely to be happy.

So far we have been exploring our common, human predicament: pain, hunger, and the dawning of freedom. The next logical questions are: How do we actually live into this full human potential? How do we learn to let go, so that love and compassion can manifest? How do we come to see things as they are, without the distortions caused by grasping? There is a great deal we already know that holds answers for us. There is much that we already do, every day, that is wholesome and generous. If we observe carefully, we will see our acts of kindness, flashes of altruism, right next to thoughts and actions rooted in selfishness. We will notice how compassion is intertwined with aversion or fear. When we encounter our friends or intimate relations, we may become aware of the commingling of selflessness and self-centeredness and of how often we choose to give.

Our experiences of generosity and kindness are landmarks on the path to the cessation of interpersonal hunger. These moments—thousands of little moments—point to a life beyond hunger. The path to compassion and freedom is wide. This path is based on our inherent capacity and urge to awaken; it is walked alone and with others, in our ordinary lives and in extraordinary dedicated practice.

> Sitting in a busy public place, watch the people around you as they relate to each other. Notice the ways friends, or even strangers, seek and offer acknowledgment.

> Make the effort to find the goodness in yourself that is interwoven with the normal hungers. Notice how kindness and generosity coexist with self-oriented motivations such as wanting to be seen or wanting to hide.

> Reflect on the good fortune of someone you are fond of. Allow yourself to feel the joy inherent in this reflection. Do you notice the mind being more awake as your joy increases?

7

THE FOURTH NOBLE TRUTH

The Full-Spectrum Path

The Nature of the Eightfold Path

A clear and powerful picture of the human condition arises when we see the roots of human suffering in unsatisfiable hungers. Pain and peace, grasping and freedom, arise dependent upon the mind. The mind's thoughts and emotions take form dependent upon what we do and how we live. The imaginings of the heart-mind determine actions, actions influence thoughts and emotions, thoughts and emotions result in further actions—and on the cycle goes. This is a poignant picture of the human condition. The universality of unnecessary hurt, and of our compassionate response, binds us together.

When grasping lessens we open naturally to compassion. But the question remains: Knowing this principle, what can we *do*? What specific actions, what lifestyle, would really put to use the power of this understanding? How can we diminish the reactive cycles of pain in the full spectrum of our lives—alone and with each other—and dwell in compassion and freedom?

This understanding of human causality points us in the direction of relief. We may not be able to stop aging and death, but we can release the grasping that makes these experiences so painful for most of us. And this is as true with respect to interpersonal pains and conflicts as it is with all other forms of hunger and grasping.

The Buddha recognized that specific actions and conditions were needed to turn the possibility of freedom into an actuality, and he described them clearly in his fundamental teaching he called the Noble Eightfold

Path, a path common to all schools of Buddhism that is also attractive to non-Buddhists. His "noble" path addresses the whole of our lives, from our everyday actions to the most refined meditative practices.

> And what, friends, is the noble truth of the way leading to the cessation of suffering? It is just this Noble Eightfold Path; that is, Right View, Right Intention, Right Speech, Right Action, Right Livelihood, Right Effort, Right Mindfulness, and Right Concentration.[1]

The word translated as "right" does not imply a judgment about who or what is good and who is bad in any absolute or moralistic sense. The statement is about the road to freedom—about the power of cause and effect. Will a certain action, way of communicating, or quality of mind lead toward the cessation of suffering? If so, it is "correct" or "right"— meaning that the action, view, speech, or other aspect of life is effective and efficient in moving us toward freedom.

Mind and behavior always affect each other; a person cannot cultivate goodness in one without the other. The individual factors of this eightfold path are of limited use in isolation: they work together. This spectrum of factors, specified by the Buddha as effective, derives from the way sentient beings actually function. Because of this, I call it the human path. It emerges from just being human.

Any factor of the Noble Eightfold Path can be practiced at any time, but because the mutual influences of mind and actions cycle through our lives, the path also specifies methods that are cyclic. The eight factors of the human path begin with the mind. Right View begins with an understanding of cause and effect. Until we see that certain actions lead to harm for ourselves and others, it is not possible to align any part of our life with the process of awakening. Right View yields an inclination of the mind: Right Intention. When the mind is inclined a certain way—toward kindness, compassion, and release—the natural results are specific behaviors: Right Speech and Right Action, and a pattern of behavior, Right Living. These three domains of action reflect our mind state. The refinement of our outward lives prepares us for more thorough mental training—Right Effort, which is the basis for the clarity of Right Mindfulness. Right Mindfulness, then, supports the steadiness necessary to discern more deeply the nature of things, which is Right Calm Concentration. This new steadiness and mindfulness help us see more clearly how things really are—and the path cycles back to Right View, which is now understood as also encompassing the nature of suffering, its cause, and its cessation. Walking this path we spiral steadily toward deeper morality, tranquillity, and wisdom. This simple teaching has been useful to people for millennia because it so beautifully follows the contours of the heart. It is usable and useful because it fits our lives.

One Path: Personal and Interpersonal

Traditionally the Noble Eightfold Path has been interpreted most fully with reference to personal life and personal practice. The path elements have been thought about and practiced primarily as individuals' solo endeavors to grow in the eight areas described by the Buddha. But our lives are not just individual: they are also relational. People live and work together; they suffer together and profoundly affect one another's mind states, suffering or free.

While not developed as explicitly, it has been generally assumed that the Buddha's path encompasses our interpersonal lives as well as our individual efforts. Any other conclusion—for example "I cultivate wisdom only when I am alone"—is obviously absurd. Monastics live in communities dedicated to awakening; the monastic context supports both individual and communal practice. In cultures steeped in Buddhism, people share innumerable gestures of mindfulness and compassion tacitly referenced to these teachings. But most Westerners have been left to their own devices when it comes to the active and communal aspects of the Eightfold Path. The situation in the West has been made even more difficult because the higher trainings in Right Effort, Mindfulness, and Concentration have been plucked from their wider context of engaged morality. People are taught meditation techniques and calm down some as a result, but the ethical or lifestyle path factors—the elements that could help them address their stress-filled and hungry lives and lay a foundation for steadier calmness—are not always taught. This can yield unfortunate results, such as isolation and the neglect of interpersonal and social maturity. Many experience the path as without the energy born of mutual support, bereft of relatedness. And even fewer teachings have explored interpersonal meditative practices. Because human beings are so deeply relational, it would be wise to understand the path as both individual and relational if we desire a practice that can impact the whole of our lives.

When we understand the path as including the relational and interpersonal aspects of life, many more opportunities and modalities of practice are possible. We see that personal suffering is most directly addressed by personal practices, while interpersonal suffering is most directly addressed by interpersonal practices.

Personal practice is practice done within the person (intrapersonally). It helps free us from personal pain; this is what it does best and most directly. It also contributes naturally to freedom from pain that arises in relation to others. Meditators often relate how individual, silent meditation has helped them to calm down, to observe their emotions with less attachment, not to believe their own reactive stories so fully. As a result they are more present with and more compassionate toward other people. Some interpersonal fruits should be evident from personal practice. Buddhadasa, a beloved twentieth-century Thai Buddhist teacher, expressed the relationship of personal meditation to our interpersonal lives: "If we are learning anything from our meditation practice, then it reveals itself in our relationships with other people."

Interpersonal practice is practice done with other people. It helps free us from interpersonal pain. The help it offers is very direct. Karmic knots that were tied interpersonally can efficiently be untied in the same way: interpersonally. One participant in Insight Dialogue described how she cast her male Insight Dialogue partner in what she called a "teacher" role and then began reacting to that role by feeling disempowered. After a stressful start, she found the courage to express these reactions to her partner. When they were met with compassion, her embarrassment gave way to relief, and she began to feel compassion for herself. This was a significant change from her habits and brought ease and new possibility. It is unlikely that this pattern of relating, and its underlying hunger to be, would have arisen so clearly in traditional solitary meditation, and it is unlikely that it would have worked itself out so elegantly. Interpersonal practice provided an efficient and effective context for working with these formations. Simple changes like this have a direct impact on the tenor of our lives: clearer awareness, greater calm, and less clinging.

The Buddha pointed to the importance of the interpersonal realm when he responded to Ananda's exclamation: "Venerable sir, this is half of the holy life, that is, good friendship, good companionship, good comradeship."

Not so, Ananda! Not so, Ananda! This is the entire holy life, Ananda, that is, good friendship, good companionship, good comradeship. When a bhikkhu has a good friend, a good companion, a good comrade, it is to be expected that he will develop and cultivate the Noble Eightfold Path.[2]

In other discourses the Buddha explained why good friends are so important. For example, he said, "Friend, there are two conditions for the arising of Right View: the voice of another and wise attention."[3] Since Right View is understood to be the foundation of the path, this advice places a very high value on wise interpersonal contact.

Many psychologists also recognize the importance of addressing interpersonal pain in a relational context. Indeed, research has found that certain qualities of the therapeutic relationship are related to positive outcomes independent of the type of treatment. In other words, relationship itself can be more important than technique. One therapist attending an Insight Dialogue meditation retreat saw that many participants assumed all their feelings were exclusively personal and inward and so treated those feelings as if they had nothing to do with the others present—thus missing many opportunities for contact, intimacy, and the release of old relational patterns. He brought a subtle knowledge that people's inner world is multilayered and takes form in relationship with the world of others.

Of course, relations between people can be understood from the standpoint of the individuals relating. For example: I see a form; it is another human; there is recognition of this person; the mind proliferates with thoughts. I hear the words this person speaks; there are conceptual and emotional reactions; the mind proliferates from there. From this perspective—which is a valuable one—the interpersonal path is entirely subsumed by the personal path.

But we are also complex social beings. Our identities took form in relation to other people. Once formed, these identities are constantly reinforced and reworked in relationships and social systems. Our hungers also arise and change shape based on interpersonal contact.

Because of the subtlety and complexity of interpersonal exchange, it is important to clarify how the spiritual path can unfold interpersonally. For many years I practiced traditional vipassana, particularly as taught to me by my Thai teacher, Achan Sobin Namto. As a result of this intrapersonal practice, my conditioned interpersonal reactions were being softened, but only slowly. As I sat in silent retreat, I learned to recognize some of the stress and confusion in my wandering thoughts; this helped foster some clarity later, when I was with others. But these changes were small and indirect.

When I began engaging in interpersonal practice and developing online Insight Dialogue with my PhD colleague, Terri O'Fallon, and again when I began teaching that practice to groups, I became aware of different issues. I noticed an urge to entertain or impress people and to fill the hole of a loneliness that I hadn't realized was present. Engagement with others, in the light of meditative awareness, brought up these issues—issues that had originally taken form in relation to others. With the support of both personal and interpersonal meditation, I maintained loving awareness of the thoughts and emotions of these interpersonal hungers. As a result, these hungers have softened, become familiar, and significantly diminished. If I had continued with only personal, individual meditation practice, I doubt that this transformation would have unfolded so quickly or so deeply

Traditionally formal meditation is done more or less alone. One may be in a room full of meditators, but there is little interaction or cooperation beyond the contact required by sharing a space, food, and so on. The energetic support of meditating in the presence of others can be surprisingly powerful, but this power emerges naturally and is usually not intentionally fostered. All the instructions are couched in intrapersonal terms: "Observe the breath. If thoughts arise, let them go. If you hear sounds, notice the hearing and come back to the breath." Or perhaps: "Let the mind rest in spacious awareness. Allow any thoughts that arise to self-liberate." Implicit in both instructions is the guidance "Do not engage with others." This means, for example, that if people bother you by moving or coughing, you might notice the unpleasant experience of being bothered, but you should not relate to those people in any explicit way. Instructions from many traditions—such as visualizing deities, staring softly at a wall, praying, or walking in nature—share this intrapersonal orientation. Such practices are what most people imagine when they think of meditation or spiritual disciplines. Individual practices are important and can be immensely transformative, but they directly address only a portion of life's dilemmas.

Sometimes we may engage in an interpersonal practice that is unilateral rather than mutual. For example, while interacting with other people in daily life, one might observe one's own mind, notice emotions that arise, and relax oneself without the others' explicit engagement with one's practice or even their knowledge of it. One may practice Right Mindfulness in interaction with family members, coworkers, or strangers. The other people need not be practicing in any similar way or even know what we are doing. A woman comes to mind who was able to bring her interpersonal mindfulness practice into her relationship with her rather distant husband. He may not have noticed a difference, but she felt more warmth and compassion as a result. In such unilateral interpersonal practice, people don't refer to the practice, share their individual observations, or support each other in the practice as such. We may be with others, but each individual is on his or her own. Unilateral interpersonal practice is not limited to mindfulness; it can include care for one's spoken interactions (Right Speech) and for the basic morality of one's behavior (Right Action). In unilateral interpersonal practice, one person brings a meditative attitude to his or her interactions with others without the others' necessarily sharing or even knowing about the practice.

Interpersonal practice shows its character most fully, however, when people interact with each other as part of the practice, with the explicitly shared intention of cultivating the path by means of their interactions. Mutual interpersonal practice goes beyond unilateral efforts in relation to others, beyond even parallel but unconnected efforts with others who may share the same or similar meditative intention. Interaction and mutual support are at the heart of mutual interpersonal practice. Quakers and others use the word *corporate* to refer to the mutual dimension of interpersonal practice—invoking an image of an interdependent whole almost like an organism or body. Independent experience is acknowledged and valued, but the challenges and benefits of mutual practice are paramount. In addition to myriad forms of mutual support, interpersonal practice offers the opportunity to tap the widely recognized, if difficult to explain, power inherent in group meditation. Interpersonal spiritual practices include interactive group meditation, collective contemplative practices, and moral action with and in relationship to others.

The cultivation of Right Mindfulness in our interactions with other people, for example, is interpersonal practice, but it can be unilateral or mutual. Even if one's companions are simultaneously but separately engaged in similar practices, the character of the practice is unilateral because its shared nature is not explicit and there is no intention to offer mutual support for the practice. In mutual interpersonal practice, the intention to practice interpersonally and meditatively is made explicit. Participants acknowledge that they are supporting each other's mindfulness; in both actions and words, they remind each other to wake up to this moment's experience. The effort is mutual and collaborative.

The collaborative element in mutual interpersonal practice can range from gentle reminders to the opening up of new perspectives about what it means to be in relationship. Cheri, who attended a weekly Insight Dialogue group in New Zealand, shared this: "I've come to see my relations with others as an indicator of whether or not I am at peace within. When I am with others, I can't hide so easily behind my own distractions; they are mirrored back to me in a feeling of distance. When I am at peace inside, I naturally feel close to others." Sometimes meditators experience the sense of separation between speaker and listener as diminished or even dissolved; sharing or creating a joint present moment, they glimpse a reality beyond the me-you, subject-object split. Such experience, not uncommon at Insight Dialogue retreats, is rare in most people's personal meditation. The feedback loop—in which two or more people support and amplify each other's mindfulness and concentration—is one of the great benefits of interpersonal practice.

Thus, mutual interpersonal meditation can enable insights that may be difficult to access through personal meditation or even through unilateral interpersonal meditation—where the support of others is nonexistent or less direct. Interpersonal meditation, especially in its mutual forms, also directly supports insight into the interpersonal forms of suffering and hunger and thus facilitates interpersonal unbinding. Practicing with others is also a powerful way to cultivate a living compassion, freed from any abstraction of "practice." Intuition and reason both point compellingly to the need for and potential of explicitly interpersonal meditation.

What are the personal components—practices, study, reflection—of your path of awakening? What are the interpersonal components? Where have you experienced fully interactive mutual support on your path of unbinding?

Ordinary and Extraordinary Manifestations of the Path

Some forms of practice are integrated fully with our ordinary lives, while other forms are undertaken in special times and places and with a heightened sense of dedication. This distinction cuts across the full range of possible practices in a way different from the distinction between personal and interpersonal practice. I call the practices that are fully integrated into our lives *ordinary* practices, and the practices that occur under special circumstances or with heightened understanding and dedication *extraordinary* practices.

For many years I practiced formal meditation at home and on retreat and tried to integrate these practices into my daily life. No matter what I did, there was a huge chasm between the two. I would return home from a retreat where I had experienced great calm, even bliss, and become tense and unhappy. After a mindfulness retreat meditation session, I would try to be mindful at home, only to find myself as preoccupied as ever. My life was, indeed, affected powerfully and positively by formal meditation. I could speak about meditation and life being one—that they could be and should be one—but I was clearly lacking the experience of this unity.

Since things were not working as I had hoped—and been led to believe—they would, I began to rethink the whole matter. Rather than continuing to focus on integrating the two, I decided to explore what I could learn if I acknowledged that there were times of special practice and times of regular living and that these two were different. Clarifying the differences between ordinary and extraordinary practice, it turns out, made it possible to clarify the relationships between the two. Ultimately this helped me arrive at a truly integrated sense of the path. I came to see how the full eightfold path is contained in each and how ordinary and extraordinary experiences work together in our lives to bring about significant and lasting change.

Two principal factors distinguish ordinary and extraordinary practice: usualness and mind state. Usualness can be understood by common sense. One can simply ask, "Is this activity a usual part of everyday life? Is this part of my normal activity, like talking to a friend, going to the store, or taking a walk?" If so, this is ordinary practice. If what I am doing is specifically or even exclusively undertaken to cultivate the path, it is extraordinary practice. By the criterion of usualness, the most notable feature of extraordinary practice is that it is done in time taken out of the flow of one's ordinary activities. It may be at a time set by the clock (such as 6:00 A.M.) or a time set by other considerations (for instance, as soon as the children are on the bus), but it is time dedicated to practice, not serving another purpose. In many instances it is also done in a special place, such as in a meditation hall or on a cushion. In this sense, extraordinary practice is formal practice. Examples of extraordinary practice include silent meditation, deep prayer, absorbed study of scripture, or any retreat that takes one out of one's everyday surroundings for the purpose of cultivating the path. In my technical use of this term, the setting aside makes it extraordinary. You sit on your cushion at home every morning—that is an extraordinary act. You mow the lawn, drive the school bus, vacation in the Galapagos, get elected president of the United States—these are ordinary acts.

The criterion of usualness yields an either/or distinction between ordinary and extraordinary practices. By this measure, when I am casually practicing Right Speech in daily encounters with family and friends, this is the ordinary practice of Right Speech. On the other hand, if I have set aside a special time to practice Right Speech with these people, this is an extraordinary practice. If I am calming down naturally in the crisp morning air as I walk to an appointment, I am practicing Right Calm Concentration in an ordinary way. If I sit down on my meditation cushion and calm the mind and body, I am engaged in the extraordinary practice of Calm Concentration. By this criterion, the specially designed living conditions of monastic life, and its special practices, make the life of the monk or nun extraordinary.

The second criterion for distinguishing ordinary and extraordinary practice is the individual's mind state, particularly the strength of Right View, Effort, and Mindfulness. Sariputta, the Buddha's wisest disciple, taught that these qualities elevate and refine every element of the Eightfold Path. He said: "These three qualities—Right View, Right Effort, and Right Mindfulness—run and circle around [each path factor]."[4] That is, these three factors are necessarily present whenever one is enacting any path factor, in even an ordinary way. It also means that as these factors increase, the "rightness" or liberating power of the path also increases.

We enter the three elevating factors with Right View. At its simplest, Right View involves knowing what is wholesome from what is harmful. One asks whether a thought, word, or action will cause benefit or harm. If a person cannot distinguish good from bad at a particular time and acts in harmful ways, that person is not on the path at that time; his or her confusion will thicken, and damage will result. Right View refers to knowing that thoughts, words, and deeds have results; this is the proper understanding of karma. This aspect of Right View is the basis of morality.

Right View has a more global aspect, however: understanding the truth of suffering, its cause, the possibility of cessation, and the path to it. If I recognize that the race to satisfy my hungers yields at best a brittle and temporary satisfaction, and that the lessening of these same hungers yields a joy that is robust and full of ease, this recognition causes me to incline my life, meditation practices, and thoughts toward freedom. With this recognition, all aspects of my practice become more extraordinary.

The daze of habitual delusion is dispersed and a new clarity nurtures courage, inquiry, and a vibrant attitude toward life. Clearer view makes the difference.

Right Effort is the second factor elevating the ordinary to the extraordinary. The Buddha counseled, "Abandon what is unskillful . . . develop what is skillful . . . [this] is conducive to benefit and pleasure."[5] Effort, here, begins with bringing more energy to the moment of experience. With this energy the body feels alert and the mind clears. Hormonal, neurochemical changes are triggered; the whole body comes alive with relaxed awareness. Such effort is inclined toward release and ease, not toward accomplishment or attainment. This energy is then applied toward purifying the heart-mind. It is used to release confused and hurtful thoughts and emotions, to remain free of corrosive thoughts and influences, and to cultivate and maintain mindfulness, clarity, joy, and ease. Old habits dissipate, and mindfulness, inquiry, energy, tranquillity, joy, and steadiness of mind all grow. Such an increase in Right Effort helps the moment become extraordinary.

Pronounced mindfulness is the third factor elevating the ordinary toward the extraordinary. When greater energy enlivens the body and mind, awareness also increases. We awaken in the moment, recollecting our active role in creating the tenor of experience. Rather than being dominated by reactive thoughts and emotions, we become aware of these reactions and let them be. Mindfulness is inherently receptive. Experiences are met with an accepting, nonidentified, and nonaversive awareness. The mind becomes aware of itself, aware of others, and aware of the environment. The moment becomes extraordinary as the factor of Right Mindfulness grows.

Right View, Effort, and Mindfulness join together to create an experience of clear awareness. There is a sense of the changing, vibrating nature of being. The body is alive with awareness; the mind is receptive. The Pali word *sampajanna* points toward this wakeful, clear-minded state. One could use the word *presence* for this heightened awareness of time and place, but it is not the presence of a self, even a transcendent self, but a paradoxically empty presence. This unfolding alertness and calm in the midst of thoughts and sensations may be akin to what Wordsworth described in "Tintern Abbey."

> . . . I have felt
> A presence that disturbs me with the joy
> Of elevated thoughts.[6]

When these three factors combine with any element of the path, that other element becomes extraordinary. For example, clear awareness together with Right Speech raises a moment of speaking to the extraordinary. One's mind state can make any activity extraordinary. By this criterion, the clear understanding and heightened effort and mindfulness that monastics try to bring to the routines of their daily lives is extraordinary and can transform their humblest routines into extraordinary practice. The same transforming effect of these factors creates an opportunity for extraordinary practice for anyone, anywhere, anytime.

After teaching a one-day retreat, I went out to lunch with a fellow meditation teacher. We were getting acquainted, talking about how things were going in his community. Then the conversation moved to the nature of meditation practice and the path in general. As we talked about being calm and mindful, about dedication and energy, the qualities we were discussing came more alive in us. Right there, in a Thai restaurant in urban America, our ordinary practice of mindfulness became increasingly extraordinary. We each had years of meditation experience behind us as well as dedication and knowledge; these things supported our simple and gently extraordinary encounter. I have had similar conversations with a friend who practices an indigenous wisdom tradition. At these times experience takes on a clarity as commonplace and as magical as any desert sky, and a doorway opens to a deeper understanding of the moment.

It is important to clearly understand that I use the term *extraordinary* in this technical sense. That is, extraordinary is defined by two criteria: usualness and mind state. By the criterion of usualness, extraordinary means unusual, removed from the ordinary—the cushion, the temple, the practice group meeting, the retreat center. Extraordinary does not necessarily mean special, however, and need not imply practices that are inaccessible or elite. For certain training it is important to be removed from everyday activities. When that's the case, extraordinary does involve an unusual setting, removed from everyday life. But when our mind state becomes stronger in understanding, energy, and mindfulness, even the usual situations of our life become extraordinary. And the other side of the coin is that sometimes a practice is extraordinary—set aside—but if it is performed in a dull way, with little mindfulness, energy, or understanding, the resultant mind states are decidedly not extraordinary.

Many meditators have described how they found themselves unusually aware and compassionate with their partners following a period of Insight Dialogue practice. After returning home from an Insight Dialogue retreat, one meditator said: "My wife keeps stopping in midsentence and saying, 'What? Why are you looking at me like that?' I say, 'I am just listening to you.' 'Oh,' she says, 'it's nice, but I'm not used to it.'" Ordinary interactions between these partners had moved toward the extraordinary, even though only one was attempting to bring meditative awareness to their relationship, and so the practice was unilateral. Another couple who attended a retreat together noticed after returning home that they continued to share their thoughts in the moment with each other without judgment and with less personalizing. They experienced their growing ability to meet difficult emotions with mindfulness as a relief and a liberation; the new awareness of the tendency to personalize things was an insight into the insubstantial nature of the self—an increase in Right View. Whenever people meet the normal human interactions of their daily lives with deepened understanding, energy, and awareness, ordinary interactions are transformed into extraordinary practice.

Ordinary and extraordinary practice, like personal and interpersonal practice, are not crisply opposed. There are gradations. It is usually easy to determine whether a given practice is part of one's everyday activities. But when Right View, Right Effort, and Right Mindfulness enter the picture, it becomes a matter of degrees. One's practice may be more or less ordinary, and more or less extraordinary, according to one's understanding and application of energy and awareness.

How does the path unfold in your ordinary life? Do you contemplate wise teachings? What activities in your life support mindfulness, wholesome curiosity, energy, joy, and tranquillity?

Experiment with transforming the ordinary to the extraordinary with Right View, Effort, and Mindfulness. Begin with mindfulness. While taking a walk alone, notice the simple act of moving the legs, and notice that you are aware of this. Then brighten the energy and attention you bring to the experience; notice any changes this brings to your felt sense of the moment. Finally, consider the impermanence of the walking body and, remaining clearly aware, gently let go into the flow of walking. How do these experiments affect the quality of your experience? Try this while you are with other people.

Transformation and Integration

Extraordinary practices open new glimpses of freedom and insight in ways that transform us; ordinary practices tend to integrate insight into the patterns of our daily lives and habits. These two movements are not wholly distinct and work together to cultivate awakening. Transformation shifts how we feel about and see the world. In the process of integration, those transforming shifts come into natural harmony in our everyday lives. Integrative practices serve to maintain the benefits of extraordinary practices; they also cultivate and instill new insights in our character and outlook, gradually and gently. Extraordinary insights become integrated into our everyday lives; bit by bit, this elevates our everyday living toward the extraordinary. The usual becomes extraordinary. There is a powerful synergy as these two types of practice nurture each other.

The door to transformation opens when we experience something that does not fit within our fabricated patterns of interpretation. In deep meditation—an extraordinary practice—we may have an insight into how mental processes patch together feelings and perceptions into an illusion of self. It may be that, forever after, habitual self-concept is open to question. But it may be that following such a transformative moment, we instead retreat into denial; however awkward, we may fabricate some patch to our meaning schemes that lets old patterns of emotion and thought remain intact. Or it may happen that we release old views and adopt another, higher-order understanding, one that encompasses both the new and the old ways of understanding the world. This is transformation. It took years of development and a whole new cosmology for people to accept the insights of Galileo, Newton, and others—to really take in the idea that the Earth is not the center of the universe. Similarly, the idea that "I" am not the center of the universe demands an equally challenging— even troubling—paradigm shift.

These are not easy shifts to make. A shift in meaning scheme transforms how we see the world and therefore affects everything we do. Transformative practices are disproportionately powerful for the time spent in practice. Even a five-day meditation retreat can alter how we feel about ourselves or how we see the direction of our lives. I have seen many people with a dread of speaking in a group shift from fear to ease, usually based on the experiential understanding that they can be received by others without judgment. Just a moment of interpersonal contact that is free from hunger can have lifelong impact and lead to less craving and fear. A life with less craving and fear will be different.

Transformation and integration cut across the distinction between ordinary and extraordinary practices, and both are necessary. In transformative practices, insight arises, attitudes shift, and wisdom and compassion deepen. In integrative practice, these changes are made real in changed outlook and behavior. Integrative practices bring transformative insights into action in our everyday lives, where they become part of our personality.

Sometimes people wonder whether the ordinary/extraordinary distinction sets up a harmful duality, robbing the everyday of its specialness and setting up a special practice surrounded by grasping and expectations. They ask, "Don't we awaken just as we chop wood and carry water?" or "Aren't we already awake and just don't know it?" But until awakening arises naturally, the habits of the heart need special attention. They need extraordinary love and extraordinary awareness and calm in order to be released. Our grasping is buried deep, protected by fear and other defenses. Intellect, everyday emotional turmoil, and the distractions of life make excellent hiding places. Deeper concentration and mindfulness enable deeper release as subtler clinging becomes known and so looses its grip. Dedicated activities, in which the extraordinary is cultivated, are appropriate and necessary. They reach beneath the surface, like digging down to the roots of weeds rather than plucking the leaves from the surface. When we are able to release grasping, our pain is really changed, lessened. A measure of serenity and love replaces that pain; when we are once again in our ordinary lives, "chopping wood and carrying water," we are a little more awake, and we know it. We experience more ease, more clarity, greater wisdom, more compassion. Extraordinary activities are efficient at bringing about this sort of change and are therefore appropriate and necessary. This is the way in which the extraordinary and the ordinary meet. The extraordinary becomes quite usual as a result of transformation, which means that the ordinary has revealed its fundamentally extraordinary nature. As this unfolds, we begin to recognize the clear, natural awareness that was always present in the ordinary.

A Full-Spectrum Path

Many people see formal meditation or prayer as the main part of the spiritual path despite the fact that even dedicated practitioners spend only about 10 percent of their waking hours in these extraordinary practices. The attraction to these practices is understandable. Something in us, sometimes hidden, yearns to release limiting viewpoints and old emotional habits in favor of wide understanding, joy, and freedom. For most of us, however, a spiritual path narrowly focused on the extraordinary is bound to result in frustration. As much as we may desire or fear transformative experiences, most of our lives are pretty mundane. We do our work, relate to people in our lives, and take care of our bodies. A vision of a mature and inclusive path offers personal and interpersonal avenues of transformative power and the means to integrate our deeper changes thoroughly. Such a path transcends the divisions fostered by the awkward meeting of Asian and Western cultures. Western individualism, emotional honesty, and worldly activity can join Asian communality, stillness, and nonattachment in a path that reflects our whole personhood. Such a path is also robust, equally suited to times of social and economic displacement and times of relative stability and comfort, such as the period that has provided rich soil for the growth of Buddhist teachings in the West.

With this wide spectrum and fully human definition of the path, we can live it in all we do. This path has four interrelated aspects: ordinary personal, ordinary interpersonal (or social), extraordinary personal, and extraordinary interpersonal. All eight path components—Right View, Intention, Speech, Action, Living, Effort, Mindfulness, and Calm Concentration—are the same for everyday practice and deep explicit practice. The eight path factors are also the same for personal practice and interpersonal practice.

Many meditation practices and guidelines for living are suggested by this wide view of the path. The ordinary personal practice of Right View would include informal reading about the human condition—reading this book in a casual way, for example—so long as there is some understanding of suffering, its cause, and its cessation. When one studies with energy and mindfulness, with a clear intention toward relinquishing grasping, the act of reading takes on the meditative quality of extraordinary practice, whether the reading material be Buddhist texts, other deep teachings, or this same book. The ordinary personal practice of Right

THE FULL-SPECTRUM NOBLE EIGHTFOLD PATH

Extraordinary
Personal

Increasingly strong Right View, Effort, and Mindfulness and/or set-aside times of practice.
Traditional retreats encompass most path factors

Right View Sequestered contemplation of wise texts

Right Intention Renunciation and compassion retreat

Right Speech Individual explicit and intense effort to speak only the truth

Right Action Living by a strong vow to selfless service and economic justice

Right Living Individual explicit and intense effort to live harmlessly

Right Effort Retreat on death (abandoning) or lovingkindness (cultivating)

Right Mindfulness Vipassana retreat

Right Calm Concentration Traditional retreat focused on breathing meditation

Ordinary
Personal

Embedded in life, with a modicum of Right View, Effort, and Mindfulness

Right View Mindfully reading about the function of the human body

Right Intention Thinking about the joys of a kind and generous life

Right Speech Personal commitment to not speaking ill of others

Right Action Personal commitment to sexual fidelity

Right Living Avoiding work that brings harm to others

Right Effort Avoiding people whose speech is crude, dishonest (prevention)

Right Mindfulness Mindfully cleaning the kitchen

Right Calm Concentration Calming down on the front porch

THE FULL-SPECTRUM NOBLE EIGHTFOLD PATH

Extraordinary Interpersonal

Increasingly strong Right View, Effort, and Mindfulness and/or set-aside times and places of practice.
Insight Dialogue retreat encompasses all eight path factors

Right View Scheduled, mindful conversations about Dhamma

Right Intention Mutual pact committing members to relinquishment (e.g., nonconsuming)

Right Speech Explicit and mutual practice sessions of useful and compassionate speech

Right Action Living in a community dedicated to peace

Right Living Monastic community

Right Effort Interactive lovingkindness retreat (maintain-increase)

Right Mindfulness Interactive mindfulness retreat

Right Calm Concentration Weekly gathering to practice interactive calming exercises

Ordinary Interpersonal

Embedded in life, with a modicum of Right View, Effort, and Mindfulness

Right View Discuss impermanence with a friend

Right Intention Long-term planning for wholesome business goals

Right Speech Work group mutually agreed to kind and true speech

Right Action Participating in a school committee dedicated to reducing consumerism

Right Living Family commitment to sustainability and harmlessness

Right Effort Group agreement to forego drugs and alcohol (abandoning)

Right Mindfulness Volunteer work group with dedication to mutual support of mindfulness

Right Calm Concentration Relaxing in nature with some friends

Speech would involve consciously speaking in ways that are truthful and harmonious—again, with a modicum of understanding of grasping and letting go; extraordinary interpersonal Right Speech might involve meeting with others in a special situation to explore speaking with deep mindfulness and concentration. The Insight Dialogue retreat is a good example of such a practice. Ordinary Right Living, personally or in community, would rest in harmlessness to others and the environment. Extraordinary Right Living would include a hermetic or monastic lifestyle, explicitly dedicated to a path of awakening. Extraordinary Right Effort might be practiced personally in silent meditation or interpersonally in the abandonment of anger or the cultivation of equanimity. The entire path is available at any time and under any circumstances. We can begin with any path factor, in any quadrant. The path is not something apart from life; it is life. As the Buddha said, "The Noble Eightfold Path, bhikkhu, *is* the holy life."[7]

We begin we understand the path as a collection of qualities that we cultivate step-by-step, spiraling time and again around to deeper understanding. As these qualities become established, however, the noble aspect of the path becomes increasingly obvious. Now we see eight qualities that converge in the life and mind of an individual, manifesting whether she is alone or with others, on retreat or in the kitchen. This is how I often experienced my teacher Anagarika Dhammadina. Her energy, mindfulness, kindness, and generosity were as much a part of her as her sturdy frame and round face. In such people, in such moments, there is no doing, no fashioning. The path is now a description of the heart-mind of the highly developed individual. This person's View is in harmony, his or her Mindfulness and Concentration established.

The ordinary manifestations of the path, both personal and interpersonal, have been well explored by people of many religions and cultures. Compassion and morality are the natural focus of explorations of the ordinary. Wherever there has been a modicum of Right View—that is, some emphasis on letting go rather than getting, on diminishing hungers rather than feeding them—I would include them in this definition of the human path. Extraordinary personal practices have been explored by Buddhists across the ages as well as by mystics in many traditions. The kabbalists of Judaism, the Sufis of Islam, the Desert Fathers of Christianity, and the sages of Hinduism are all exemplars of the extraordinary personal path. Again, when Right View is present, all such practices are part of this full-spectrum human path.

But with few exceptions—for example, Quaker meeting, Tibetan debate, Sufi dancing, and certain forms of the meditation teacher-student relationship—there has been little development of extraordinary practices that are interpersonal and interactive. Such practices, I have found, hold immense potential for helping us realize our inherent capacities for wakefulness and ease, for happiness, and for wisdom and compassion. They contribute this fourth quadrant to our path, the interpersonal extraordinary. The four quadrants taken together do not constitute separate paths but one full-spectrum human path.

Part Three

PRACTICE

— 8 —
ELEMENTS OF AN
EFFECTIVE PATH

WHAT WOULD an extraordinary interpersonal practice look like? What would life look like if our interpersonal lives were infused with tranquillity and letting go? In the Buddhist tradition, the path rests upon morality, tranquillity, and wisdom.[1] If we build a practice upon these elements, we will be building on a time-tested tradition. Still, a practice built on interpersonal experience would have to include interpersonal contact. It will have some distinctive features, and the forms of such a practice may not match our preconceptions about meditation.

Interpersonal practices will involve speaking or otherwise interacting with others and will therefore leave behind the most obvious feature of traditional meditation: the bastion of silence. We must add the element of mutuality to the traditional elements of morality, tranquillity, and wisdom. Then we will be able to discern the outlines of a well-grounded extraordinary interpersonal practice.

Morality is the terra firma of any path of awakening, ordinary or extraordinary. The Buddha was among the sages who were very clear about this.

Bhikkhus, just as whatever strenuous deeds are done, are all done based upon the earth, established upon the earth, so too, based upon virtue, established upon virtue, a bhikkhu develops and cultivates the Noble Eightfold Path.[2]

Without the human consideration that underlies morality, without the ease brought on by a clear conscience, all deeper wisdom remains an idea—another delusion in our collection of attachments. As a consequence, the path, whether considered from a personal or interpersonal perspective, simply must be founded on morality. The moral factors of the Eightfold Path—Right Speech, Action, and Living—refer primarily to how we encounter and treat others. Speaking, along with listening, implies relationship. Right Action corresponds to the moral basis of nearly all religions: abstaining from killing, stealing, and sexual misconduct—these are all relational issues. Right Living and Right Speech refer to the honesty and decency of our livelihood—or of our entire lifestyle. Morality is foundational for any wholesome mutuality.

One specific element of morality has special application to our exploration of extraordinary interpersonal practice: the Buddha's teachings on Right Speech. This element of Insight Dialogue is most clearly represented by the guideline Speak the Truth. As we will see, this also implies kindness, mindfulness, usefulness, and other good qualities of speech. Because Insight Dialogue practice can transform our patterns of everyday conversation so greatly, people sometimes refer to Insight Dialogue as a practice of Right Speech. Insight Dialogue is an adaptable and wide-spectrum practice, however—no more limited to Right Speech than traditional meditation is simply a practice of "Right Silence."

The second element of an extraordinary path is tranquillity. A mind at ease, a calm heart, is essential to happiness and to seeing things as they actually are. Tension distorts the lens through which we see the world by framing everything in terms of that which makes us tense. Without tranquillity the mind cannot dwell with any experience long enough to know its nature. Without knowing the nature of experience, we are unlikely to abandon self-centered fabrications, and we cannot be fully compassionate to others or to ourselves.

Right Effort, Mindfulness, and Concentration are all understood to be part of the tranquillity portion of the traditional Buddhist path. They all have to do with cultivating the mind, including refining our emotions, enhancing moment-to-moment awareness, and setting up serenity and lucidity. As we have seen, the energy and commitment of Right Effort and the receptive clarity of Right Mindfulness are necessary for any practice to be designated as extraordinary. These two factors are primarily represented by the first Insight Dialogue guideline, which is Pause.

This leaves the tranquillity factor of Calm Concentration. At first glance it may seem ill-advised to try to foster calm concentration in a practice where people are engaged with each other. After all, other humans are generally our greatest source of stress, and there are highly developed systems of silent, individual meditation that are well suited to cultivating calm. The Buddha often spoke of the "rapture of seclusion,"[3] and mystics through the ages have extolled the values of silent solitude. One could easily argue that the very fact that other people are such a source of stress makes it imperative that we learn to meditate with others; that way we can begin to calm down while in relationship. But since we are talking about extraordinary practices, it also makes sense that leaving stimulating elements behind for certain periods of time can be helpful or even necessary for deeply transformative work. I agree with this and highly respect and value deep stillness in personal meditation. I have learned, however, that profound calm is possible in interpersonal practice. I found a key to understanding this possibility in the teachings of the Buddha; it all rests on the relationship of happiness to concentration.

The eighth factor of the path, *samadhi,* is one of the Buddha's most misunderstood teachings. Concentration is often taken to imply a volitional placement of the mind upon an object, a tightly focused state of mind. Many teachers and practices are influenced by this view. In fact, the Buddha taught that the mind is concentrated—naturally unified and settled—when it is happy and calm. He said:

> For one who is joyful, there is no need for an act of will: "May my body be serene!" It is a natural law that the body will be serene for one who is joyful.
>
> For one of serene body, there is no need for an act of will: "May I feel happiness!" It is a natural law that one who is serene will feel happiness.
>
> For one who is happy, there is no need for an act of will: "May my mind be concentrated!" It is a natural law for one who is happy that the mind will be concentrated.
>
> For one who is concentrated, there is no need for an act of will: "May I know and see things as they really are!" It is a natural law for one with a concentrated [calm and unified] mind to know and see things as they really are.[4]

This teaching points us toward the ease and calm inherent in *samadhi.* For this reason I usually refer to this aspect of the path as Calm Concentration, not simply Concentration. This kind of tranquillity is usually practiced individually. The Buddha exhorted monks to go to the roots of trees or to empty huts and apply themselves with diligence. This makes sense: thought, emotion, desire, and aversion arise as we listen to, look at, touch, and otherwise encounter people.

Interpersonal meditation can and does support the arising of a happy, calm mind state, however. The central guideline addressing this is Relax. I experience and observe in others significant calm at every Insight Dialogue retreat I teach. Tranquillity is also a key support in integrating our interpersonal practice with our everyday lives. Stress fosters reactivity and interferes with mindfulness. Conversely, the intentional cultivation of a calm mind and body will incline one toward careful responses to others and mindfulness of present experience. We grow in our ability to recall the serenity suggested by the meditation guidelines at critical moments in our lives; as we do so, we become more able to stay present with anyone. When we are tranquil in our relationships, we will be happier, healthier, and more empathic. When the heart is calm, reactive habits soften and lose their power. The calm mind is also naturally more concentrated, and we can stay on-task longer when we are relaxed than when distracted or stressed.

In everyday practice, tranquillity will not usually mean the utter still-ness of meditation. More often it is revealed in a calm face, easy smile, and relaxed voice. When serene, we tend to be patient, clear minded, and emo-tionally balanced.

Wisdom—seeing things as they actually are—is a third basic element of traditional extraordinary paths. In the Buddha's teachings, the wisdom factors of the path are Right View and Intention. We have considered the nature of a harmonious, fitting view, but we only touched upon how one might cultivate such a view. There are specific practices that support the development of Right View.

Right View, O monks, if it is helped by five things, has liberation of mind as its fruit . . . Right View is helped by virtue, by wide learn-ing, by discussion, by tranquillity and by insight.[5]

This call for virtue, tranquillity, and insight is in alignment with most images of meditation. What is less expected is that learning and discussion are included in this teaching. The wisdom aspect—Right View—will be supported by the contemplation and discussion of teachings that reliably reveal that nature of things. Listen Deeply and Speak the Truth are guide-lines that support this aspect of the wisdom factor. These practices fit nat-urally into extraordinary interpersonal development.

Throughout his discourses, the Buddha taught contemplations, posing questions such as "Would this action . . . lead to my own affliction, or to the affliction of others, or to the affliction of both?"[6] "Is there any obsession unabandoned in myself that might so obsess my mind that I cannot know or see things as they actually are?"[7] Such inquiries stand beside the classic contemplations on impermanence, suffering, and impersonality. In Insight Dialogue, the use of contemplations and the guideline Trust Emergence supports these aspects of wisdom. Study and contemplation are venerated as a road to wisdom in nearly all spiritual traditions, both Eastern and Western. The Western knowledge traditions of science, psychology, and philosophy also seek wisdom through study. Most wisdom traditions include contemplations on the body, death, transience, love, compassion, and the sanctity of life.

It stands to reason that these and other contemplations could play an important role in an extraordinary interpersonal practice. It is also easy to see how bringing carefully chosen contemplations into our daily lives can nurture understanding. While Celia was on retreat, a group contemplation on impermanence in relationships led to a powerful insight about the nature of moment-to-moment experience.

Six of us sat in a circle. It was nearly sunset, and as we talked about change in our lives, nature put on a display of change outside: yellow to pink to red to near darkness. We became more quiet as we contemplated changes in relationship. Not one of us had the illusion of stable relationships; we were all too seasoned—that is, too old, I guess—to even imagine a relationship that doesn't change from day to day and year to year. This greased us up for change in the very moment of our practice.

Jack started the spiral that was to take us to the point, the instant, of our being together. All he said was, "My knee hurts." Then there was a pause, and he said, "Now it doesn't." That was it. But like dominoes lined up, each of us seemed to experience all of our sensations as passing. "I'm watching the mind as it doesn't know what to say . . . now that thought is gone." Then, "The reddish light on Lisa's face is beautiful . . . now it's just reddish." Everything we attached to seemed to vanish in every moment, like the daylight had vanished into night. By the time we broke for dinner, impermanence was no longer a contemplation, it was a simple and obvious fact of being.

In its most direct manifestation, wisdom can grow in extraordinary interpersonal practice by bringing about a direct experience of interpersonal suffering, hungers, and freedom, as it did for Celia's group. No intellectual experience can replace the direct apprehension of stress and freedom. Grounded in this insight, practice is oriented toward releasing rather than feeding hungers. This is no different from the way Right View is fostered in traditional, silent meditation: meditators see how their thoughts and emotions are impermanent, stressful, and impersonal; they experience firsthand the ease that arises as the mind ceases its habitual clinging. The primary difference is that this insight unfolds in mutual rather than solitary practice.

Mutuality, including communication, is the fourth key element of an extraordinary interpersonal practice. This is most directly represented by the third Insight Dialogue guideline Open, as well as by the instruction pair Listen Deeply–Speak the Truth. I pointed out earlier that the support of spiritual friends and community was considered by the Buddha to be the most important element of the holy life. Even so, mutuality was not called out as an explicit factor in the Buddha's Eightfold Path. Indeed, one could say that the most insurgent aspect of Insight Dialogue, from a traditional Buddhist perspective, is its collective nature. But if we look closely, we see that mutuality is inherent in the cultivation of morality— Right Speech, Action, and Living—even though it is only indirectly considered in relation to tranquillity and wisdom. But if we are to arrive at a practice, or indeed an entire path, that includes the relational, we must address mutuality in all components of the path.

Listening and speaking must be included in a comprehensive mutual practice, as this is a defining feature of being human. Also, verbal communication is uniquely well suited to cultivating Right View. It enables understanding to be collectively evolved and emotions to be disentangled. Despite the use of language, such release can unfold at a prerational level, where the limbic brain—the brain of bonding and emotion—is reconfigured in dialogic encounter. Transformation at this level is not solely an individual affair. Interactive meditation opens up new avenues of evolution.

Because speech is a uniquely powerful force in our relational lives, and so much of our life is relational, the inclusion of speaking and listening in an extraordinary practice enables the power of practice to infiltrate our entire life. Language brings into our practice the force of intellect, the associative power of words, and its own potential to reveal limiting beliefs, desires, grasping, and fears. Language is a powerful tool for both constructing and deconstructing such formations. A well-designed interpersonal meditation, if practiced diligently, could bring about profound transformation in individuals and groups.

Any interpersonal practice, ordinary or extraordinary, must have its roots in compassion. Speaking and listening, we will hear each other's pain. When we rest in compassion, our attention can easily shift out of self-reference, and this becomes the basis for insight into the nature of the relational mind. Rather than focus on subject and object, me and you, we become attuned to encounter itself, to the ever-emerging fact of meeting. We have no way of knowing the world other than through a view forged in the presence of others. Humbled by this fact, and with compassion as the basis of an interpersonal path, we will more readily be able to accept the impermanence and stress inherent in the relational life.

Such a practice must also be rooted in lovingkindness; that is, a heart-mind that is caring and receptive. A kind heart is central to interpersonal practice for one simple, practical reason: if people are to present themselves to each other in the clear light of mindfulness, they will be comfortable doing so only if they know they will be met with kindness and understanding. The open heart of love gives birth to compassion; an extraordinary interpersonal practice will not merely rest on a foundation of already developed compassion—it will also naturally increase compassion. This is the inevitable result when meditative awareness reveals our shared humanity.

So we see that an interpersonal practice rests on the four elements of morality, tranquillity, wisdom, and mutuality. For such a practice to be potent, each element must be significantly developed and must support the other three. Ideally such a practice would lend itself to cultivation in both everyday life and dedicated settings, capable of extraordinary practice in each setting, without compromise. The impact of such a practice must be discernable by the wise and reflected in the human decency of the practitioner. Insight Dialogue is an interpersonal practice that meets these criteria.

Insight Dialogue can unfold both in set-aside circumstances and in our daily lives. In Insight Dialogue retreats or groups, two or more people gather in silent personal meditation, then extend that practice into an interpersonal mode, including listening and speaking. When the practice is embedded in life, the meditation instructions function as guidelines for wakeful engagement with others. In both cases the practice leads to the fading of hunger and ignorance.

Like traditional, individual meditation, Insight Dialogue in retreats and groups is an extraordinary practice in that people gather at times set aside just for this practice. Meditators anticipate that this practice will influence their everyday lives in positive ways but recognize the transformative potential of explicit extraordinary practice. Practice in our everyday lives helps shift the ordinary to the extraordinary by arousing the transformative factors of Right View, Effort, and Mindfulness. In both cases we aspire to meet the moment with some understanding of the futility of feeding hungers and with the intention to let go of cravings.

Just as various forms of traditional silent meditation benefit from different instructions, Insight Dialogue likewise has meditation instructions, or guidelines. These have evolved to support meditators as they migrate from habitual ways of interacting with others to ways that are in alignment with the path of virtue, tranquillity, wisdom, and mutuality. We will explore the Insight Dialogue meditation instructions: Pause-Relax-Open, Trust Emergence, and Listen Deeply–Speak the Truth. We will also look at the contemplation component of the practice, which channels and contributes to its power. Different practice forms are discussed, as are some of the ways practice can go awry. Finally, we will see how such a practice touches our lives. The proof of any meditative practice, and of any guideline for living, is both in personal liberation and in our behavior with others. For certain, an interpersonal meditation practice such as Insight Dialogue is an exceptionally effective means for developing what Daniel Goleman calls social intelligence.[8] But it offers far more than this.

～ 9 ～

INSIGHT DIALOGUE
MEDITATION
INSTRUCTIONS

Six instructions provide the scaffolding for Insight Dialogue. They are

Pause
Relax
Open
Trust Emergence
Listen Deeply
Speak the Truth

These guidelines remain the same whether Insight Dialogue is undertaken as a formal meditation practice or is embraced as a path for wise living. They can be easier to remember and implement if thought of as three groups: Pause-Relax-Open, Trust Emergence, and Listen Deeply–Speak the Truth.

Taken together, these guidelines offer essential support for awakening amid the rich challenges of interpersonal encounter. Each guideline calls forth different qualities, and all of them are complementary. In brief, Pause calls forth mindfulness; Relax, tranquillity and acceptance; Open, relational availability and spaciousness; Trust Emergence, flexibility and letting go; Listen Deeply, receptivity and attunement; and Speak the Truth, integrity and care.

In everyday life, the guidelines can be taken up as needed to support a kinder and more mindful way of relating. In meditation groups or retreats, these instructions are introduced individually in an atmosphere of dedicated practice and mutual commitment. Practiced diligently, the Insight Dialogue instructions help guide the meditator toward deeper practice, insight, and release.

— 10 —

PAUSE

To PAUSE is to interrupt a movement, to step out of the habitual rush forward. Pausing allows reflection, reconsideration, rest. In Insight Dialogue, the movement that is interrupted is the sensitive body-mind's incessant grasping at whatever contacts it: sights, sounds, touches, smells, tastes, and thoughts. The habit of grasping is very strong in the interpersonal realm. Seeing another person, the mind grasps to hold or to push away, to know or to be known, to touch, to fix, or to adjust. Yet, strong as these urges are, it is possible to step outside them momentarily, to bracket their driving concerns: to pause.

Interrupting automatic habit is the first step on any path. For anything new to happen, conditioned patterns of thought and emotion must be interrupted. The first instruction in Insight Dialogue is Pause. We carry this instruction with us while meditating with others or engaged in every-day affairs. By interrupting automatic reactions, pausing opens the door to nonclinging. The instruction Pause is an invitation to step out of our reactions and identification with our own and others' stories. It is the same basic movement as returning to the breath in individual meditation. It is an opportunity to get off the train and look around, to dwell a moment with immediate experience before speaking or while listening. To let the mind take a break. To come home to things just as they are.

I invite you to slow down, to find the present moment, and explore Pause—here and now. You don't need another person's presence to Pause from habitual thoughts and reactions. Pause from reading and from thinking for a moment and notice the body. What is the posture of the body now? What is the shape and form of the body? You can ask, "How am I feeling right now?" You can notice any sensations or tensions. At this first level, the Pause is a definite gap in our activities; it takes time. Notice the sense of letting go of whatever you were doing or thinking. Pause.

In interacting with another person, we can pause before we speak, while we are speaking, or after we are done speaking. We can pause as we listen, in the midst of speech, or as we sit in silence. Such reflection involves stepping back, mentally, from the flow of speech. Internally, to Pause is to step out of engagement with an emotion or thought and to become aware of the experience, in the moment, without identification. Habits of speech—indeed, all relational habits—pour forth into the moment automatically, without awareness or choice. The process is the same whether our habit is to express judgment or to continually offer reassurance. We are predictable, and predictably stressful. Without choice there can be no meaningful change: we remain enmeshed in our webs of identity, loneliness, fear, and wanting. The Pause is a break in this cycle, a pivot point to freedom.

In an Insight Dialogue retreat or group, I invite the meditators into a conversation in which we collectively contemplate the essential truths of our lives. These contemplations can be stimulating and engaging; they can foster emotional reactivity as they reveal attachments and fears. Periodically I interrupt these conversations by ringing a bell. At the sound of the bell conversation stops and meditators are reminded to step out of reaction and into awareness. This externally induced pause is a literal pause, a temporary stopping of the conversation. It helps participants understand the nature of the Pause and supports their early attempts at practicing it. In this pause we can see and release the old run-on habits of the mind and develop a tendency toward mindfulness. This is mindfulness in the moment of interpersonal contact; pausing is the technique, the practice.

Laurie came to a daylong retreat in New York City bearing the burden of years of anger and in a state of intense reactivity: suffering painful stress-related physical symptoms and full of judgments about other meditators. Her experience at the daylong Insight Dialogue retreat was moving toward a crescendo of self-generated stress when she had a moment of more detached mindfulness.

As I sat in that silence my judgments and my desire for closeness became a crushing cycle that I keyed into. But then I was able to see for a moment what the anger really does: how it racks my body and takes me away from the possibilities of being present and letting go. I was able to see that there were two ways I could live, two choices: open and loving or angry and distant. This was the first time I was able to stay with my anger long enough to get a good look at it. The Pause helped me to stay with the rocking anger in myself. I don't believe I could have been present long enough to get these insights were it not for the pace of the retreat and the Pause.

For Laurie the Pause created a momentary space in her emotional turmoil in which she could be mindful and unidentified with her anger. In that moment she could glimpse its consequences in her life. The Pause also opened the possibility of choosing differently, less automatically. It offered her a choice, a way out.

When painful and habitual thoughts and emotions rush upon us, it can be very difficult to Pause because the turmoil feels so solid, so real. We need something stable and immediate to help us find the moment. Mindfulness of the body provides an anchor in Insight Dialogue. When we get lost in the fabrications of the mind, carried away by emotions, we can take a moment to become mindful of the body—we feel its shape, its form; we notice how awareness seems to vibrate in it. The body itself reveals where the moment is; here is that elusive "now."

This body is also the clear sky in which every thought and emotion leaves its trace. As we learn to rest in mindfulness while these weather systems play across the body, we find ourselves able to avoid identifying with every emotion. We observe the pleasant and unpleasant qualities of experience or the rising and passing of the thoughts and moods; we notice that we are not, in fact, these phenomena that come and go.

Phenomena that are primarily mental, like reactions to other people, move even more quickly than bodily sensations. To be aware of them without falling into identification takes agility and practice. At first the Pause requires effort. It is an interruption of a lifetime of habitual forward pressure, driven by the mainspring of tension and fueled by the juices of emotion. As one woman said about trying to Pause while she was with her sister, "It seemed every time I paused I was greeted by my judgments of my sister. But when there was awareness of these judgments, I saw the judging mind was just a habit. I could see my desires were the same way: habits. When I learned what it felt like not to be wrapped up in the judgments, I could start to see all kinds of things." Just as it takes energy to alter the momentum of a massive moving object, it also takes energy to interrupt the forward push of habit-mind. This energy is our right effort to wake up and relax. Effort is essential if we want to steer our wheels out of deeply worn ruts.

Strong intention is essential to the cultivation of greater mindfulness. But even strong intention needs some way of working with how things really are in the heart-mind. How does this remembering, this Pause, happen? Without the support of a practice, it is difficult to do anything other than what we have always done: live in the trance of conditioned emotions and thoughts. U Pandita, a respected Burmese meditation teacher, specifically points to perception and previous moments of mindfulness as the factors that give rise to mindfulness. That is to say, previous moments of mindfulness foster future moments of mindfulness. It is difficult to find traction on the gravel hills of habit. Even if we have been committed to traditional meditation, waking up in the Pause of Insight Dialogue will challenge us to still greater commitment, because it challenges us to awaken and release clinging while engaged with other people.

> As you Pause, I invite you to release, for the moment, automatic and habitual reactions. Feel the lightness as the clinging mind releases its grip on your present thought or feeling. Step into mindfulness. As you pay attention to your body or look around, you might ask "What is this?" When you Pause, you may notice a certain freshness about things. In this freshness you may notice the habit-mind at work. You might also notice new thoughts.
>
> If you are with another person, I invite you to Pause before speaking to him or her. Inherent in this pause is a silent wondering: "What is unfolding in this moment?" I invite you to try pausing after speaking, to notice what the mind is doing—perhaps you will find it thinking about what to say next or wrapped up in an emotional reaction to an earlier statement. You can also Pause while you are speaking—you can become mindful of yourself and of the other person. You don't need to actually stop speaking to do this, though initially this may be helpful. It is the quality of mindfulness, the interruption of automatic habits, that is the Pause.
>
> You can also Pause while listening. Just step out of identification with the story or topic of the moment and arrive here and now, fresh. Perhaps you touch in again with awareness of the body and find that listening becomes grounded in this moment rather than in some mental fabrication about what's being said.

Even though the Pause doesn't require stopping, if you are feeling more reactive, you may want to give the Pause more time. It can take a while for the body to calm down, for the mind to come to rest. If you are mindful and relaxed, the Pause is an easy slip into the moment. In an instant we can release attachment to whatever occupies us and arrive in the present. As you practice, pay attention to the lightness associated with letting go, with the nonclinging of the Pause.

The Pause is not about time; it is about mindfulness. It can be long or short according to circumstances. When the emotions are strong, we may need to take longer pauses, to allow their power to drain away. This is where we get the maxim "When you are angry, count to ten before speaking." For this practice, we might say more generally that when the emotion is strong, the Pause is long. This is not a rule, however, only a guideline or starting point.

When mindfulness is well established, the Pause takes essentially no time. The mind is already at the cusp of the moment, and the slightest recollection enables the release of attachment. The mind lands lightly in the present, stable and alert as the conversation unfolds. The meditator has been engaging in conversation, moving in and out of identification with his own thoughts. Mindfulness is interleaved with the abstract thought required for using language, and the slightest reminder, generated internally or externally, results in clear, moment-to-moment mindfulness. The Pause that is mindfulness is integrated with other experience. It takes no time.

The subtlety of the Pause is essential if we are to integrate it into our everyday lives. If we take a noticeable amount of time during everyday interactions to pause, people may think we are not paying attention or that we are being sullen, or perhaps that we are simply dim-witted. This isn't so helpful. Also, people can get upset and indignant that the pace of the conversation, or argument, is not what they expect. This certainly happened when I was first developing the practice and tried to bring the Pause into heated discussions with my wife. So we may want to first experiment with shorter pauses, or practice in relaxed situations.

Another bridge between formal practice and everyday life is mutual practice with a friend or two. Just agree that each will talk about things that matter to him or her and that each will pause before and after speaking to establish mindfulness. A half hour might be a good length of time to start. It is surprising how in even such a short time, and without a lot of fuss, a shift can occur toward mindfulness and ease.

Group practice can sustain mindfulness. If we pause while in an Insight Dialogue group, our co-meditators might rest mindfully in the moment, open but not eagerly unbalanced. This will support the mindfulness of the Pause. Now the moment may expand, come alive with mutually supported awareness. Some of our reactivity, clearly known but not fed or encouraged, may come untangled. It is still not easy, though. Especially as we begin the practice, the internal mental note "Pause" can help us let go. When Krista was singled out by a fellow meditator at a retreat as being callous, the reaction to grasp was automatic.

At first I felt attacked and very fearful. My whole body flushed with an enormous surge of emotion, which signaled me that this was a time to pause. I watched the defensiveness, the urge to understand. My mind was trying to grab on to anything that would help me get through this thing. This made me pause again and try to relax around all of the tension in my body and in the group. At some point I felt my body start to soften and relax. I found myself attending to my breath, and I began to hear my truth and open to whatever came next.

Krista's story is an example of a strong emotional reaction, one that could benefit from a longer pause. In the context of a group committed to Insight Dialogue practice, that pause could be explicit and obvious; Krista was able to take the time she needed, with the group's understanding and support. She was not just trying to alter her behavior by preventing an angry response. She was practicing mindfulness in a very difficult situation. She herself understood what was happening and was able to keep pausing until her emotionality passed.

The body-mind, with its emotions and thoughts, does not easily yield to interruption and will reassert itself in the very next moment. The person or people we are meditating with can either be a reminder to rest in awareness or a magnet for the assertions of personality. If we are talking with friends who want to hear our story, even our intention to Pause may be overwhelmed by the excitement in their eyes. Our own urge to be heard or to rediscover our story may pull us forward into reidentification and emotional agitation. We dive into the familiar pool, and the clarity of mindfulness is again obscured.

The Pause can seem awkward and artificial until we become familiar with how it feels to pause into awareness. Our culture has conditioned us to expect movement, sound, quick interpretations, and quick decisions. Stillness, silence, not knowing, and indecision seem all wrong at first, triggering anxious responses. One meditator observed, "At first I felt obliged to fill the empty space." Meditators engaged in extraordinary personal practice encounter the same issues, of course.

Pausing can also seem contrary to spontaneity, disruptive of what we believe to be a "natural" way of interacting. We don't have to look too closely, however, to see that what we call spontaneous and natural is usually habitual and conditioned. If the pause feels like an interruption, it can be helpful to realize that what is being interrupted is the assemblage of fabrications we take to be reality: "my" emotions. Our responses are not quick and thoughtless because they are devoid of onrushing mental habits. They are quick and thoughtless because they are predetermined by our past. What we call spontaneity is usually just knee-jerk reaction. Cause and effect dominate the moment; we listen this way or respond that way because in the past we have had such and such interactions and, well, this is what comes out of it. "Call me an idiot and I'll call you a jerk." There is no choice, no presence of mind, no creative response. There is only reflex.

The Pause, on the other hand, paradoxically opens the door to true spontaneity. By stepping out of reactive habit, we enter the moment afresh. Anything can happen once we have even temporarily escaped the shackles of the past. It is true that the Pause feels unnatural until it is established as a new habit, but it is also true that the unnatural moment is soon behind us and we are here, now, in this freshly running stream of the present. It is at once restful and exhilarating.

Of course, when reactions such as liking, disliking, or other emotions are very strong, we are not as aware of what is going on around us or of our own inner responses. The Pause may reveal judgments, anger, stress, fear, or longing. Perhaps we will be ready at that moment to release these painful reactions. But positive reactions, reactions that feel good, can also unfold and take us over. We may be in a reaction of excitement, or enjoying something that someone said—but in our enjoyment we are identified and clinging. We may actually be moving into our own automated story, habitual and conditioned. It's like a push coming from our past or from some emotional motor ready and waiting to be switched on. When something pleasant is switched on, we don't particularly want to notice it and let go; we just hang on to it.

When you Pause, notice how it feels to release clinging. In the very moment you step into mindfulness, you are stepping out of identification with all of your reactions. If the mind is still buzzing with emotions, don't worry. This is natural. For your entire life the mind has been pushing forward into what's next, and that won't stop right away. But notice the quality of knowing the thoughts and emotions without identifying with them. The emotions are interrupted, and something fresh can now happen.

As your practice ripens, this Pause becomes essentially continuous. We feel steady and awake. The mind is clinging less and less. Even a drop into habit-mind is just a temporary excursion. Notice how the mind takes up its old burdens but then drops them again. So the mindfulness of the Pause goes right through speaking, listening, silence, and thought. You may notice a kind of vibrating silence when you pause. Even when someone is speaking, or a thought arises, that silence is there. Stepping out of the mind storms that usually occupy us, we find this wakeful silence is available at any time: in retreat, in life; it is all the same.

Two things are happening when we Pause. First, we are stopping. We not only stop speaking, stop ranting inwardly, we also stop the momentum of our conditioned tendencies. Discontinuity with past habits is a huge change. Technically the Pause is the shift from clinging to nonclinging. At the same time, we sow the seeds of a new future, create a new tendency—the tendency toward mindfulness and nonclinging. We are inclining the mind to dwell wakefully in the moment. By pausing in the midst of reaction and not feeding emotional habits, we drain the energy out of old patterns. As we practice the Pause at home or in retreat, it becomes more likely that the next time we are triggered we will Pause into mindfulness naturally, without volitional effort. Because we Pause in the context of an interactive relationship with another person—a context that has been the source and provocation of so much habit—that context is being transformed toward clarity. You awaken me; I awaken you. We awaken each other—together.

Rather than based in obligation, force, or an outwardly imposed responsibility, the presence of the Pause is rooted in joy. This joy is born of the lightness of the nonclinging mind. The Pause can yield reverence for the moment and for other people. It can come with a quality of expectancy and the delight of discovery: something new can arise. There is joy in the moment of making the choice to commit, because our dedication is to greater happiness and freedom. Energetic commitment in no way conflicts with ease and naturalness. Indeed, it is born of the natural urge for happiness.

As practice deepens, the power of the silence grows. At first the Pause will primarily reveal reactivity: conditioned responses, automatic and unfree. In the mindful pauses, we find a complex web of conditioning rising into the moment. Relaxing, we do not turn away from the tension and conditioning. When we stay with them, it becomes possible to apprehend the silence that underlies reactivity. The Pause becomes continuous, and we experience the essentially fluid nature of things.

This is a natural awakening. One does not have to try so hard to be mindful. When torrential thoughts and feelings are not fed by our identification with them, mindfulness is the natural result. Rather than try to be mindful, we let go into the mindfulness that arises from our intention. When someone speaks, it is as if words rise out of silence and descend back into it. As in a "gathered" Quaker meeting, it feels as if the silence continues unbroken. Whether one speaks with the voice of God, as the Friends believe, or comes to know the Unconditioned that underlies all conditioned things, it is the Pause that hints at the infinite. From the demanding activities of work and family to the subtle awakenings of a meditation retreat, the Pause offers a touch point of sanity, a reminder of stillness. During the Pause we can know awareness and the phenomena that touch it as coarising. In simpler terms, pausing inclines us to calmness, to slowing down, to seeing ourselves in a broader frame of reference. When we Pause, we can lessen our grasping at pain, momentarily cease reactivity to anger, realize the emptiness of phenomena, or perhaps know peace.

More than just a welcome respite, the Pause is also transformative. It is a basic dynamic of Insight Dialogue that when stillness meets reactivity, unbinding occurs. The karmic pattern that generated the reaction is interrupted, cut off from its source. Unfed, energy drains out of the reaction. In the brain, the patterns of neural firing associated with the moment's emotion or thought continue to fire but do not find resonance and reinforcement in the feedback loops of proliferation. Their firing is met by the cortical intervention of mindfulness; the neural networks of stress defuse. If we lack sufficient mindfulness just then, perhaps our partner remains mindful and calls us to the moment. Supported internally or externally, we dwell at the boundary of clarity and fabrications; we may even move into and back out of identification. Our choice becomes clear: constructions and delusion or mindfulness and wisdom? We come to know the nature of the mind to create and believe its own stories. We do not push all of these constructions aside. Rather, in the Pause their grip is released, and there is knowing. This is the freedom toward which we are oriented. This is the spark of wisdom.

What does the mature Pause feel like? The answer is revealed in traditional silent meditation, in the personal practice of mindfulness and resting in awareness. In our interpersonal practice we recollect and step into the riches of our personal silent practice. As one meditator describes it: "I noticed when I paused, for the first time, even after years of regular meditation, a deepened sense of openness, relaxation, and permeability with attention to the body. There was greater stillness, perhaps even a lightness. It was an exquisite way to dwell in awareness and be present with others." We recall the clarity, the pristine stillness, the lightness and joy of personal meditation, only now it is not solitary and internal. We are awake in relationship. But the incisiveness and discernment, the nonclinging, the mindfulness and emptiness of awareness are the same in personal and interpersonal meditation. We may even find that this wakefulness can be enhanced in the mindful presence of others.

Any given Pause may be noisy or exquisitely still. Stillness for its own sake is not a goal. Rather, we seek to know things as they actually are. When mindfulness is touched by any level of activity, the experience is known as it is, clean and simple. In that moment we stop building the world. There is no past or future, no mine or yours, no breaking or fixing. Knowing exists side by side with the mind's fabrications. We know these constructions as changing and insubstantial, and we recognize the constructing nature of the mind. Just now there is only the bare experience of this moment. The body sits. The body breathes. Thoughts rise and fall. Emotions break like waves on the shore and retreat again to the sea. There is knowing.

~ 11 ~

RELAX

WHEN WE pause into mindfulness, how do we meet the experience we find? Often the Pause catches us in habit-driven thoughts or emotional reactions. The body is agitated, stirred by the spike of a recent interchange or by the ongoing rush of thought. If we do not meet these experiences skillfully, we will be flung back into unaware and identified activity. The wakefulness of the Pause will have been brief. If it is brittle, mindfulness alone is not enough. We need further support.

The second part of the core interpersonal meditation instruction is Relax. We Pause into awareness and Relax the body and mind. At its basic level, this instruction is as simple as it sounds. We bring mindfulness to those parts of the body where we tend to accumulate tension and allow the tension to relax. Becoming aware of the body as a whole, we give ourselves permission to let down, to let go, and not grasp at the reactive state we find.

In this practice we recognize tension and choose ease. There is no other practice, really, than this letting go. We only need to choose the ease. Choosing the ease over and over again is itself the practice. Our formal support for making this choice, for remembering that this choice is available to us, is the simple instruction Relax. This word of guidance is offered not only to the body nor only to the mind. The body and mind move together; they are not two. The body relaxes, the mind calms down. The mind calms down, the body relaxes.

When you Pause, what do you notice? Is there tension around the eyes? Let it melt away. Are the lips or jaw tight? Let go. How is the neck or throat? Is the belly tensed? Let it soften, inviting it to release the grip of anticipation, fear, wanting, and other excitements. Relax.

As you relax into the moment, you may become even more

aware of the body: its tensions rising into the moment as subtle discomforts. You may also notice how thoughts continue to arise even in the Pause, and these thoughts register on the body as sensations or tension. Invite the body to let go into the tensions, not to fight or resist but to soften, to yield.

When you encounter another person, it is normal for the mind to become excited or for the body to tense. When you notice this, you can invoke this same sense of inviting ease: simply pause for a moment and give yourself time to relax, let go. Gradually the heart can become settled and peaceful even as you are engaged with others. Time and again, as you practice, remind yourself to relax.

At a time of stress during a retreat in Korea, Mi-Ja worked with the first two meditation instructions in a very explicit way. She said her emotions were blocked by an "oppressive power." She continued, "I concentrated on my body and repeated 'Pause' and 'Relax' in order to let my sorrow and agony flow out of my body. Now the water pressure of my tears went down and the tension of my body eased." The image of an emotional moment that was blocked points to something important: these reactions are impersonal, they are not initiated by a self. In an experience like this there is no decision to block emotions; it is a conditioned reaction. The implications of this are profound. It shows that we are all constantly at the whim of the events and reactions that have led up to this moment. It is not me exercising control over my life but me controlled by a lifetime of conditioning. Invoking the meditation instructions Pause and Relax, Mi-Ja's "oppressive power" vanished. Such is the potency of relaxed awareness.

Mi-Ja's image of pressure also reveals the tension in experience. We may identify tension as happiness—"I was bursting with excitement"—or as stress, but there is a tautness about it. A good way to understand this tension is to compare it to a time of deep stillness—perhaps on retreat or at an exceptionally quiet moment. A phone ringing or a chance encounter in the hallway seems startling. We can easily recognize the tension of our response because it is in contrast to such deep quietude. But when we are in the midst of lives that are already tense, it can be difficult to recognize that tension is not calmness because we have no reference point to real tranquillity.

A background of tension obscures the details of our experience, separating us from each other and from ourselves. Think of a noisy restaurant where it is difficult to hear the person next to you. Even if the person speaks loudly, you have to strain to hear and understand the speech. The speech signal is overwhelmed by the noise of the room. If the room becomes quiet, you can easily hear a voice, even a whisper. During a workshop dialogue, Gail observed how the noise of her background tensions separated her from others: "When I became emotional, I could not even hear what was being said because I was swept away by my own mental tide of thoughts." Such habitual tides of reactive thoughts and feelings drown out our own experiences, separating us from others, from our more subtle thoughts and feelings, and from more subtle tensions within us.

Calming down improves the signal-to-noise ratio. Polly discovered a basic hunger behind her tensions when she was able to relax out of them.

> I was amazed that a simple comment by Jon about what I'd said could trigger such a strong reaction in me. Insight Dialogue really can slow the pace of input and output—in the "normal" world I might not even have noticed these sensations. Pausing, I had the opportunity to feel the sensations without any pressure to respond. Relaxing with these sensations, I realized they were based on fear, and I was able to share that. Later I realized that the fear was an old bogeyman of mine: behind it was the need for approval.

As she slipped out of automatic reactivity and relaxed with her sensations, Polly was able to perceive subtler tensions that were usually hidden from her, and the driving power of one of the hungers behind those tensions.

The tranquillity cultivated in personal meditation may be deep, but is often too fragile to sustain during interpersonal contact. The individual meditator may feel temporarily happier, but relationships disrupt that ease; society is left wanting. In interpersonal meditation, we practice tranquillity in the presence of others and as part of a larger system. If we cannot relax with others under good circumstances, how can we expect to relax in the rolling seas of relationship? If we cannot be at peace in our relational lives, how can we contribute to a healthy and peaceful society? If our society cannot be at peace, how can we expect global peace to arise?

It would be nice if we could just tell our bodies to relax and they would obey. Most of our headaches and ulcers would vanish; we would be happier and live longer. But it just doesn't work like that. Usually by the time we notice that we have slipped out of mindfulness and into habitual ways of relating, our thoughts are excited and our emotions are simmering, perhaps ready to boil over. Because mind and body are interconnected, this reactivity has already sent neurotransmitters and hormones surging through our systems. Anger, fear, despair, and delight all have correlates in electrochemical activity. While the mind is infinitely light and may be able to turn quickly and let go of the past, the body's mass inhibits this. Tense muscles take time to release. Adrenaline takes a while to flush out of the bloodstream. A request (or order) to "relax" cannot be obeyed immediately by our bodies and brains, despite our best intentions. Patience and practice are necessary.

This momentum is not just physical, however. Thoughts also continue to push forward, even after we have become aware of them; so do the mental components of emotions. We may invite ourselves to relax out of our intense and identified interest in someone's story, but the desire to know something or to be entertained carries the tension forward. Habits of the mind run deep and fast, with a lifetime of momentum behind them; without a great depth of practice, stopping and settling into the moment is not easy. For many the only time we experience the natural clarity of the calm body-mind is when we have awakened from an unusually good sleep. If undisturbed by restless dreams, the interlude of night can naturally provide both Pause and Relax.

As the heart calms down, we become more mindful; as we become more mindful, we calm down. With a supportive practice, the fresh perspective of morning can be available to us more than once a day. Many forms of yoga help calm the body and bring about ease. Progressive muscle relaxation enables us to become aware of our patterns of holding tension and what it feels like to choose to relax contracted muscles. Biofeedback can also help us identify and cultivate deeper states of calm. Practices of bodily awareness—whether breath, posture, or movement—contribute to mental and emotional tranquillity. Traditional personal meditation is an excellent way to develop deeper calm. This integral link between mindfulness and calm is at the heart of many traditional meditation practices, including vipassana. Any of these can support Insight Dialogue's instruction Relax.

As Relax deepens and you become aware of more subtle tensions and emotions, it becomes clear that these graspings and grippings are not all going to vanish suddenly. "Relax" becomes "accept."

Receive things as they are, with a yielding mind and heart. Whatever sensations, emotions, or thoughts arise into the moment, simply receive them. There is no effort to change or get rid of them; we release resistance and Relax, accept.

When, in the Pause, you notice your bodily posture, just let this be met with an accepting awareness. If you notice the mind racing with your own or someone else's stories, accept the ongoing stream and its inherent pushing motion. Let the heart-mind yield to experience. Even if what the moment presents is strong, like great sadness in the heart or fear in the belly, time and again meet the moment's experience with acceptance. You can notice how this pain touches awareness—touching, touching, touching, and each touch is met with accept, accept, accept.

If you are with other people, Relax and let in what they say with this same receptivity. Accept their words and accept any reactions that may come up. If, when you are touched by others, you feel eager or critical or become attuned to deep longings, meet all of this with acceptance. Time and again, invite yourself to relax into the moment and accept things just as they are. Relax. Accept.

When we relax, we can let others in. We can also accept our own inner landscape. Gail—who noticed how her emotional reactions kept her from hearing what others said—was surprised by this dynamic.

At the start of the workshop I was very tense. It had been an emotionally difficult year for me, with health problems and a marital separation. I thought the workshop might help my conversations with others but did not expect the lightness and easing of tension I felt by its end. The weekend drove home the importance of taking care of myself, accepting myself, and cultivating equanimity and peace. When I love myself and I am calm, I see that my relationships with others are also filled with love and calm.

While tensions leave us separated from others, ease is a doorway to availability. Gail experienced the link between personal calm and being present for others. When we Pause, we step out of reaction and into the moment; when we Relax, we meet thoughts and feelings with acceptance. Accepting is to the mind what relaxing is to the body. It is how the mind relaxes. Having awakened to this moment's experience, we rest in a quality of awareness that is accepting, yielding, nonresistive, and available.

Such acceptance is an inherent quality of mindfulness; it has only been obscured by the habit of tensions. Awareness that is relaxed and stable can know the present moment intimately, neither grasping nor backing away. Having consciously given ourselves an initial reminder to "Relax," emotions may continue to rise into the moment. All is received and accepted. We don't run away from discomfort, confusion, fear, unhappiness, or ugliness—even our own perceived ugliness. When we notice a tightness in the belly or the sinking feeling of sadness, relaxed awareness has the stability to remain soft and present as the feeling unfolds. When the automatic tendency to fly backward in aversion is interrupted by the reminder to Relax, the mind stabilizes. Relax sustains nonclinging.

In this change the old habit of continuing or amplifying tension is supplanted with a new habit of ease and acceptance. Joan was surprised and delighted to discover a measure of freedom in this ease and acceptance.

> I felt so tense at first. As my meditation partner and I spoke about past unconscious relationships, I kept Pausing and Relaxing and began to settle into more ease with him. Then I had an insight: that I was accepting myself. It didn't matter whether he liked what I said or not, whether he accepted or rejected me, because I accepted myself. I accepted each thought and feeling as it arose, as well as the whole composite "me." Wow, the experience of self-acceptance in this very moment, rather than as a personal growth goal! How freeing.

As Joan accepted the tensions that arose in dialogue practice, she was also letting go of the grasping that sustained them. This easeful and light letting go was the source of what she called freedom, a foretaste of deeper liberation. The mind that can accept is more stable than a mind that grasps or pushes away; it can rest in the flow of ever-changing experience. Such a mind is adaptable enough to dwell in the unfolding moment. Relax gives stability and continuity to Pause. Excitements come and go during interpersonal engagement, but the Pausing mind does not identify with them. Willful attention is unnecessary. When the mind is happy and at peace, it naturally rests in the moment, contented and alert. Ease is the seed of concentration.

The relationship between Pause and Relax in Insight Dialogue is identical with the relationship between mindfulness (*sati* in Pali) and calm concentration (*samadhi*) in traditional Buddhist meditation. As mindfulness (Pause) becomes more steady and acute, the body-mind becomes calmer and more at ease. When the body is calm, the mind is happy and it, too, calms down. As this tranquillity deepens, the mind can become very still. It is content to rest easily on whatever is before awareness, and this ease-filled one-pointedness is Calm Concentration (Relax).

Calm Concentration supports a more refined mindfulness. This natural steadiness, without any attempt at peering or prying, can reveal tremendous detail about the subtle contours of the heart-mind. Mindfulness is very clear but absolutely without judgment or any of the other sharp habits of our everyday cognition. The mindfulness of Pause and the calm concentration of Relax are balanced; this enables deep insight into our internal world and the external world that includes other people and mindfulness of the *between* of relationship.

As this steady awareness reveals subtle truths about ourselves and the people we are with, desires and hungers are recognized, as are compassion and kindness. Because this awareness is yielding and adaptable, we are less likely to make the rigid flip back into reactivity, though this remains a possibility. New thoughts still arise; the urge to identify still arises. But these thoughts and urges are met with mindfulness and acceptance. They are known and released, not acted upon out of reflex. After we have met thoughts and emotions with acceptance, we can choose whether to pursue them or to act upon them. Just as there is no clinging to the thought or emotion, there is also no judgment. These activities of the heart-mind are simply known for what they are: conditioned responses that, unheeded, cause pain and lead to unskillful action and further pain. Met with acceptance, however, they lose their power. We may be able to answer the meditator who asked me, "What would it be like if we didn't retreat into anxiety? It supports everything we know." If we are asked, "Is life possible without anxiety?" we may be able to answer, "Yes."

Before Camille's first Insight Dialogue retreat, fear often overtook her when she was with new people. Afterward she shared the following: "All the intellectual understanding in the world could not repair my fear response. The actual experience of profoundly relaxing in the presence of silence while interacting with others created an opening of my awareness that made peace a reality. This experience continues to inspire and stabilize my practice." Camille experienced a basic dynamic of Insight Dialogue: Relax heals what Pause reveals. That is, the ease and acceptance of Relax enable profound wholesome shifts in one's internal landscape. Camille's acceptance and ease arose not only from her efforts but also from her mindful engagement with others who were also receiving the moment with calm acceptance.

I invite you to notice, as Relax and accept become steadier and more complete, that at its base, this meditation instruction points to a practice of lovingkindness. This is something you'll see emerge naturally. As you encounter internal experience—your own thoughts and emotions, your bodily tensions—the acceptance ripens into love. Let the mind, the heart, be fully receptive to experience just as it is. Any aversion, any pulling away from discomfort, is known as simply another layer of tension. Meet any pulling away with acceptance, and as the mind softens, notice the natural emergence of lovingkindness.

This is the lovingkindness of the mind with no aversion. Meet each thought with kindness and receptivity. In the Pause, let this lovingkindness saturate the body. There is no need to manufacture something called love. Just receive the moment fully, kindly receive whatever touches awareness, and remain awake as love naturally emerges.

If you are with others, in speaking or in silence, receive external experience—the other people—just as you receive the internal experience of your thoughts and emotions. Their faces touch your eyes and, being received without resistance or fear, kindness arises. Their voices touch your ears, and their words touch your mind, and there is no aversion, only lovingkindness. If the habit of fear or withdrawal arises, meet this, too, with kindness; this is a natural and deeply conditioned response, and we just meet it with acceptance and kindness. We let it go. Again we meet the moment, internally and with others, with Relax. Again we accept. Naturally, love emerges. More than an act, this is a shift of the heart-mind: let that lovingkindness set the tone of the moment.

As Relax and accept deepen, they lead us further into the engaged meditative experience: acceptance ripens as love. Acceptance is nonaversion; complete acceptance is the basis of love. This is not emotional love but *metta,* lovingkindness. Indeed, traditional practices that foster selfless love

—for example, holding others in awareness and wishing them well—are tremendous supports for Insight Dialogue. In Insight Dialogue such practices are not abstract; they are experienced as energies of the heart, states of the mind, as experiences of sending and receiving that are dynamically lived with others. When we pause into mindfulness, we also relax and accept whatever presents itself to awareness. We meet this experience with love, with kindness, with a yielding and pliable mind that enables exquisite proximity with that which is known. With relax-accept-love, feelings are not judged, and so they cease to hide from awareness. This is intimacy with experience. Internally, it is intimacy with our own experience; externally, it is intimacy with and availability to the other.

Loving awareness also reveals more deeply what is in our hearts. Imagine a light outside a house, connected to a motion sensor. If we approach the house fearing discovery—as intruders—we will run away when the light goes on. If we approach as travelers in need, who see the light as a welcome break in the darkness, we will come all the way into the house, undefended. The truth is, we are both the wary and the weary. We can make of this light of mindfulness a searchlight for encroaching evil that we imagine dwells within us; this is what the habit-mind often does. Or we can make this mindfulness the light of lovingkindness, gentle and hospitable. Experience can be known and met warmly. Dwelling in the glow of relaxed, loving acceptance, the chill is warmed, the strain unwrenched, the grasping released.

Just as the Pause is where stillness meets reactivity, in Relax love meets suffering. When this occurs, healing happens. It happens on the spot. Awareness is yielded in love; the confused and hurting heart loosens its tight bindings. Loving awareness permeates the fibers of the aching and confused body-mind, and the protective grip softens. As the heart begins to yield, basic hungers diminish and the rigid sense of self softens. The hole of wants no longer needs to be filled; shame no longer insists on hiding; without fuel, the flames of anger have nothing to burn. *Love meets suffering* also means *love meets nonstillness.* Tension and change are accepted. They often transmute to stillness, but whatever remains can be accepted.

In individual meditation both stillness and love are internally generated. In interpersonal practice stillness and love can also be within oneself. But it is part of the magic of the practice that the reactivity of one person can be met by the stillness in another. The suffering within oneself can be met by the love of another, or of the group.

This love, we realize, was here all along. The background noise of tension was so great we could not hear the voice of lovingkindness. Habits of clinging, older than anything we can remember, release when met with steady, loving awareness. In the nonclinging that is characteristic of the aware and accepting mind, there is ease. In the steady calm of the tranquil mind, the heart easily releases whatever is held. The maturation of this meditation instruction might be described as relax-accept-love-unbind. When self-concept is released, hatred, hurt, and self-protection soften and dissolve. The heart rests easily, steady in its tranquillity. We begin to see things as they actually are.

12

OPEN

PAUSE AND RELAX establish the traditional meditative framework of mindfulness and tranquillity. In Pause we step out of habit and meet the moment afresh. Aware of the body, emotions, and thoughts, we awaken out of identification with reaction. In Relax we meet with acceptance whatever presents itself to mindfulness. Whatever the experience might be, it is met with receptivity and kindness. The third part of the core interpersonal meditation instruction is Open. In Open, awareness extends to the world around us. Open invites us to extend the accepting mindfulness developed in Pause and Relax to the world beyond the boundaries of our skin. This extension to the world outside ourselves opens the door to mutuality: it is the basis for interpersonal meditation.

When we extend awareness beyond the skin-encapsulated self, our meditation grows to include other people and the environment. The Buddha's central instructions on vipassana meditation included the guidance to contemplate experience "internally . . . externally . . . or both internally and externally."[1] Focused internally, mindfulness emphasizes sensing this body, these thoughts, these emotions. Expanded externally, mindfulness includes the world that is sensed and reacted to: the physical world and the appearance, words, and actions of others. We meet other people with the same mindfulness and calm acceptance with which we are learning to meet our internal experience. If we are meditating in dialogue with one other person, we meet this person with wakeful acceptance. If we are meditating with an entire roomful of people, the same awareness opens wide to receive the whole group. With mindfulness of both the internal and the external, we are cognizant of the relational moment—what Martin Buber called "the between," the incessant flux of self and other.

With Open our practice ripens into mutuality. Just as we are extending awareness to encompass the other, our meditation partner or partners are doing the same. This is where we meet, encountering each other in mindfulness of both internal and external. As I extend my awareness outward to include another, I have a sense that that person is, in this same moment, extending his or her awareness outward to include me. This move is delicate and powerful. Some traditional meditation practices encourage wide-open awareness, such as Tibetan *dzogchen* or Christian contemplative prayer, but most do not extend that awareness to specific humans who are physically present and so do not open the door to encounter in co-meditation. In Insight Dialogue we open this door intentionally.

It is easy to begin to explore the instruction Open. We begin with the awareness cultivated in Pause and Relax. I invite you to become aware of the body right now, sitting just as it is. This is mindfulness established on the body: we inhabit the body, and inhabit the moment, in acceptance and nonclinging.

Now, beginning from that clear and stable inward awareness, find a particular place where sensation draws your attention—perhaps the touch of the body on the chair or cushion, or a point of discomfort in the hip or knees. By bringing focused attention to that area or point, mindfulness stabilizes there. Now, right at that point, we meet the sensation with acceptance. This awareness is very precise but very kind. We observe the receptive quality of awareness and allow ourselves time to become familiar with it. Sensation simply touches awareness.

Now begin internally to expand and extend that kindly awareness so that it fills the whole body. The entire body is saturated with receptive mindfulness. Let this become stable. Now, we do not stop there. To explore Open, we allow this awareness to extend beyond the body. We may first notice the expansive quality of a wider sense of hearing. Sounds come from the whole environment and touch awareness. If our eyes were closed, we might gently open them and notice that the visual field, even the entire room, is in our field of awareness. We may notice that other people are also in our field of awareness. If someone is in front of you, just keep the quality of seeing soft and general. If we meet another's eyes, we do not try to force any special experience—for example, by holding a steady gaze. The same kindly, accepting, mindful awareness that was offered internally to our own body-mind now encompasses the other. It is wider and more spacious. With Open, mindfulness encompasses the external as well as the internal. This is the step into mutuality. Open.

This quality of opening can be cultivated in many ways. It may be wise to explore it first in ways that do not involve other people, or to do so in parallel with our work with others. One of the easiest ways to know the spaciousness of external awareness—part of the spaciousness of Open—is to awaken in nature. As we walk in the forest, our consciousness may extend spontaneously to embrace the trees or the sky. Sitting by the seashore, we may find our minds wide like the sea, and this sense of expansion naturally takes us out of our habits of smallness. The hugeness, beauty, and utter uncontrollable aliveness of nature invites us, lifts us, out of our constructed inner world, giving us the sweet taste of freedom for a roofless moment. In such simple ways we extend beyond our little selves and step into a spacious relationship with the natural world. We may even discover how completely we are one with and not apart from nature.

Opening our awareness to include other people is not always easy. In many practices and practice settings, we are sequestered from another's face or voice or opinions so that we may more easily attain peace. Some practices, such as traditional lovingkindness practice (*metta*) or the boundless heart of compassion practiced as *bodhicitta,* can give profound support to Insight Dialogue's instruction Open. But on the threshold of extending our awareness to others present with us, we may find ourselves uncertain and afraid. At the moment of meeting we open a door: to both reactivity and possibility, selfishness and generosity, fear and freedom.

Extending our awareness to others, we open ourselves to the interpersonal hungers and the tensions they spawn. Annie, a meditator in California, described her first encounter with the process of opening. "Because I avoid intimacy, staying with this process was a transformation. At the thought of interacting with a stranger, my gut wrenched and my back tightened in knots." On the other side of the planet, a meditator in India, Stefan, said he felt as if he were "roasting in a fire." He experienced his anticipation as a pressure, wondering what he would say. Going back and forth between this pressure and the instructions Relax and Open, the stress of the first day precipitated a headache. Annie's fear and Stefan's roasting took root through years of conditioning. Their feelings arose automatically because there were other people present to trigger the conditioning. In the context of Insight Dialogue, the pains of encounter could be recognized more clearly because there were few distractions and because a degree of receptive mindfulness had been developed. Together these conditions—the triggers for the old hungers and graspings, the mindfulness of the Pause, and the acceptance of Relax—allowed unexpected release. Annie noted, "I still have a long way to go, but I felt that a great chasm had been spanned with this simple but monumental leap into silence." Stefan realized that his habitual search for the correct technique was unnecessarily effortful. "I may be simply surprised! There was a lot of energy, lightness, and spaciousness in the moment of Opening. Everything felt fresh and new and possible."

Not everyone feels fear at the prospect of opening to others, but even those who do not may not know how to open to another person in meditation. For example, Mike wondered, "If you've become aware of a heartache in yourself, how are you supposed to be present for, say, someone else's joy?" Mike is a therapist and an experienced vipassana meditator; both forms of training inclined him toward awareness that is either internal or external but not both. Also, his mind is very precise and accustomed to knowing, or thinking he knows, exactly what he is aware of at any given moment. But the Open component of Pause-Relax-Open does not incline us toward spatial precision, toward awareness of you or me. It suggests a flexibility that can move with ever-changing experience. Explicitly internal awareness, explicitly external awareness, and awareness that is both internal and external—all of these are valued and practiced. The mind unencumbered by clinging becomes malleable and learns to navigate internal and external freely, without distinct boundaries or transitions. We enjoy vibrant rest amid the wide sea of experience.

> As you practice Open and your mindfulness becomes more steady, you may become aware that you can notice thoughts arising as easily as you notice bodily sensations. It is just like looking at a tree and the next moment giving your attention to hearing some insects or birds. You can attend just as easily to internal or external phenomena. So I'm inviting you to cultivate a malleability of mind. See how it is to be mindful of rising and falling emotions and then attending to the words or facial expressions of people around you. Sometimes your attention may be very focused; at other times, quite wide. Sometimes it may be internal, sometimes external. Let the reminder to Open be an invitation to you to move

freely through the field of awareness, without clinging to anything whatsoever.

Inwardly directed mindfulness is extremely valuable to Insight Dialogue, especially its capacity to reveal details of unfolding experience that would otherwise be missed. One meditator described how he was able to observe his own physical responses during a period of intense emotional reaction to another participant's attitude. "After my belly tightened, I could see how judgmental thoughts started popcorning, and the urge to speak was like a bursting pressure in my head. As I continued watching, these thoughts had less impulsive power and I could relax again and open to him." By shifting his attention to internal phenomena, he was able to ride out the intense stage of his emotional storm, and he learned much about his patterns of reactivity. Once the storm was past, he could extend his awareness to the external world again—and, in particular, to the person whose comment triggered his reaction.

With both internal and external awareness, the mind is wide but still generally in touch with the flow of sensations and moods. Greta described an experience in which her attention moved between the internal and the external with ease.

The room was quiet. Everyone was still. The same stillness that was "out there" was "in here." Dave said he felt friendly and uncharacteristically relaxed with our group. Hearing him and knowing what he said did not interrupt my mindfulness of my body or of my emotional state. The hearing and the mindfulness were all part of the same experience of knowing the moment.

Greta experienced a pliable mind state. This is important to all meditation practice but particularly necessary in Insight Dialogue, where awareness may shift between the internal and the external, moment by moment. Mindfulness can move a great deal during practice, even during the course of a single conversation. When someone speaks, awareness may open outward in the hearing. Latching on to emotions or ideas may momentarily pull us into identification and reaction. Aware of our reactivity, we can Pause back into bodily awareness. Opening again, perhaps as our partner is still speaking, the awareness may now include both our body and the speaker's voice, then the sensations of emotional response and the sight and sense of our partner's emotional responses. In the silence that follows, awareness may move inward, noticing the delicate reverberations of thought that were aroused by what was said, then settling into a wider awareness of the silence, until a third person speaks and we are drawn again to outer perceptions of words and moving lips and expressive eyes. As we speak we may touch into mindfulness of our body and feel the moment come alive as both internal and external are known. We recognize awareness that has no self center. Openness and sensitivity to the fluidity of the moment are key.

As we practice like this we are developing the capacity to navigate easily between internal and external awareness. We see that Open is a spatial extension of nonclinging. The nonclinging mind does not need to land anywhere, not on our emotions and not on anyone else's. Meditation teacher Joseph Goldstein speaks well of the problems of unbalanced practice. He notes that practicing only focused mindfulness can tend to leave us narrow and tight, while cultivating only wide, spacious mind states can leave us ungrounded and spaced-out.[2] Insight Dialogue is a way to become familiar with and move between different qualities of awareness—internal and external—not privileging one over the other.

This kind of movement requires some stability and calm if we are to avoid shooting into agitation and reaction. This is why some foundation in traditional silent practice is so important to the maturation of Insight Dialogue. In Insight Dialogue our individually developed calm concentration is repurposed for relational meditation. We can now remain grounded and at ease as the quality of momentary experience changes. Inwardly or outwardly, objects simply touch awareness. This very touching is relationship. As the mind becomes more facile, we invoke Relax and the inclusiveness stabilizes.

For Amy, opening was, at first, a lot of work.

My desire to connect and Open was great, as was my desire to close and withdraw. I was moving constantly between the two. Attempting to Pause, Relax, and Open whenever I felt myself closing down exhausted me, but it also excited me and gave me hope. After a while I was able to stay open for a longer period of time.

Amy's exhaustion may have been the result of the fear of being seen. It may also have been the consequence of unspoken constraints that go with a belief in separateness. Most of us in the West grew up in a very individualistic culture. We were encouraged to form a strong sense of self: "Think for yourself." "Be your own person."

Open invites us to let go of this isolated and heavily bounded sense of self. At first it may seem like a fabrication to open the mind wide. In fact, intentional opening offers balance to the unrecognized construct of a contracted awareness. Locked in this construct, we may experience some friction as we open. Another meditator, Linda, did not feel exhausted at first, only confused.

> The internal mindfulness was very familiar and precise. It was just my usual meditation practice, only we were talking, too. And the external awareness was easy to comprehend—it was like being at my home and looking across the lake; very spacious. But it took me several days to experience these two simultaneously. Over time my awareness became soft but clear, engaged but dispassionate. This is where I learned what this whole teaching means.

The learning process Linda described unfolded quite naturally. Relaxation yielded openness.

Opening can begin as a rational process: we guide ourselves between specific internal sensations and a wide, spacious awareness. But it may also happen that we find ourselves effortlessly opened to the world when we simply Pause and Relax. In our everyday engagements with the world, the mind is always going back and forth—one moment lost in thought (internal) and the next watching out that we don't get hit by a bus (external). These inner and outer shifts can be known by mindfulness without grasping and identification. Over time we may find these shifts quite effortless, even when they are intentional. We may notice our own feelings or the outer expression of someone else's—the sound of the voice or quiver of the eyes—and it is all just phenomena, known as it rises and falls. Whether it is internal or external, we remain aware. Whether it is pleasant or unpleasant, we remain aware—not caught up, but aware.

> When you Open in meditation, let the mind relax out of any sense of agency or control. As the mind relaxes more and more, and as Open becomes very wide and familiar, you may find yourself settled in an awareness that is both internal and external. If you are with another person, you may notice that there is not such a rigid

divide between what that person is saying and what you are thinking; both just arise and are known. In here and out there is not such a big deal. As you become comfortable with this, you may begin to notice the between, the relationship itself as it manifests between yourself and others. The subject, me, and the object, you, or it, are joined in the relational moment. Let the Pause reveal this I-Thou quality of Open.

In this practice, as in individual meditation practice, we do not seek a fixed state but cultivate adaptability of mind, the malleability that enables opening and reopening to changing experience. As mindfulness moves inward and outward, over and over, this movement becomes easier and more familiar. The constructed self softens at the edges, and relationship shifts from contact between discrete objects to two people finding the moment together—opening touching opening.

When two people meet in meditative intimacy, clinging is reduced to a flicker. Content still arises, but the completeness of the relational moment is primary. Wanting, seeking, and grasping are not activated. If they become activated, we recognize this and release as we can. The more we release any grasping, the greater the intimacy. Because of our conditioning, at first this may seem counterintuitive. We are accustomed to a form of intimacy constructed around the content of our lives, our shared experiences. We have learned to treasure, to crave, this constructed intimacy. As we release grasping, though, the relational experience becomes very immediate. The word *im-mediate* means there is nothing between—that is, the hungers and fears do not separate us. This immediacy is not personalized. Because it is not constructed by a hungry personality, I call it unconstructed intimacy. In unconstructed intimacy, much is revealed by virtue of the empty field in which experience unfolds; whatever unfolds is accepted. This is cling-free connection, connection as nonseparation, empty presence.

Such nonpersonalized, natural intimacy arises on the basis of crystalline mindfulness and requires steadiness to be sustained. While it may be easy to open to silence or to nature, opening to the complexity of human contact is more challenging. Resistance to opening is a natural and lifelong habit. It is part of the defense system the self established to survive in family and society. So we must be patient with ourselves. Time and again Pause-Relax-Open invites us to wakeful calm. Time and again we meet internal experience with acceptance. We ask ourselves, "Where does the mind grip? What makes the heart recoil?" We may experiment with stepping courageously into Open when we are in conflict with another or feeling attacked. Aware of the person and his or her hostility without shutting the person out, we may find compassion arising. We may be able to observe our own urge to withdraw; perhaps we will discern the presence of clear awareness. As we learn that each of us lives in the shared human experience of vulnerability, and each of us is capable of great love, the emotional body begins to relax and allow this opening.

We will be able to sustain openness only when we dwell with acceptance and love. If we are pulled inward in the search for the safety of the me capsule, shrinking even from a silent intimacy free from expectations, then we can invite awareness out again, in the spaciousness of compassion. The gravity that collapses our star is the sad habit of smallness and separation. But if we Pause, Relax, and Open, letting the heart be guided by joy and compassion, we may find the experience described by the Quaker writer Douglas Steere: "a readiness to respect and to stand in wonder and openness before the mysterious life and influence of the other."[3] In this stance we are stable and awake; our awareness encompasses the personal and internal as well as the other and the world. This touching defines the boundary of self and moment.

> In those times when you feel at ease, stable, and present, let the mind be wide open, and see how it is to rest in the vastness. The heart is at ease; there is no inner-outer divide, no firm self and other. And you can dwell there. Even though you may be with other people, and you yourself may even speak into this vastness, any contraction that may come with speaking quickly passes. Again you rest in spaciousness. Experience rises and falls, and there is just knowing. Just openness itself.

We find that the fundamental experience of awareness is one of contact and of consciousness arising from this contact. It makes no difference whether it is awareness of an internal thought or of something external, such as hearing another speak. It is still "me" experiencing this. But right at the point of contact, this subject/object relationship vanishes. It is not experienced as "me knowing." The once rigid boundaries of self and other soften; both are known simply as experience. There is simply knowing. The flexible mind, grounded in mindfulness, moves freely between sensations, thoughts, and wide awareness. Or the mind can simply know all phenomena equally touching awareness. Bodily sensations appear to awareness almost synesthetically, as no different from sounds and thoughts. We are released from the burden of sustaining a self. We find that the separation of phenomena and experience is a construction; we can simply experience the knowing.

> Touch—wanting.
> Touch—fear.
> Touch—excitement.
>
> Touch—love.
> Touch—compassion.
> Touch—equanimity.
>
> Touch—just touching.
> Touch—just knowing touch.
> Just knowing.

The open mind, just knowing, is not caught. It is receptive and non-clinging. Our self-concerns are not so total and compelling. As self-concern quietly drifts away, opening becomes more complete. Complete internal opening unfastens the portal within to the unconscious, the ground of being, silence, and love. Complete external opening is universal extension and what some may call contact with the divine. In full completion there is no boundary between these two. The mind is wide like the sea. The particulars of experience are empty of substance; they are known as change itself. When the subject-object split disappears, looking outward and looking inward are the same. All phenomena share the quality of openness—the heart has opened fully outward and encompassed the inner; the heart has opened fully inward and encompassed the universe. The only boundary was the sense of self, which we find is an illusion, a by-product of stress. Eliminate the illusion and there is only being, "experiencing experience," as Venerable Punnaji calls it. All that remains is the purring engine of presence, which is awareness itself.

~ 13 ~

TRUST EMERGENCE

W E HAVE established the core of the practice: the mindfulness of Pause, the calm acceptance made possible by Relax, and the mutuality that comes with Open. With these instructions we meet the moment awake, loving, and spacious. But what if we find the present moment changing uncontrollably? Or what if it hardly seems to be changing at all—predictable, dull, and habit driven? The next meditation instruction in Insight Dialogue is Trust Emergence. With this instruction we are invited into the numinous but observable impermanence of all experience.

Trust Emergence is rooted in the wisdom aspect of Insight Dialogue. That is, it supports our seeing things as they are—unstable and far more complex and fluid than the mundane glance can know. The dynamic quality of experience demands robust practice and provides the object of that practice: change itself. The instruction Trust Emergence invites us to dive headlong into the tumbling moment by providing guidance for how we relate to each other and to the totality of experience. To *trust* is to make the leap of faith required to enter this seething sea of change. *Emergence* refers to the process by which the complex things we experience arise spontaneously from underlying contributing factors.[1] We can verify the fact of emergence by observing impermanence in the world around us, and especially the way conscious thoughts arise from a cauldron of sensation, memory, and emotions. Similarly, we can directly observe the incessant changes of social encounters as conversations and other interactions emerge from the complex conditioned personalities of the participants and the societies they inhabit.

To Trust Emergence is to let go into the changing process that we call "now," replete with its uncontrolled sensations, thoughts, emotions, interactions, words, topics, energies, and insights. Whether on retreat or in our daily lives, practicing Trust Emergence can help us stay with the insecurity and ambiguity of the changing present. *Emergence* and *renunciation* both come from the same Sanskrit root, originally having meaning related to leaving the household life. Both meanings point to the same inner gesture: letting go of the tendency to cling to conditions that are forever changing, ceasing to orient oneself in the world by reference to them. Paradoxically, attending to impermanence gives us a certain stability. It involves renouncing a pseudosafety and releases us from the pain of fearing change. In Tibetan Buddhist teachings the spirit of emergence is seen as reinforcing calmness. Our daily lives benefit when we stop resisting inevitable change —to our bank accounts, relationships, or health.

In Insight Dialogue we bring this attitude to meditation. To Trust Emergence is to enter practice without the bias of a goal. This does not mean we do not hope for better communication, wise relationships, or the emergence of collective intelligence, compassion, or peace. Rather, we recognize that we don't know what these things really are or how they can be attained, and we give our full and energetic commitment only to this moment of experience. The images and judgments that hinder clear and fluid awareness are set aside, freeing our natural intelligence. We recall that Insight Dialogue, like personal meditation, can point us toward clear understanding, and we commit to awareness. Good things like personal freedom and interpersonal harmony will emerge; we need not pursue them.

> You can explore Trust Emergence here and now. When you Pause out of preoccupation and pay attention to this moment, do you notice any sense of having plans for the day, a sort of ongoing to-do list? What is it like to invite yourself to release those plans, to let go of the push of your own agenda? Perhaps you are carrying the weight of other people's agendas, or you feel some pain associated with the fear of change. Right now, invite yourself to enter the moment with nothing to accomplish, with not having to be anyone special or attain anything. Invite yourself to drop the burden of attempting to control things.
>
> If you are with other people, you can remind yourself to Trust Emergence anytime you notice yourself planning what you are going to say or wanting to gain some specific outcome from a conversation. Meet others in a spirit of not knowing. Acknowledge that you don't know what is going to unfold in the next second, in

the next hour, week, or year. Meet the changing moment. Trust Emergence.

A group gathered expressly for meditation provides a rare opportunity to meet life in a radical way, stripped of social norms regarding productivity and accomplishment. From such a practice we learn new ways to live. The guideline Trust Emergence calls us to experience what it is to just be with another person or group of people in the present moment, not trying to make something happen nor looking forward to something that may happen in the future.

Participants in Insight Dialogue retreats often tell me that the meditation instruction Trust Emergence was the most confusing initially, but later it became the most useful instruction in their practice. For a while, the instruction Trust Emergence seemed silly to Klaus. His dedication to learning a precise practice caused him to resist letting go of plans and expectations.

> Then, I was with a group that totally lost its way. We were just chatting and laughing. It was fun, but I didn't see the meditation at all. Then I thought of this Trust Emergence. All at once, all of the chatting became just changing experience. When I shared this with the others, they seemed to understand this also. Then, even when the talking slowed down, the impermanence was still totally obvious.

There is an evolutionary basis for the wisdom of emergence. The human organism evolved to meet the world and not only survive but learn. Ever more mental capacity, however, created both opportunity and obstacle. We developed the capacity to reflect on experience and learn about how we learn. This has helped us learn certain things faster or more thoroughly. This same mental horsepower, however, has become the basis for an intricate sense of self and for confusing concepts and social norms that separate us from what we do best—move through the world with sensitivity, closely attuned to our environment. Trusting emergence, you might say, has been cultivated out of us. If we are clear about the nature of practice, we can remember and reestablish a naturally fluid way of being. We do not come to Insight Dialogue to reveal our conceptual knowledge and gain more knowledge but to know the nature of the conceiving mind and to drop its burden. We enter practice expectant, alert, ready for anything or for nothing, hunters and gatherers walking in the unknown—calm, alert, patient, and ready.

Trust Emergence is a powerful aid in our active lives in this busy modern world. I often invoke Trust Emergence when I find myself stuck in thoughts about where I want my life to go or when I attach to long-term plans. Just as we meet experience without attachment to a long-term goal, Open and Trust Emergence also call us to release short-term attachments and the personal agendas that hide us from each other. It often happens that as we speak with others, much of our mental activity is taken up with planning what we will say next and, especially in larger groups, how we can interject our contribution. When we pause in Insight Dialogue, we become aware of this microplanning, relax the tension behind it, open to our partner or the group, and—right in that very moment—let go of even these little plans and trust emergence. Kim experienced it as like putting down a weight.

> At the retreat, as my attention became more subtle, I could feel in my body the small muscle contractions that accompanied any tiny thought of "I don't want that; I want this," including my response to what others were saying, worries about too much or too little eye contact, and so on. I saw the way I was clinging in even the most minute and unimportant of thoughts, the way I began to compose my response before my partner was finished speaking—not trusting in the moment. Guessing ahead, cringing at an expected pain or embarrassment whether it happened or not.
>
> There is a great relief in the phrase "Trust Emergence." The mental and even physical tension involved with the tiniest craving and aversion are a burden I carry around so continuously that I don't even notice it until I find its absence. Then I get a glimpse at the relief in putting it all down. And to me a sense of space in which I can relate to others more directly and immediately.
>
> By bringing my awareness to my thoughts, speech, and actions without getting bogged down in self-recrimination when I do slip up, I am better able to Trust Emergence the next time.

This last point, that Kim found she could improve her capacity to trust emergence, is important. It is the habit of the mind to cling to sensations, thoughts, and emotions, even when we find them unpleasant. If we can, like Kim, see without judgment this clinging as it arises and let go time and again into the flux of emergence, this becomes a new tendency of the mind. Because of this practice, in the future letting go comes more easily. Most of us typically carry a great burden, a burden of personality, an obligation to inform or to entertain or to respond to others in expected ways. The feeling of setting down this burden is an immediate reward of trusting emergence.

> As you let go of plans, you are perched on the edge of possibility. Let the reminder to Trust Emergence arouse curiosity. What is happening now? Feel the truth of contingency and let it pull you out of any comfortable certainty. Attune to the unfolding moment and let your mind become nonresistive and pliable; let it move with experience. You can't predict what someone will say, what will happen tomorrow. So you are waiting, relaxed in expectancy. Dwell in the moment lightly, with patience. If the mind wants to run ahead, to figure things out, remind yourself of the unpredictability of things. Let all plans fall away. Ride the moment. Locate the wisdom in not knowing. This leaves you open to anything, and not fearing change. Trust Emergence.

We don't know what thought is going to come up next in our minds; five minutes of silent meditation will convince all but the most obtuse of this truth. We don't know what is going to arise in the mind of our dialogue partner; we don't even know what is in his or her mind right now. How can we possibly know what will arise from our complex interactions? Humans are remarkably subtle, unpredictable, capricious, mysterious, and endlessly varied. Each of us arrives at the interpersonal moment deeply conditioned, with our bodies in certain states, our emotions and thoughts already careening down the mountain of the moment. To think we can understand, let alone predict, what will emerge in any given conversation is a folly with a price. Prediction fills us with assumptions rather than truth. Rather than experience others, we experience our own projections, and the subtlety of emergence is lost.

It's funny how things move so quickly but can seem to be changing so painfully slowly by worldly standards. Letting things unfold naturally goes counter to the "make it happen" attitude so ingrained in the West. When I first started teaching Insight Dialogue retreats, I had to tell myself constantly, "Nothing appears to be happening. It will. Trust Emergence."

In those days I may have been the greatest transgressor of this guideline. I knew how powerful this practice could be, and I wanted people to have meaningful experiences. When things seemed slow, I was often tempted to shift groupings, throw another guideline at people, or exhort. "Feel your emotions well up into the moment," I might say, or "Is this silence stressful?" I wanted people to "get it" immediately. I found that every impatient intervention I made resulted in awkwardness and tension—precisely what I was attempting to avoid! I didn't recognize, yet, that the awkwardness all groups go through is a necessary stage and that important processes unfold beneath the seemingly pointless meanderings of the group. Then, it wasn't exciting for me to watch people grow more comfortable with pauses in conversation or notice how their mind's petty judgments were causing them stress. Now it is.

It became a personal creed for me to follow the guideline Trust Emergence. When things did not go as I wanted in my life, I would invoke this teaching and be continually surprised at how powerful it was. As I began to understand and trust the process of emergence, I became more patient on retreat. Also, trusting emergence meant getting any personal agenda out of the way so I could remain sensitive to the unfolding of the teachings and act with integrity. I knew I was not in control, and time and again I was called to surrender to that truth. I was able to model patience and nonattachment and thus encourage it in others. This was an unexpected gift of trusting emergence: patience opens doors that effort finds frozen shut.

Thinking we know costs us all we don't know—which is nearly everything. Knowing is a veneer our minds create and lay over the landscape like a painter's drop cloth set upon a forest floor. Its uniformity protects us from the pine needles and beetles, but it also obscures them, as well as the soft moss, fragrant soil, and teeming complexity of nature's bed. Our knowing is nearly always tinged by the filter of our conditioned outlook, and what we see as "true" is determined by our expectations, preconceptions, hopes, and fears. In short, the things that define the self stand between our awareness and our environment as such. In moments, however, we catch glints and feel the breezes of something more direct, something outside that self system. It may just be a clearer view of a mountain range, as it was once for me in Hawaii, or it may be something with a strong impact on our lives.

We can meet this world immediately, but as Brigid found, we sacrifice security. She said:

Every time I reminded myself to Trust Emergence, I felt like I lost everything I knew how to do. I lost how to have a regular conversation; I lost the solidity of my own body. I felt that my relationship with God was also being thrown up in the air, because God is supposed to know what is coming next. Where was the control? I lost my bearings. It was scary. But I also felt exhilarated. Somehow I felt God was more present in this not knowing and fear than was the case when I thought I knew what to do.

Brigid was touching on what Alan Watts called the wisdom of insecurity.[2] By sacrificing the frozen silhouette of life in favor of the never-the-same-river-twice reality of lived experience, Brigid touched the numinous, but she also touched fear. Her ability to speak according to norms was temporarily gone. Gone, too, was the safety of a stable sense of self and the feeling of reliability of social contracts. Brigid was called to enter what Suzuki Roshi called beginner's mind,[3] where possibility replaces safety and interest replaces delusion. In such a state the roots of who we think we are loosen. I recall seeing a sign outside a Christian church that said: "If you do not like the way you were born, try being born again." Trust Emergence is a way of being born again, fresh in each moment. In this radical act we leave behind personal baggage, emotional and intellectual. Such release may be temporary, but the universe cracks and spills its copious jewels when we penetrate the shells of certainty and glimpse the vast potential of uncertainty.

The senses are our gateways to recognizing impermanence. Just as the body is the terra firma of the Pause, ever-changing sensations are the most reliable way to reconnect with emergence. This can be directly experienced in the body by bringing awareness to changing bodily sensations. The Buddha taught this as an insight practice: "Or else he abides contemplating in the body its arising factors . . . or its vanishing factors . . . or both its arising and vanishing factors."[4] We can bring this same practice to all of our feelings, perceptions, mental and emotional fabrications, and to consciousness itself.

To explore Trust Emergence in a subtle, moment-to-moment way, it is helpful to attune to the senses. You might notice where your body touches the chair or cushion. If you look closely, you'll notice that the sensations are constantly changing. Whether that sensation is focused or diffuse, pleasant or unpleasant, it's changing. Subtler than this, you might notice that the sensation itself is vibration. Touching, hearing, seeing: these sensations are all made up of electrochemical change. They arise and keep arising; they fall, they fade, continuously. The sensations rise and fall dependent upon the stimulus and the working sense organ, for example, our skin or ears. This is known by consciousness, which is also constantly changing along with what arises. The knowing "I am feeling this" is a spontaneous, emergent result of this contact. Notice the change. Notice the emergent and changing experience of "hearing arises" or "feeling arises." Here, at this very point, we can reliably contact the truth of impermanence and so practice Trust Emergence.

If you are with other people, notice that hearing and seeing them also reveals this quality of change. Attune to the speaking voice as a song of impermanence. Let Trust Emergence remind you to come ever closer to the unplanned and unknowable aspects of this relationship.

The truth of change is part of the magic of music. Sound itself is vibration, and music is constantly changing, so music is changing change. It invites us to let go into its insubstantiality, defining the edge of the moment in shifting pitches, rhythms, and timbres. But as happens in the rest of our lives, our brains help freeze these ever-shifting sensations so that we may make sense of them. Pure sound becomes melody and resolution. Changing faces and vibrating voices are likewise frozen by the mind into something predictable. Even our moods seem to unfold in chunks rather than continuously evolving experiences. All the better to name and control them. The simple reminder to Trust Emergence reveals continuous change internally and externally. It invites us to let go of any illusion of control and relax, to drop the weight of being in charge of what is beyond the grip of the rational. Things are beyond our control and unpredictable; we may as well trust our ability to perceive and act clearly once the mind is unshackled.

In our highly rationalized society, this movement of surrender can seem quite alien, even though it is universally recognized as the heart of mystical experience. Ironically, meditation can reinforce the illusion that we can completely know our own minds, that there is no mystery that mindfulness cannot fathom. It took many unexplainable experiences—emotional, energetic, nonrational—for me to acknowledge the unknowability of mind and to accept meditative experiences that I had for years put on a shelf. My mother's death, for example, presented me with energetic shifts in my body that I did not understand. Following her passing I also experienced a shimmering aliveness in nature that did not fit neatly into my belief system. My insistence on knowability and control had demanded that I set aside such experiences. To trust change is to surrender into the flux of being, to release the rational. We resist it with the same energy with which we hold on to the self. We must be patient. As another meditator put it, "It took me some time to really enter Trust Emergence, because my lifelong habit of repression worked so well."

We have fled from change and mystery for many good reasons. We have needed control in order to deal with the insecurities of our physical and emotional environments. All of us have been let down, hurt, and left confused or lonely when we trusted people, institutions, or God to take care of us. To Trust Emergence in Insight Dialogue does not mean we are expected to abandon these habits of distrust immediately or give ourselves up to whomever we happen to be in practice with. As awareness of change, Trust Emergence is not about trusting people; it is about trusting that when we meet the unknown with mindfulness and acceptance, we will emerge from the experience wiser and more compassionate than we entered it. Put another way, it is about trusting life not to destroy us but to move through us in an enhancing way.

Trust Emergence is not the same as personal irresponsibility. It is far from any claim that we have no role in the unfolding of life and therefore may as well just sit back, watch, and do whatever pleases us. Rather, Trust Emergence involves both the wisdom inherent in recognizing impermanence and the strength necessary to meet this truth head-on. When we are trusting emergence, our perceptions are more true and more accurate because they do not originate in delusions of stability. When we Trust Emergence, our decisions are more trustworthy because they are not directed by a grasping heart or a controlling mind.

As the mind become clearer, lighter, and more attuned to the moment, let Trust Emergence become an invitation to surrender to the change itself. When you remind yourself to Trust Emergence, notice those moments of release. The mind rises and falls with phenomena. We are beckoned to the lightness, the freedom of nonclinging.

> Notice how you don't know what will happen next in the news, in your own next thought, or your next moment of interpersonal contact. You can't know. So meet that with courage and ease, and surrender to the not knowing. Each moment, everything rises and falls. Trust emergence. Trust dissolution, too. Be awake as phenomena fade. Remain aware as the present dissolves.

When mindfulness is strong, certainty is gone. In the absence of certainty, spontaneity emerges. The channels of habit are flooded by the river of rising life. As Lao Tsu said:

> The Great Tao flows everywhere.
> It may go left or right.
> All things depend on it for life, and it does not turn away from them.[5]

Despite the uncertainty as to where the Tao will flow, there is confidence that it does not become unavailable to anyone. Likewise, if we summon the courage and flexibility to Trust Emergence, we will function with a freedom beyond certainty—it is the freedom itself that will not turn away from us.

Behavior we had come to believe was spontaneous, when seen in the midst of trusting emergence, reveals itself as dull and predictable. Where mindfulness at first appeared to foreclose naturalness and the unexpected, we now see it is essential for what is truly fresh to emerge from the mud of the conditioned. We are usually like billiard balls on a table, obeying the laws of personality physics—until nonclinging wakefulness intervenes and enables something new. The winds of the Tao cannot carry the heart heavy with selfishness or preoccupation. When we are mired in self, Trust Emergence can help us become unstuck. Trust Emergence is nonclinging through time.

We are not alone on this passage through the unknown. We are trusting emergence together. Which brings energy and alertness. This helps us notice when the hooks of clinging catch on the fabric of experience. Out of that snag, moment to moment, we make what we call the real. Here emotions, thoughts, and sensations are frozen by the grasping mind, becoming "your" experience and "my" experience. In these moments we support ourselves and each other by recalling this meditation guideline.

We attend to the between and ask, usually internally, "What is emerging now?" Or we may ask, "What is dissolving now?" We dwell at the meeting point of doubt and wonder. What is arising in this heart-mind, what is emerging in this relationship, what is emerging in this group? What can I say, we might ask, that issues from the tip of the instant? Can our inquiry together reveal the next flower of the constantly blossoming present? Is there something latent in this between that, when attended to, might reveal a truth subtler than routine psychology? Surrendering to the flux of being transforms static experience into pure process, and we let go fully into wonderment. My thoughts become thinking. My emotions become feeling. The self becomes simply knowing.

When all members of a group Trust Emergence, there is spontaneous flow, and the group functions well. In many fields—team sports, theater, musical ensembles—people have recognized this spontaneous flow, when entire groups function as one. Each individual surrenders to the flow of the moment, so every interaction is free to manifest higher-order relationships, relationships not bound by habit and expectation. A ball is passed, a musical phrase is handed off, a comic opening is provided: everyone is riding the emergent pattern, but no one is making it happen. Birds flying in formation form beautiful patterns as they respond to the birds adjacent to them. The higher-level pattern is neither thought out nor preordained.

We can be where we are only if we can set aside where we've been and where we're going. In this setting aside, we still experience the ongoingness of being, and perhaps of individual awareness. But impermanence itself is greater than the personality, and so we yield to the arching sense of change. To cling is to suffer; to Trust Emergence is to surrender to the mystery of being conscious. We can only attend to the rising and falling, recognizing the pain that arises when we grasp and the ease that arises when we release. This becomes our navigational beacon. Trusting emergence together, we allow ourselves to be supported by the milieu of love. And when we withdraw because of habit or fear, this, too, is met with acceptance and love. Again, we practice patience. If we pay attention, it is always an impermanent moment. Flux becomes fixed as personalized experience when sensations are segmented into perceptions and the flow of perceptions congeals into the constructed self. The fleetingness of each experience is the living manifestation of the fleetingness of the whole of life. We ride the moment like a wave: we know the direction, maybe even the distance to shore, but not when the wave will break into turbulence and foam and be sucked to the re-forming sea.

～ 14 ～

LISTEN DEEPLY

PAUSE-RELAX-OPEN establishes the mind state for being fully present in the moment. Trust Emergence helps us develop this presence further in the active unfolding of mutuality. Into this vibrating and aware moment, we listen and speak. The Insight Dialogue meditation instructions that directly address this are Listen Deeply–Speak the Truth; we will focus first on Listen Deeply.

Listen Deeply opens the senses, heart, and mind to receive this moment fully. To listen deeply is to listen with mindfulness, surrendering fully to the unfolding words and presence of our co-meditators and others in our lives. We are a receptive field touched by the words, emotions, and energies of our fellow human beings, grounded in clear awareness and sensitive to the speaker's offering.

> When you call to mind Listen Deeply, let it be a call to awaken more fully into the moment. That is, step into mindfulness with particular attention to what is being said. As you listen, mindfulness is alert with a question something like "What is happening now?" The ears are attuned, but the heart, too, is open. You are listening to a fellow human being. Listen with kindness. Let the words, the stories, touch a compassionate heart. So we see that Listen Deeply is a reminder to allow ourselves to notice fully and be touched by the experience of another.

Communication is an act of mutual gift giving. We offer each other the gift of presence, of the particular wisdom of the moment, and of the muscled and softly textured heart. We receive the spoken word with appreciation for this gift. We listen with the generosity of patience, unhurried by a personal agenda. We aspire to the type of generosity Thoreau suggested when he said: "The greatest compliment that was ever paid me was when one asked me what I thought, and attended to my answer." With the mind expanded by Open and Trust Emergence, we are touched; tranquil, we do not interrupt our listening with an internal dialogue. For the moment we are free of the fixation on how we might respond to sooth, fix, impress, or dominate. We listen with kindness, compassion, and responsiveness.

As the words of another touch us, the astonishing and mundane loop of communicative contact is closed. What began as an emotion and thought in the mind of the speaker has landed in our heart-mind. For the voyage, the speaker's thought was wrapped in conditioned language uttered as speech sounds. Our ears were touched in the contact of raw sensation; then our minds instantly interpreted these sounds, touched in mental contact. Now the associative machinery of our conditioning has taken this input and proliferated it into ideas, emotions, and images. All of these reactions yield the experience we call understanding, as in "I understand what you said." The constructed and subjective nature of that understanding is rarely observed in action, but it makes up our felt sense of everyday conversations.

In meditation, mindfulness reveals this process of mutual contact and the reactivity that is all but inherent in verbal communication. One of the first things we see is how compelling we find each other's stories. We are attracted to the words and the cadence of our companions, as some part of our psyche is filled with the sweetness of apparent contact. We inhabit the story we are being told, internally creating its images and emotions in an effort to understand and empathize. We are taking it as our own. Here is what a meditator named Emma noticed during retreat:

> When I involve myself in someone else's story, I am no longer present as the listener. I am less available to support them and less aware of myself. I especially noticed this when the stories were powerful, like listening to Li tell of her shame of having been rejected by her family. My reactions and emotions claim a piece of the story and take me away from my center.

So what at first felt to Emma like generous and empathetic listening migrated into a kind of self-involvement. She felt taken away from her center in this moment of experience and unavailable for Li in her moment of pain. With Listen Deeply we acknowledge the value of momentarily inhabiting our internal fabrications of others' stories; this is, after all, our richest source of empathy. However, we also cultivate the ability to reestablish nonidentified mindfulness of the body, feelings, mind states, and thoughts, and this allows us to sustain a grounded presence even when stories are fascinating or relationships heat up.

Until we establish a stable, unidentified awareness, listening deeply can be experienced as teetering between empathy and self-involvement. As I hear your story, my first doorway into its truth is resonance with my similar experiences. So your words, in effect, trigger my story; we call this empathy. If I am mindful, though, I become aware of identifying with my fabrications, and this awareness itself becomes the defining element of my mind state. So I remain available to your words and my empathic reactions but not lost in a cascade of proliferations. I dwell at the boundary of empathic response and nonidentified awareness.

If the pictures we formed internally were completely in accord with what the speaker intended, perhaps miscommunication would diminish so much that the drop in mindfulness would not be too high a price to pay. But the sad fact is that we mold and taint what others share by projecting our own stories onto those of our speakers. Doing so, we take our conditioned interpretations to be the other's truth. Whenever listening is devoid of mindfulness, we "hear" and react to the roles and expectations we bring, not to the person in front of us.

Listen Deeply calls us back to the instant, out of all these reactions, with the question "What is happening now?" As Zen master Seung Sahn would say, "What is this?" This meditation instruction, together with the nonattachment that comes with Trust Emergence, moves us to investigate the moment more fully. At a time when we are with family or friends, we might try relaxing into a wide, receptive listening—and noticing any tendency of the mind to grip with interest or aversion or to impose its fabricated understandings. We begin to open ourselves to any new understanding the streaming present may bring. As Thoreau notes, "It takes two to speak the truth—one to speak and another to hear." We are that "other," ready to receive the truth in whatever form it presents itself.

As you listen, I invite you to give particular attention to several layers of what is being conveyed. Begin by attending to the meaning. Listen deeply to the content the speaker conveys. Listen to specific words and phrases, and watch meaning unfold in your mind. To listen deeply here means bringing clear and precise mindfulness to these words and the emergence of meaning.

After exploring content and meaning deeply, shift your attention to emotions. Pay attention to your own body as it responds to the words and images. Also, listen with your eyes and mindfully observe the body language of the speaker. Listen to the tone of the stream that carries the word meanings. Where are the pauses? Does the voice crack? Notice the rise and fall in pitch and loudness. Mindfully receive this rich stream.

Now I invite you to listen to the subtle messages of your body. What sensations arise as you allow the other's voice to touch you. To Listen Deeply here is to dwell mindfully, receptive to the energetic presence of the other.

Begin to notice how sometimes you listen in a focused way, attending to details of the words or voice tone, and sometimes you listen in a wide-open way, attuning to the overall flow of language, sound, and human movement. Explore moving among all of these ways of listening, as mindfulness becomes light and steady, not clinging to any particular moment of meaning. Listen Deeply.

There are exploratory and receptive qualities to Listen Deeply. In explorative listening, we apply the energy of attention to the many qualities of experience. We seek understanding, absorb detail, and navigate the inlets and bays of the ever-shifting coastline of verbal relating. The receptive quality of Listen Deeply emphasizes the stability and sensitivity of awareness. There is no reaching out, no going anywhere. We are calm and vigilant as the sounds and sights touch us as they will. In both types of listening there is no grasping at what is heard.

Explorative listening, as I use the term, is simply another facet of active meditation. I am not referring to communication techniques that stress such tools as acknowledging what we've heard, reflecting it back to the speaker, summarizing, reframing, supporting, checking perceptions, and the like. I simply mean the act of listening itself as a dynamic and fully engaged mindfulness practice. Just as we can explore the internal world of the body and thoughts in personal meditation, we can explore the external world of vocalized words and gestures in this mutual practice. This quality of listening brings the moment alive with the energy of inquiry.

There is always something to listen for, even if it is not contained in the apparent topic of conversation. When the topic of death came up, it was unappealingly familiar to Dmitry, who had worked with this topic extensively. His response was to turn, quite naturally, to an awake and energetic form of listening.

Rather than turn my mind off, I began to just look at people's faces. There was an electricity of life in them—sadness, happiness, confusion, all kinds of things were expressed. Watching this heightened my awareness further, and I started to listen to their voices. Even where there was fear in their words, there was strength in their vocal tone. I also heard doubt, even when the words spoken were confident ones. The topic, frankly, was old hat to me. The mindfulness that came with this listening was new and very alive.

The quality of Dmitry's listening sustained his alertness at a time when his attention could have dribbled into polite indifference. Rather than turn off, he became more attuned to his senses and more fully present for his co-meditators. If they were alert to the quality of his attention, they may have been invited more deeply into the clear awareness of that moment and perhaps even experienced a more subtle contemplation of the topic.

Listening can be a bona fide meditation practice, revealing something of the nature of experience. This is how it was for Brenda.

Lisa and I were talking about relationships/loneliness/ways of avoiding the feelings of isolation. At one moment during our dialogue I had the experience of Lisa's words touching the boundary of my awareness. I told her it felt like drops of water touching a still pond . . . it was like no moment I've ever experienced before . . . and then it was gone.

This brief and simple experience is interesting because, despite the psychological nature of their topic, Brenda's experience was devoid of personalizing. She was receptive, like a still pond, and the words touched her stillness. It was pure process; Brenda was actively attuned purely to being touched, not simply to verbal or emotional content.

We are not always graced with the qualities of listening that visited Dmitry and Brenda. In the complexity of relating to others it is so easy to become caught up or distracted. When this happens, Listen Deeply can be a reminder to explore other qualities of listening. We may listen closely, attending to the details of experience, or widely, zooming out to the greater flow of communication. Listening closely can be approached in many ways. Because listening and speaking in meditation can be so nuanced and challenging, at Insight Dialogue retreats I often separate the two and lead meditators through increasingly subtle approaches to the close aspect of listening deeply: listening to meaning, emotions, and presence. These three are interrelated. Words carry meaning, have an emotional valence, and suggest a quality of presence. Pauses and facial expressions that show emotion also help convey factual content. A sense of presence is carried in words, inflections, and gestures. But it can be useful to explore these individually.

Words and phrases carry content; close listening to words hones our ability to receive that content more precisely. Although we have each learned different meanings and associations, there is usually enough overlap that the words and phrases convey a sense of what the speaker intends. By closely attending to word meanings, we can become aware of ambiguities, questions, and metamessages that we might otherwise have missed. We might be drawn to note our subjective reactions to certain words that are particularly rich or pivotal to the conversation, or to words that indicate something about the mind state of the speaker. In interpersonal meditation we seek to establish a clear, receptive awareness; we are not actively seeking communicative benefits. But obviously, communication will become more precise and clear as a result. Such close listening requires energetic commitment and consequently supports the vitality of the practice.

Word meanings may convey emotion-laden content, but emotion is more directly revealed in prosody, pauses, and vocal timbre. Most of us are acutely sensitive to vocal nuance; we began to develop this sensitivity before birth, and it has enabled us to pilot the shoaled waters of our relational lives. What our mothers meant by "Come here, please" was carried more by vocal tone than by the meaning of the words themselves. A pause can indicate thoughtfulness or forgetfulness, insecurity or distraction. Cracks in the voice; emphases; and changes in loudness, talking speed, and rhythm form a stream that carries emotional content—content that is revealed to close, active listening.

Visual cues, too, are part of listening deeply. The subtleties of hand gestures, body postures, and facial expressions can all serve as foundations for mindfulness. We can easily understand that "I did it" might be perceived as a confession, a boast, or a lie, based on the glance of the speaker's eyes. Indeed, the psychological science of facial expressions reveals their role in the unconscious mind reading that naturally occurs among people in conversation. In meditative dialogue, listening closely with our eyes can reveal meanings more nuanced than the words being spoken. Craig experienced this in meditation with far more subtlety than he had ever noticed in daily life.

> My meditation partner was telling me of her concerns about changing jobs; for some reason I can't recall, our conversation came to a place of silence. We were looking at each other without any fear or wanting, just looking. My awareness got deeper in the sense that my senses were acute and my mind very still. I saw a wave of sadness brush across her eyes. I couldn't even tell you specifically what I saw, like eyebrow movement or a squint; I just knew it was sadness. I told Jane what I saw. Her eyes briefly pulled away, but then she came back. After a few moments I saw it again and told her so. I was feeling compassion but also a real curiosity that this could be happening. I mean, her face didn't even seem to move. She said to me, "Yes, there is a deep sadness in my life right now, but I don't want to talk about it." I could see the pain in her face much more than I heard it in her voice, but I honored her privacy and didn't ask about it. In fact, I felt I had to soften my attention so as not to pry. I didn't want to use this gift invasively.

Craig was wise to soften his attention. Fully present listening can lay bare matters that our fears would prefer to keep hidden. In meditation we can become conscious of exquisite sensitivities that may often be present but are usually overlooked. Such awareness enhances compassion. At the same time, the same subtlety and steadiness of awareness, when turned toward the impermanence, stress, and impersonality of our experiences, will yield the gift of seeing things as they actually are.

Just as we can listen for meaning and emotions, we can "listen" to the energy and presence of an individual or group. This kind of listening can be done with the ears, for example by noting the overall loudness and speed of a group's conversation, but the body is the more sensitive instrument for this kind of close listening. Perhaps our hearts vibrate with sensation as a large group settles into the moment. Perhaps our skulls swim a bit as we attend to the clarity of our partner's countenance. It may be that our whole body is felt as the sensitive organ it has always been. Such things are not easy to describe; language falls short in describing that which shimmers but never lands. Whatever the channel of sensation, we attend to these energies with the steadiness of Pause-Relax-Open and the nonattachment of Trust Emergence. Rather than land on any particular perception, we remain aware and attuned to the flux of experience.

When we shift from focused listening—to meanings, emotions, or energetic presence—to a wide listening, the overall flow and direction of the dialogue is more readily perceived. Rather than attend to individual words, we allow the river of sound to pour over us and reveal its larger contours. Changes in pitch and loudness become more musical than linguistic in nature, and energetic changes simply become part of the fabric of changing sensation. The different facets of our communication may merge into a gestalt, or whole pattern, of changing experience. As we dwell in this gestalt, we attune to others.

Each quality of listening has gifts to offer, and we can navigate between these qualities intentionally or as they naturally present themselves. There is not one right way to Listen Deeply. Focused listening to content and meaning via words, focused listening to emotions via sound qualities and visible bodily changes, focused listening to energies and presence, and wide gestaltlike listening can all function as foundations for mindfulness and thus reveal impermanence and emptiness. Deep-listening meditation teaches us to discern the rising and passing of experience in all sound; this is wisdom. It also teaches us to discern the specific pains and joys of our common, human experience; this is compassion. All of these qualities of listening share the quality of inquiry; all can extend well after the other has stopped speaking. Meanings continue to unfold within us in the silence. We trust emergence as different qualities of listening are called forth.

I recall an experience from my teens when I was at a workshop that took place on a college campus in Maine. While wandering during a break I found the music conservatory, a beautiful room with a domed ceiling and a wonderful grand piano. After playing for about an hour, I sat with my fingers placid on the keys as the sounds of the long, wound strings rang with the last notes played. It was a contemplative moment, but my mind wandered from the sound. I played another note and listened as it died away, but again thoughts entered my mind. I resolved to remain in the hall until I could remain in fully absorbed listening while one grand piano note faded beyond audibility. As the day darkened toward evening, I played one note, time and again, until, about an hour later, I had remained with a steady mind, listening as the note faded into emptiness. I looked up. Early evening entered through the windows atop the dome, and the large circular room delicately glowed in the soft gray light. Visually, objects were acutely defined. Internally, my mind was at peace. This was listening as a path of concentration, a path to clarity.

Listening to people is considerably more complex than listening to a single musical note. Whether close or wide, all forms of high-quality listening take as their object the complex other. Our experience is likely rich in attraction, aversion, energetic bursts, and the intensity of transience at the full human scale. It is good to remember that even as mindfulness migrates between close and wide and among meanings, emotions, and energies, we can always come home to the body or to the recognition of mindfulness itself: to simply knowing. Pause-Relax-Open reveals this basic movement among the internal, the external, and the internal and external combined. The body remains as a pointer to now; clear awareness can always be recognized.

As your listening deepens further, I invite you to listen to the silences between words or between speakers. Rest quietly and receptively in open awareness and listen to emergence itself. Your attention may be drawn to someone's face or to something someone says. This is fine. But then remind yourself to Listen Deeply and let go of all particulars. Dwell in receptivity. Let the heart rest in this receptivity as it ripens into lovingkindness. Words, other sounds, faces, and other sights are all received; they are just phenomena touching awareness. Rest in this presence. Allow the rising and falling particulars of human contact to be gathered into continuous presence. Listen Deeply.

As we become increasingly sensitive to each other, we see that our inquiry often takes on the quality of lovingkindness. Indeed, our love of inquiry itself motivates the practice to finer attunement. A sense of possibility and creativity arises that is synergistic with Trust Emergence. A participant in a four-day retreat shares her experience of the connection between emergence, listening, and creativity.

Gregory was answering a question about speaking from silence, and suddenly I realized that as he answered he was actually doing this. The creative nature of speech was revealed to me in this demonstration. I have a habit of interrupting people and completing their sentences. This may be motivated by a desire to dominate, but it mostly comes from a desire to be so attuned to the other that I share the same thoughts and to demonstrate that by speaking "their thoughts." What I saw was that each person needs to be free to give more space to that creative aspect, to allow what comes next to be unknown. In dialogue we draw something forth from the unknown together, but taking turns.

When Listen Deeply leads to this quality of creativity, we find that everyone has something to teach us. Loving, careful attention to the moment will reveal what this might be. Our energetic presence is rewarded with new understanding and insights. A Tibetan saying goes, "You may not hear something new, but you may learn something new." When we work with Listen Deeply, we are always learning something new.

Explorative listening offers many rewards, but it also presents us with dangers. Our trying may itself create tension and distance, which is not uncommon among people new to practice. I hear from people how exhausted they get "trying to listen" and "trying to pay attention to everything." They criticize themselves for not being mindful and clamp down into a stressful effort. Fortunately, most people soon realize that this is not a helpful approach to practice and that it is much easier and more joyful to relax into listening than force ourselves into it. As in all meditative paths, we need to balance energy and calm. The mind that is alert and tranquil, susceptible, responsive and available, is naturally engaged in receptive listening. Where active listening yields the benefits of doing, receptive listening shares in simply being. Deep listening that is receptive settles agitation. Silence is the basis of this listening, and this silence also becomes a gift to the speaker. Through Insight Dialogue practice, Thea discovered wordless listening.

I felt keenly aware of my internal desire to speak and acknowledge to the person speaking that I heard her. Instead, I paused and merely offered her my eyes, which said I was present with what she just said. There was silence and then she continued. I appreciate now that listening can be done silently, without words; this allows for the speaker to go even deeper into the process of awakening.

Being present for others takes internal silence as its foundation, yet when this listening ripens, it takes on an active role in the spiritual life of the group. Douglas Steere, a Quaker thinker, described the act of receptive listening as disclosing "the thinness of the filament that separates [people] listening openly to one another, and that of God intently listening to each soul."[1] In Insight Dialogue every meditator participates in listening the others into presence. This is a salient feature of mutual practice: receptivity powerful enough to draw forth from others a full participation in the moment. When I am listening in this way, it feels as though inquiry and love have begun to glow, nourished by the energy of calm concentration. I can feel the attractive quality, the way this listening is so receptive that something essential in the speaker lets go into it. There is no hunger in it, only awareness fully willing to be touched.

The exquisite sensitivity of receptive listening broadens the intersubjective field. When someone is speaking the truth through the conditioned medium of words, and these words are received via our conditioned minds, the overlap between the other person's intended meanings and our received meanings can grow. This is because the listening itself reaches into and beneath the word meanings, phrases, intonations, gestures, and energies and thus arrives at the immediate and shared experience of our humanity. We perceive each other as sharing the fact of embodiment and the silence that underlies this embodiment. In a group where many are listening to one person, we are joined in this listening. Even the speaker is listening. There is the shared intention toward release, toward cessation of confusing hungers, and we are joined in this intention. In Quaker corporate prayer, it is said participants listen and speak as a body. It is like this. We are joined in love. Listening to the between, we become sensitive to its movements. As an African proverb puts it, "Much silence makes a powerful noise."

Listen Deeply may reveal a collective intelligence, if this is our orientation, or when a meeting is "gathered," as the Quakers say, we may experience the presence of God, if our heart-minds are inclined in this way. In Insight Dialogue we just refer to the waiting, and we trust emergence. We allow what comes next to be unknown. We trust that others are doing their best to speak from empty presence, and we listen deeply, with a sacred expectancy. Our listening now reveals the more refined facets of wise attention. Taken as an ethical practice, wise attention simply means withdrawing attention from those encounters that corrupt the mind. In extraordinary practice, wise attention also encompasses listening to the radiant field of change itself, the faint echo of emptiness detected between the spoken words.

Listening is not only about sound; it is the natural action of receptive awareness. All of our senses, all of our being, listens. Listen Deeply rests on personal silent practice, such as the many forms of sitting meditation. Listening is stillness and the vibrating of that stillness. When stillness deepens, the "me," presumed to be at the center of this experience, is decentered. Receptive listening dissolves selfishness. Its inherent stillness allows the cries of the internal self-making voices to die down. Attention is not gathered around me and my needs. Even so, listening deeply includes a delicate inward listening that enables receptive listening to the other. One meditator put it this way: "The more I pay attention inward, the more able I am to listen to others. If I am not present with me, I cannot be present for others."

In empty presence, receptivity continues, but the one who is receptive does not. Analysis naturally diminishes, and the natural world is simply known. A Buddhist nun named Vayama shares a hint of this experience from her Insight Dialogue retreat.

> For one of the dialogues, I sat in the back corner next to the small pond. The windows were open and the frogs began to sing. Being with the singing and in meditative dialogue, joy arose. I had never heard the singing so clearly before. It is the voice of the Buddha that sings. I cannot describe being with the frogs and with the silence. It was like a beautiful symphony. The birds also sang, like a wake-up bell.

The simple and direct perception described here required no effort. Sister Vayama had already done her "work." This quality of awareness was the natural fruit of her practice. There is mindfulness but perhaps for moments not the sense of "I am mindful." Sandra speaks to this:

> This retreat opened me up to the qualities and power of listening without self. This experience provides for a sense of connection—as

in we are all one—and a felt sense of lovingkindness and compassion. As a professional therapist I thought I understood and practiced "good listening skills," but this experience goes beyond this.

The experience of "we are all one" arises not by dint of effort or by shoehorning our egos into a newly assumed nonself belief system. Rather, oneness is simply the temporary dissolution of the self through yielded, generous, and boundlessly receptive listening. The Pause, then, is ongoing and infinite. Relax is accepting and replete with love. Open is extended and centerless in mutuality. Trust Emergence is realized as the living surrender to lucidity. No-self Listens Deeply as the Truth speaks itself.

15

SPEAK THE TRUTH

U P TO THIS point we have been exploring how we can dwell in meditative awareness with others. As we Pause, we can Relax and accept what we find and Open our awareness to encompass external as well as internal experience. In that moment, we Trust Emergence, resting in the flux of experience. We meet the impermanence of things and experience both the delight and the insecurity of change and not knowing. We attend to what the next moment will bring. Listening Deeply to our inner voice and to the voices of others, our meditation brings us to the precipice of outward action. Attuned to the moment, we *Speak the Truth*.

Communication inevitably arises in the moment of emergent interpersonal contact. With or without the use of words, seeing and being seen yield an emotional interchange. Mere bodily proximity generates a flow of energy between people. It is uniquely powerful, however, to meet each other through the power of language. When we speak, some bit of the heart-mind is revealed. Every day, through the mystery of language, we touch each other: mind to mind, heart to heart.

As we begin to explore Speak the Truth, I invite you first to consider the basics: we don't lie; we tell things as we actually perceive them to be. At the same time, there is no pressure to say anything you don't want to say or that somehow doesn't feel appropriate. This is always your decision. And we don't say what is not useful. There is economy about our speech. We say what is appropriate, not more. We also approach speaking with an attitude of kindness, or non-cruelty. Just as we listen with kindness, we speak with kindness. Even the difficult things that must be said are spoken with goodwill.

With this basic understanding, please consider what it means to Speak the Truth. This is the subjective truth, the truth of your internal experience. Because it is subjective, it can be known only by mindfulness. You can explore the exquisite challenge of speaking with mindfulness, speaking the truth of this moment of experience. You know thoughts as they come and go; you are mindful of sensations in the body. Bring this same mindfulness to speaking. Notice the rising and falling of thoughts: before, during, and after speaking. Be aware of the physical act of speaking—breath, tongue, lips. Let this mindfulness help maintain the sense of the moment, the sense of truth. Speak the truth.

Speak the Truth most obviously embodies the morality and mutuality of our practice; it also contributes to the element of wisdom. Speaking the truth in meditation also involves the factors of the Noble Eightfold Path that heighten practice into the extraordinary: Right View, Effort, and Mindfulness.

Virtue makes our social lives livable and lays the groundwork for happiness and ease. Morality inhibits detrimental actions such as harsh speech and helps create harmony. When harmony is established, peace can be cultivated. With Insight Dialogue we are committed to ethical speech, to truth and kindness. The Buddha's words on this are simplicity itself:

> Monks, a statement endowed with five factors is well-spoken, not ill-spoken. It is blameless and unfaulted by knowledgeable people. Which five?
>
> It is spoken at the right time. It is spoken in truth. It is spoken affectionately. It is spoken beneficially. It is spoken with a mind of goodwill.[1]

At a very basic level, Speak the Truth is Right Speech that will do no harm.

The wisdom element of practice unfolds naturally in Speak the Truth as we share with others our observations and insights. Also, when we contemplate a specific topic together, we are infusing our minds with thoughts about things that matter, things that can transform how we see the world. The mutuality element of practice is obviously manifested here, because listening and speaking involve more than one person. In this simple act of communication, we invite each other into the moment.

Given the human propensity for reactivity and the power of language to spin us out of present-centered awareness and into self-centered habits, it is no surprise that most extraordinary practices do not include speaking. Many people have come to assume that words have no place in spiritual practice. With Speak the Truth we are invited to bring our highest intentions and our most refined perceptions into language, the workshop of our conceptual lives—invited to include the rich process of interpersonal communication within our expanded field of awareness. This may seem foolish or even arrogant. But to ignore the opportunity to bring the power of extraordinary practice into speaking would be unnecessarily limiting, possibly even irresponsible.

Speak the Truth invites us to reexamine the process and function of verbal communication. To speak the truth we must know the truth. Because we are referring to the subjective truth, the truth of our experience, we must listen internally in order to discern this truth. Thus, speaking enters meditative practice through the door of mindfulness. The other Insight Dialogue guidelines support and sustain mindfulness in the presence of others. Clarity arises when the mind is energetic, mindful, calm, and spacious (Pause-Relax-Open) and when it is unattached (Trust Emergence). Only by means of this clarity are we able to discern the truth of the moment. Speak the Truth supports our mindfulness as we act and interact with others.

The truth we speak is not static. When we Speak the Truth, the story changes as we tell it, evolving in each Pause as subjective experience unfolds. You can experiment with this unfolding in your daily life by noticing the different thoughts you could express in any social situation, all the different directions you could go in your sharing. Behind these directions it is possible to notice the motivations for your choices, often compounded of elements of hunger, generosity, curiosity, and wisdom. Also, we can never speak the whole truth, in the sense that words are not the whole felt experience. For example, the word *sunrise* may refer to a time of day but not to the suchness of one's experience of the blushing blue chill. Even so, the moment of communicative contact between people, the suchness of *that* experience, is true and whole, especially when reciprocated with Listen Deeply.

It is not easy to establish mindfulness while speaking. One meditator spoke for thousands when he said: "I felt really present when I was listening and really challenged when I was speaking." Words are conceptual representations of experience; when we speak, we can easily jump into the river of ideas and loose the moorings of presence. It can seem as if the very act of expressing ourselves necessitates abandoning mindfulness, calm, and all the meditative qualities we have been cultivating. Maintaining mindfulness while speaking takes practice. Two friends might decide together, for one interaction, to take the time to speak only the deeply felt sense of what is necessary and true. Even a small amount of this kind of practice, undertaken with energy and commitment, has power. Those who try this experiment might also inquire as to the quality of their own speaking: is there any sense of freshness? Of familiar cliché? How does it change the relationship or the quality of awareness?

When we use words, we wrap the coarse cloth of language around the subtly textured surface of experience. Do the words *emotion* or *heart* even begin to capture the nature of mind? Can words express the experience of the death of a loved one or how it feels to see a newborn baby? Every time we communicate with words we enter a domain as slippery as it is powerful. Language is culturally situated, and each of us brings a lifetime of conditioning to its use. The meaning of each word, each phrase, is therefore highly subjective. When two people meet verbally, the overlap of subjective meanings provides some intersubjectivity, and this becomes the basis of communication. One immediate benefit of bringing verbal communication into meditative awareness is that we can vanquish the delusion that clear communication is easy or common. Sheila offered this reflection after attending a couple of weekly Insight Dialogue group meetings:

> We spent an inordinate amount of time laughing uproariously at our assumptions, misperceptions, and self-centered natures as they were revealed. I found it both ludicrous and astounding, bordering on scary, to realize how tangential "communication" and "relationship" really are when compared with actual internal experience.

When the conceptualizing associated with speaking pulls us out of the moment of experience, mindfulness of bodily sensations can help us return to the immediacy of experience. For example, noticing the posture of the body or the sensations at the point of contact with our seat will reconnect us with the moment. The mind has the capacity to do this while speaking, just as we can know our emotional state or thoughts as we speak. This quality of speaking, however, is possible only with mindfulness, and mindfulness is often challenged by the forces of clinging and reactivity. When we say something with attachment to a certain outcome, we are not fully present with our thoughts or environment. An effective way to be more mindful is described by Elizabeth, who explained:

> From Insight Dialogue I gained a much deeper understanding of the difference between thought and feeling. Thinking seems synonymous with believing, but feeling comes up from within; it is more certain, more authentic. To speak out of feeling is to speak out of inner experience.

The certainty to which Elizabeth refers reflects the centrality of bodily sensation to how we understand the world and make decisions. Business people, artists, therapists, indeed all of us at one time or another, report going with "gut" feelings when faced with difficult decisions or trying to deal with an unfamiliar situation. Neurocognitive research has solidified this by connecting limbic (emotional) and cortical (cognitive) involvement in decision making.[2] In the practice of "focusing" developed by philosopher Eugene Gendlin, careful attention to inward bodily sensations is developed as a way of understanding our relation to particular life situations.[3] Philosophers and cognitive scientists speak of embodied knowing, even suggesting that we can understand the nonphysical world only through metaphors that link concepts and moods to the felt senses.[4] Examples include "He has a sharp tongue," "I'm clinging to this idea," and even the "full" in mindfulness.

Mindfulness of the body and feelings helps bring us into the moment and is especially important when we are in reaction. Madeline was in a group with another woman and two men and began to boil as she saw that "again, the women were attending to the men."

> I told the group I needed to say something. The group fell silent. I felt heightened energy and awareness and the realness of the moment. The energy of the group became charged in that moment. I was unsure how to say my truth.
>
> I took a breath, intending to speak, then realized I was not calm enough; I was still angry. I let the breath out. I took another breath. It wasn't enough. I closed my eyes, took a breath, waited, focused again on my body, and with some fear and tension but some groundedness and calm, too, I told the group about the irritation I was experiencing as a result of the group's stereotypical behavior.

The group was open to hear what I said, including the men. Everyone became very alert. It brought all of us right into the present.

Madeline was reacting to an external stimulus—the words and gestures that, to her, conveyed the marginalization of women—and recentering in her body was helpful. External input, however, is only a small part of what drives reactive speech. Conditioned hungers and mental and emotional constructions drive speech in ways that are often invisible to us. Speech itself is just the tip of the tornado where mind touches down on the interpersonal terrain. With all sense perceptions our minds are continually dancing with proliferations: a red rose reminds us of a red car, the touch of a stranger on the bus arouses disgust or erotic thoughts. Language is part of this dance, and we are easily thrown into the insane mélange of thoughts that we call the normal mind. Just as personal silent meditation reveals once-hidden inner tendencies, so does bringing meditative awareness to speech. To observe ourselves as we speak can reveal much, as it did for Ryan.

> It was sometimes difficult for me to avoid infusing irrelevant information into my statements that might impress the person/people I was talking to. This was my ego talking, I want people to think I am a great guy. Instead of "I'm a perfectionist and don't want to be," it was "I'm a perfectionist; I have won a lot of sales awards because of it but I don't want to be a perfectionist."

Ryan discovered that his hunger for being seen interfered with his conveying the simple truth to his meditation partners. Our words are drawn from a huge vat of memories and views, and because speech flows from the mind and we think and feel much quicker than we speak, we often speak from conclusions. Listening to such talk, one meditator in Australia said she felt like she was being served frozen rather than fresh vegetables. The poor thing was malnourished! Our frozen vegetable words are fully conditioned and simply emitted into the interpersonal moment. This is not a bad thing; it is efficient and often necessary. It is not, however, extraordinary. When we speak quickly or for long unbroken stretches, we are more likely to speak from habit. Calling on the Pause to interrupt such a flow, speech transforms from novellas into haiku, abundant with subtlety, meaning, and clarity. Without the Pause, which is more about mindfulness than about time, truth is rarely spoken.

Such conditioned speech actually leads us into reactions, interreactions with others, and tremendous confusion and pain. Our hungers get in the way of speaking the truth, either the objective or subjective truth, as they drive us toward speaking for entertainment, to get what we want, or to protect ourselves.

Even when we are speaking in ways that are not overtly harmful, much of our speech is simply to relieve stress, as this meditator discovered.

It became clear, in right-now-real time, how much of what comes out of my mouth is just an attempt to do something, anything, about my own internal stress. That "caught in the act" seeing is pure gold. Especially if one can manage not to seize up when it happens. And a couple of times it became pretty clear, in just-barely-past, wow-look-at-that time, how much of some other people's annoying ways were just the same: attempts to maneuver themselves out of the direct line of fire of their own stress.

Words spoken from hunger and stress have great power to harm. This is because words are an index to our intellectual and emotional history. When a wife says to her husband, "You *always* do things like that," with just the word *always* she is referencing perhaps thirty years of hurt. When we say "American" or "cancer," we tap into not only emotions but a knowledge base that can evoke numerous associations depending upon the context. There are countless communication techniques, for example the Nonviolent Communication practice developed by educator and activist Marshall Rosenberg,[5] that can help us deal with the often unskillful speech behavior produced from hungers and stress, then amplified and launched by the power of language. Many of these are of immense value. Self-regulation, assessing power, offering support to others, using "I" language, reframing disagreements, and other such tactics all have an important role on the front lines of human interaction. Extraordinary practice, and meditation in particular, invite us to also explore other possibilities.

In interpersonal meditation we are revealing and transforming the fundamental dynamics from which speech emerges. We are invited to slow down and perhaps find some fresh words among the reactive. There is no delusion that we will never speak from habit. If complete nonreactivity were a rule, we would all be mute! But what doors open when we practice mindfulness? Like Cindy, we may begin by seeing how speaking inclines us toward identification, which can open new opportunities.

I love silence and am usually more willing to listen than speak. It's been difficult to be silent and speak this weekend. Mindfulness so quickly shifts into runaway self-analysis. Some of the reluctance around speaking comes from not wanting to tell my story—again. Not wanting to identify with it or have others identify me with it. Practicing speaking from awareness of the moment helps.

Cindy found that mindfulness offered relief from the identification so rampant in her conversations. The roots of speech communication show us that along with delusion, language offers us some distinctly human gifts. The power of speech, together with its nuance and delicacy, constitutes a double-edged sword forged from years of evolution. Verbal communication evolved from animal communication for survival. The squawking bird warning other birds of danger is one such predecessor, and this same message was abstracted in some animals as the gesture of a pointing muzzle or perky ears. While grunts and gestures could describe a danger and issue a request for help or command to run, with the explosion in the size of the cortex, humans greatly enhanced their capacity to express tenderness, compassion, anger, desire, and fear. The abstract thinking that language makes possible also formed the basis for complex societies that include legal and monetary systems, ideas of justice, rapid accumulation and sharing of ideas, and transmitting those ideas across time. Language enables complexity.

As we explore speaking the truth, we're going to look at different facets, different layers of the truth. I'd like to invite you to begin by paying attention to meaning, to the actual content you mean to convey, and to the words used to convey it. When you consider the contemplation topic, or as you simply meet the moment, what thoughts arise? Be mindful of these thoughts. Making use of the Pause, take the time to notice how you put these thoughts into words. Choose your words carefully, mindfully. Do they say what you mean to say? Or are you sharing a story born from habit, speaking in prepatterned ways? Pause even as you speak and ask yourself whether these words you are sharing accurately convey the images and ideas arising in the mind. Is this the truth? Is it true right now? Let the meanings be as clear as possible.

As you settle, I also invite you to explore speaking the truth as it is known in the body. This is the truth as revealed in the belly, solar plexus, or throat. As you prepare to speak, attend to your emotions and your mind states and find the truth of the moment. This is what you speak. Watch carefully whether you are simply running on with old ideas, old feelings. Watch for the words that spill out without mindfulness and care. Speak the truth of the heart. Dwell with thoughts and feelings before speaking. How do they reverberate in the body? How do these feelings unfold as you speak? After you have spoken? This is a subtle aspect of the truth of the moment. Take your time. Mindfulness will know the small stirrings that define, here and now, what has the truth power to be spoken.

As the heart-mind becomes steadier, you can explore what it is like to speak the truth underneath these thoughts and feelings. What is the truth that comes from silence, from the energy of just sitting here now? What truth do you perceive in simply being aware? Let the moment, the energetic attention of others' listening, form what is said. There is no right or wrong, there is only the intention to be fully present in the moment and, as moved, to allow consciousness to speak. Speak this truth.

While language is a fertile source of conceptual traps and misunderstandings, it also carries great positive power. Words can convey simple interest, embody kindness, point to wisdom, or share presence. They can even be used to deconstruct themselves, to deconstruct the very misunderstandings that words can weave.

The wholesome potential of words is multifaceted. With words we communicate care, offer love, and express joy. Marcel had this experience with his wife: "The next morning, when I apologized for what I'd said, I was deeply mindful. It seemed that from the power of this, Eve and I could feel how our situation was so much a part of just people being married. It was just human." With words we share what we know and even convey insight. Spiritual teachers across the ages have left a trail of words that have uplifted and healed. Words are, indeed, necessary—but not alone sufficient—for the awakening of wisdom. Sometimes the power of words is squandered and wisdom cannot see its way through to others.

Insight Dialogue practice can sometimes be as paradoxical and inaccessible to rational understanding as the teaching riddles, or koans, of

Zen tradition. The power of conceptual thinking is sometimes turned in on itself, and the underlying relativity of language can cause the conversation to dissolve into absurd circularity and groundlessness. Whether hilarity or discomfort results, practitioners are offered a uniquely clear view of the absurdity of believing in the logic and validity of their own fabrications. They may be coaxed into an intuitive understanding of the human condition.

The walls of our internal prisons are built with the mortar of words, but in Insight Dialogue, words can serve to break apart our sad confines and direct our minds toward the wholesome, as happened for Frank.

A moment of insight for me occurred during dyad dialogue. My dialogue partner from Korea made a comment that touched me, and I told him so and thanked him. In response, he looked into my eyes and stated, "You are welcome."

There was such intensity and presence in his words that I not only heard them but felt them in my gut. The experience woke me to the understanding of the power that comes from words spoken truthfully and mindfully. I felt welcomed into a new awareness.

The power of the words spoken by this man's partner issued from the strength of the partner's intention to be present. As speech arises in the mind, it opens a window into the subtle emotional basis of intention. The meditation instruction Speak the Truth steadies us as we cultivate Right Intention, "right" in the sense of leading toward release, love, and compassion rather than toward grasping, hatred, and cruelty.

While Insight Dialogue is an extraordinary practice, it still rests on the same foundation of kindness that is the ground of ordinary human decency. The golden rule—speaking and listening as we would like to be spoken and listened to—provides a basis of ease and safety. Observations and jokes that have no real point beyond establishing a friendly relationship, that occur outside retreat settings as small talk, still foster relaxation, camaraderie, and happiness. Kind speech, no less than wise speech, conditions the future by cultivating wholesome mind states.

Real life is messy, however, and Insight Dialogue is not intended to be a shield behind which we hide from our anger and fear. So we return to intention. If everyone understands that we are in practice for higher purposes, then our words can express difficult emotions with confidence that the group can maintain mindfulness, love, and receptivity as we do so.

When a group of meditators ripens in this way, it becomes possible not only to realize and diminish the tendency to speak unskillfully but also to transform our reactions to others' doing so. Meagan was at a retreat where another meditator spoke harshly about her. Accustomed to feeling self-critical and insecure, she found that something had shifted after several days of dialogic meditation.

> After Jenna let loose on me, I began to realize the impact of words and the great responsibility we all have to use words with care and respect. I became aware that at times in my life I have spoken about matters that I know nothing about—which is what Jenna was criticizing me for. There was some truth in what she said. But whether I knew about that stuff or not wasn't relevant to what I had shared.
>
> Through the process I began to feel truly free and open. My emotional habits were not present. I was free of self-judgment, anger, remorse, and all the emotions that usually dog me. I could really see that Jenna's reaction wasn't about me. I also felt a lot of compassion for Jenna. I could see that she was hurting from the pain she may have caused me.
>
> I had been wondering if I was "getting" this meditation practice: if I would experience it here. I do get it; but it doesn't just look like quiet, peaceful talk. I feel gratitude and joy.

Meagan's observation that Insight Dialogue is not just about quiet, peaceful talk is important. To carry the notion that speaking and listening meditation is supposed to be purified of all difficult emotions is as harmful as believing this about personal, silent meditation. Both yield repression and turn spiritual practice into another way to bypass the messy truths of our lives. Speaking the truth encourages emotional and intellectual honesty as an inherent component of the path to freedom.

Wrong speech, on the other hand, hurts. It puts a painful clamp on emotions, arouses agitation, and leads to confusion. Lying, cruel, contentious, and frivolous speech all disrupt this meditation practice. Speaking the truth does not mean selfishly indulging in unbridled emotionality. If we find ourselves with the urge to stretch the truth or speak cruelly, we pause and take the time to ask if what we are about to say is based in greed, hatred or delusion or in generosity, love, and wisdom. Are we speaking to excite and entertain or to express the truth of this moment?

This brings us to the matter of discernment. Of all the possible things we could say, to what do we give voice? Much of what we might say is not wrong or cruel, but does this mean it should be said? Here we come to the greatest challenge of Speak the Truth. As we learn through practice to perceive directly the instantaneous truth of our own experience, we begin to realize that the mind is awash in thoughts and emotions. When a thought or feeling presents itself, we can instantly speak it or observe it and let go. What do we *do*? What does it mean to speak the truth?

> Now we're going to explore a subtler layer of the truth. This is the truth that emerges with discernment. This is speaking from emergence itself, in the same way that we looked at speaking from presence. But now, we attune to the delicacy of recognizing what is right, what is true, now. Here, I invite you into the paradox of knowing and emptiness, of speaking and of a silence that continues even as you speak.
>
> As you join with others in practice, establish the moment: attend to the body, feelings, and mind states, and to the flux of experience. Notice the luminosity of awareness itself. I invite you to relax and let go into this changing moment. Take your time. What is revealed in this flickering impermanence? Of all the thoughts that might arise in the mind, which rings with truth? Is this the truth for now or for later? Is it the truth of the conditioned self, or is there something else presenting itself? Don't be concerned with how this should look. There is no right way to do this. Just attend to that delicate sense of rightness. Drop, time and again, into the moment and speak from the energy it presents. Watch that energy to speak rise up. Is this the truth?
>
> Allow yourself to be baffled, to surrender to not knowing. What is the truth of meditative contact? What is in and beyond language? Whenever you are lost, be silent and attend to the listening of your partners. Allow this listening to draw you out, to define the present moment as it arises between or among you. Open to meditative contact. There is no need to force anything. Even your silence speaks. Live in the question presented by Speak the Truth.

Insight Dialogue invites us to examine and practice the heart, the essence, if you will, behind what would be spoken. When asked to Speak the Truth, we are called to examine not only what is true but what is useful, and even what is in some way fitting for that moment. We are speaking the subjective truth, that which has a rightness about it. The Buddha set a high bar when he said:

> I will engage in talk that is scrupulous, conducive to release of awareness . . . [to] direct knowledge, self-awakening, and Unbinding [Nibbana].[6]

Quakers talk about discerning what to speak and what to let go by unsaid. For them discernment sets a very high bar: speaking in the group meeting should not express the limited self but the voice of God as it moves through the group in the moment—Quaker discernment is being able to recognize this voice. The instruction Speak the Truth in Insight Dialogue, while not framed as worship, also includes the intention to discern and express the words that belong to the moment and that are free of the self's constructed concerns. This sense of rightness includes speaking from a place other than mundane thoughts and emotions, but it also encompasses our conditioned selves, when that is the truth of the moment. Discerning that rightness, we are called to all the elements of our path: morality, tranquillity, wisdom, and mutuality.

We may choose to ignore or suppress a thought, perhaps feeling it is too private, unkind, or simply not worth sharing. If the urge to speak what has arisen persists across mindful pauses, perhaps—trusting emergence—we feel our words will be of real value in this moment. The felt experience of discernment varies with our mind state and circumstances. At times the words of truth will present themselves with intensity. At other times we may feel relaxed; speech drops like ripe fruit from a tree. The truth may emerge from interest or as the result of being touched emotionally. The question "What do I speak" cannot be answered by any formula. Speak the Truth calls us to live with the paradox set up by simultaneously honoring both emergence and mindfulness. Thoughts blossom moment after moment, while mindfulness remains poised like a sage in a cave: action and stillness in the same moment. Asking, "Is this the truth that would be spoken," we find we are also asking (with the Quakers), "Is there life in it?" How would I recognize life, or truth?

We come to recognize meditative speaking as something that has less to do with words than with the source from which the words emerge. We learn to recognize the truth as we develop an intimate relationship with our own speaking. Lucidly present with the moment of experience, we watch speech emerge from the body, thoughts, or the unknowable unconscious. Perhaps, then, we touch the level of truth the Buddha refers to:

> Truth, indeed, is deathless speech.
> This is an ancient principle.[7]

Recognition comes with practice—just as it does in listening to music or appreciating poetry or fine art. Through trial and error we learn when favorable conditions increase or decrease. We find ourselves confronted with ambiguity, extreme subjectivity, and even mystery. No one answer about what to verbalize can be given. We share those inner experiences which, for whatever reason, feel right to share. They may sparkle with the light of recognition. One does not have to defend such thoughts; they are spoken as simply the truth of that moment.

Recognizing the truth of the moment, we speak it naturally, with confidence. Sometimes when I am with my wife or a close friend and speaking about delicate things, I pause for long periods of time, even midsentence. During these pauses I might turn my attention to my belly and see what the sensations there suggest about what I have to say. Then perhaps I'll notice the thinking mind, as if to ask, "Is this what needs to be said now?" I may enter into an empty silence and then turn to the solar plexus, or to the whole felt sense of my emotional state. Moving around like this, I find, the truth emerges of its own accord. Sometimes it just takes time. At other times I feel clear and empty as I speak, and gently allow my mind to follow the thread of a topic, trusting that each moment will reveal what needs to be said next. I'm speaking while truly not knowing what the next sentence will be. But because I am comfortable in the moment, no pauses are necessary. I trust the rolling forth of truth. When I am offering teachings, I might notice as this thread draws from a knowledge base, and then dip back into the truth of that moment's experience. But often, in teaching or in my everyday life, I find I have to release references, release knowledge, and track only the thread of experience, gently following the moment.

We can learn to trust our discernment. Sometimes we are tentative; we experiment. But even then, we can learn to recognize that the truth has about it a sense of stability, fortitude, and rightness. That rightness can be discerned even in the little truths of each moment. These, too, can be spoken with confidence. Underlying the feeling of confidence is a sense of centeredness that accompanies the nonclinging heart. The voice that speaks is not simply the voice of a separate self. It is also the voice of the circle or of the relationship emerging through us. We are encouraged to feel at ease with ourselves, confident of the group's lovingkindness. There is a boldness in this, a boldness far from aggression or ego promotion. It is simply trusting the thoughts, intuitions, and inspirations of the moment. In this sense Speak the Truth involves learning to recognize and trust the receptivity of others.

With this essential basis of acceptance, we may find the courage to speak the truth in ways we never have before. There is so much we do not say, and the practice of truth speaking can reveal what has been hidden. In the safety of retreat, met by the acceptance of our fellow meditators, we may find the courage to speak out as never before. Simply saying, "I was hurt by that" or "I need time to take this all in" can represent a liberating moment for someone who has shrunk from uncomfortable truth.

Speaking the truth refines discernment. Words spoken in truth and in a context of spiritual practice have the power of bearing witness. The power of mutual truth telling is beautifully revealed in Claudia's story.

> I told my partner that I wanted the intention behind my artwork to be investigation. I soon realized that speaking this intention in the context of retreat deepened my commitment to it, even though I say this often in discussions and lectures. Saying it to her felt like a vow. She responded, "I wonder why that is?" She began investigating in that moment! So we explored why that might be: words as carrying another kind of meaning, someone bearing witness, the intention going further than the sphere of oneself, the larger energy field holding it, the depth of truth being evoked by the dialogue, the extraordinariness of the context giving it extraordinary weight, including the renunciation of less noble goals, and knowing that the statement is being heard deeply. There was an answering reverberation of the intention in the listener.

In Claudia's story we see communicative relationship directly impacting the constructions of the meditators. Ideas and emotions are constructed, and words play a powerful role in that process. When the language is fitting and spoken from wisdom and love, the mountains of accumulated debris shift like a feather; the rusty chains of patterned thinking fall away. Words can change us.

A participant at a retreat in India reflected about the importance of truth speaking in the context of trusting emergence: actually speaking the truth in and of the moment.

> I've known for a long time that there are consequences for wrong speech. But it hadn't occurred to me that there might be consequences as well for withholding. So now I understand. It is not only "Speak the *truth*" but also "*speak* the truth."

When we speak the truth we refrain from taking Mark Twain's satirical advice: "The truth is the most valuable thing we have. Let us economize it." Truth speaking can free both ourselves and others. It can be an act of generosity and compassion, as when the Buddha decided, after his enlightenment, that he would teach.

The clearest truths are spoken from silence. Even when the mind becomes very calm, which certainly happens in retreats, mental processes are still occurring. We do not experience the stillness of total absorption as defined by a strict Theravadan interpretation of *jhana* (absorption). According to early Buddhist psychology, for speech to arise, there must be both an initial thought and the follow-on force of subsequent thought to propel this complex and powerful act. The precise observations made possible by insight practice help reveal these processes. Especially when we are sparing in speech, mental clarity arises, and we become witnesses to much of what has been hidden. The clarity and beauty of this process can heighten our energy. Attention may be directed inward and outward again, noticing the particulars of the mind that would speak and opening to that which is beyond these fabrications. Perhaps we notice the breath and calm down again—then open once more to attend to the between.

As awareness becomes more refined and still, we are moved to ask, "Can we even speak from silence?" Most practical spiritual advice regarding speech is on kindness. When confronted with the mystery of speech, we are brought time and again to "don't-know mind." This state, or attitude, is often referred to in Zen practice; it arises at the intersection of mystery and innocence. I cannot offer a formula for just how delicately words can brush the base of silence. But I frequently observe meditators attain profound states of *samadhi*—calm concentration—sufficient for the dissolution of the subject/object split and therefore of the self concept. Based upon experience, and upon what I've seen in retreat, I know it is possible to speak from great stillness, and there is more subtlety and power in words than is commonly thought. In one of his talks, the Buddha described how he was able to meet people and remain in a powerful and deep meditative state, or as he put it, "to enter and abide in voidness internally by giving no attention to all signs." It involved going in and out of various levels of extraordinarily deep absorption but not entering into the voidness possible with such absorption. Finally he would arise from these solitary dwellings to dwell with others and offer such talk as "favors the mind's release."[8]

Insight Dialogue neither requires nor rules out this degree of facility or stillness. Rather, when we are invited to Speak the Truth, we have the opportunity to become intimate with our own potential for speaking from something other than ego. Nigel wondered about the source of spiritual insight.

On rare occasions, I voice the truth in a dialogue or have an insight on the spot. Much more often the insights come afterward, while I am assimilating the experience. How do we know what is true? In my tradition it is the psychic being that has the power of discrimination. In Buddhism, does the truth simply arise spontaneously from the ground of being? I don't feel any conflict about this, I just see our dialogue go deeper and deeper.

As Nigel saw, speaking the truth transcends the boundaries of any particular spiritual tradition. The dialogue that goes deeper is not only the dialogue between individuals but also the dialogue between cultures and traditions. And beyond the constructions of culture and tradition, we find a common mystery.

Perhaps we are presented with the paradox that language can open doors beyond self-concept. Juan felt himself as a channel, or witness.

Language can open doors. Often I only have to connect loose ends and the thing is done. When I am only a channel for an energy that gives me the words and expressions, words come into my head/mind, but they are not my own. It's like being a messenger, without ego interference. This is very fulfilling.

Without ego interference, the mindfulness of Pause and the calm love of Relax and the boundlessness of Open move right through our words. Speaking does not interfere with our dwelling in the flux of emergence. Speaking from that which is not personal opens a portal to collective experience.

A coherence can arise in co-meditation that engenders very deep conversation. Many practitioners have reported speaking or hearing the voice of the group rather than a sea of separated people-points. Speaking the truth of the moment, the subjective truth, we encounter an intersubjective truth broader than the tiny overlap usually permitted by the everyday use of words. When Speak the Truth and Listen Deeply meet, the between comes alive as a shared experience. Communication becomes meditative contact. Hearing and speaking in compassion become the same act. We accompany each other to the edge of emptiness; doing so, we meet each other more fully in this human experience.

> presence is transparent.
> when i am present words are transparent.
> when i am transparent words have presence.
> when presence is transparent there is no "i am."

16

THE GUIDELINES
WORKING TOGETHER

THINKING ABOUT these meditation instructions reveals unexpected details and distinctions. A careful practice of them also reveals they are one in experience.

- *Pause* is essentially accepting (Relax), spacious (Open), and given over to impermanence (Trust Emergence). Reception and expression (Listen Deeply–Speak the Truth) issue from it.
- *Relax* yields easy mindfulness (Pause) and a wide or even unbounded (Open) awareness. It moves easily with changing experience (Trust Emergence)—speech blossoms and is received (Listen Deeply–Speak the Truth).
- *Open* invites the mind to be undistracted and alert (Pause), tranquil (Relax), and to encompass all emergence, including listening and speaking.
- In *Trust Emergence* the mind is fully present (Pause), nonresistive (Relax), unhindered by fabricated boundaries and not clinging to self-concept (Open). The mind trusting emergence listens with the lightness, agility, and curiosity of not knowing and speaks from the moment.
- In *Listen Deeply* we are mindful and fully present (Pause), steady and profoundly receptive (Relax), permeable to receive the external as well as the internal (Open), and poised on the tip of the moment (Trust Emergence)—where sound becomes hearing, hearing becomes listening, and contact occurs.
- *Speak the Truth* necessitates mindfully knowing the moment of experience (Pause), resting with acceptance of what arises (Relax), listening internally and externally (Listen Deeply), opening our awareness

to share with others (Open), and surrendering to the truth that is emerging in the moment we would speak (Trust Emergence).

The interoperation of these meditation instructions is suggested by the way they are grouped: Pause-Relax-Open is often presented as one guideline, Trust Emergence as another, and Listen Deeply–Speak the Truth is the third. We could present the whole as a single instruction—or as six. Each approach would emphasize different and important aspects of the practice. Considering them individually as six separate instructions or guidelines encourages us to focus on each and find nuance and depth. Thinking of them as three not only helps us remember them, it also reveals the flow between Pause, Relax, and Open; the centrality of letting go in Trust Emergence; and the reciprocity of Listen Deeply and Speak the Truth. The guidelines also function elegantly as pairs: Pause and Relax are the meditative core of mindfulness and concentration, Open and Trust Emergence are the extension of this mind state through space and time, and Listen Deeply and Speak the Truth bring the qualities of practice into interaction. Taking all the guidelines as a single instruction reveals the all-at-onceness of meditation, the concurrence of qualities that is the hallmark of the mature heart-mind.

Keeping the Insight Dialogue meditation instructions in mind as six elements provides a strong support for our practice, especially at the beginning, and whenever greater energy or clarification are called for. At the beginning we simply need the support of particular instructions to counter our habits of interpersonal encounter. Singly the guidelines are also easier to migrate into ordinary, daily practice. For example, it is not so hard to tell ourselves to relax anytime, or to trust emergence in diverse situations. When our commitment flags, our mind is scattered, or our heart is agitated, a specific focus can help us find the meditative moment. For example, a specific focus on Pause can help us step out of the preoccupations of a frenzied mind. It may just not be the time to expand into the spaciousness of Open because our distracted state would only become more diffuse and unpresent. A mental note, "Pause," can call up the clarity of our prior practice—personal and silent or interpersonal and engaged—and transform agitated energy into wakefulness. If this doesn't work, we might move to Trust Emergence, riding the wild wave of agitation as a fresh and adaptable foundation for clear awareness.

When emotional attachments arise—anger, desire, fear, and the like—we may benefit from the specific suggestion to calm the body and to meet pain and grasping, our own and others', with acceptance and love. This is Relax. Perhaps in these moments, Listen Deeply will open us beyond the shrunken patterns of self-concern, as we open our hearts to receive the humanly spoken words of whomever we are with. Perhaps Trust Emergence, at any of its levels of subtlety, will reveal the changing and insubstantial nature of the emotional reaction to which we have attached, opening the way to the transformational movement of letting go.

If we find ourselves locked in lethargy, perhaps the energy and commitment inherent in the Pause will invite us back into full participation. Perhaps Open will reveal the support of our companions in practice, as their energetic presence enlivens us out of torpor. If we can call forth a deep enough contemplation, the wild energy of Trust Emergence may lift us out of our sleep, reveal the contingency of all things, and maybe banish boredom with the sword of wise insecurity. Perhaps our commitment to Speak the Truth will call us out of our slump, inviting us to offer the gift of our momentary truth to the group, which is listening for the expression of this particular instant. If our torpor remains, perhaps we can Relax and, in offering ourselves this internal instruction, invite acceptance of the torpor and disclose a quiet, mindful stillness inside it.

The various guidelines can be called to mind to support specific difficulties in our practice or in how we meet others in life.

- Remember to *Pause* when you need to slow down, to drop ignorance, to see more deeply, or to brighten the mind.
- Remember to *Relax* in moments of stress, when facing challenging truths, and to bring ease to the body-mind.
- Remember to *Open* when you need to move out of isolated practice, loops, contraction, or selfish patterns.
- Remember to *Trust Emergence* to call forth energy, to end doubt, and to help you ride the moment.
- Remember to *Listen Deeply* to increase receptivity, to heighten inquiry, and to extend the heart.
- Remember to *Speak the Truth* to end stasis, to enhance generosity and courage, and to bring meditative interaction.

At the heart of Insight Dialogue is the ever-deepening mutual support of Pause and Relax. Mindfulness engenders calm, and calm concentration brings steadiness to mindfulness. Together these guidelines draw us toward increasing subtlety of insight: deeper calm helps us become more aware of what's going on in any given moment, and as the associated tensions are accepted and released, tensions diminish and the moment comes naturally into focus. As mindfulness and tranquillity come into balance, they infuse all the other guidelines, whether employed in special groups or in our everyday lives.

The guidelines can also work together as clusters of two or three to reveal other beneficial qualities of practice. We have already seen how Pause and Relax combine to yield clear, loving awareness. Combining the empathy possible with Listen Deeply and the moment-to-moment detachment of Trust Emergence, we find an elixir that helps us be fully yielded to another's story yet cognizant of its impermanent and insubstantial nature. We live in the paradox of human pain and emptiness, compassion and wisdom. When we combine Pause with Trust Emergence, our practice takes us to the edge of a cliff, where we are shocked into the energy and aliveness inherent in being fully awake. This combination also opens us up to humor as our vista reveals the edge of absurdity and the flailing of our everyday insanity. Together, Open and Trust Emergence condition the essence of surrender, while Open, Trust Emergence, and Speak the Truth show the essence of interpersonal courage. The combination of Pause, Trust Emergence, and Listen Deeply brings us face-to-face with the vibrating mystery of things, while Relax, Trust Emergence, and Listen Deeply sink us into the undulance. Relax with Listen Deeply engenders patience and receptivity; Relax with both Open and Listen Deeply so fully decenters us that we come to the brink of selflessness and emptiness.

As we take the guidelines into our lives, it can be helpful to play with them a little. What combinations touch us? What happens when we Pause and Trust Emergence while engaged in sports? In a dynamic conversation? Is it different from pairing Relax and Trust Emergence? We experiment to learn what supports us in different situations and different frames of mind. Eventually we find that all the guidelines manifest simultaneously. As they do so, they all disappear in the simple truth of being. This is the practice: fully interactive, relational, and mutually committed. There are no reminders here, no cues; just presence with each other. We have taken care of mindfulness, and now it takes care of us. And if there is a lapse in mindfulness, that's just part of being human. We accept our humanity with humility and love, and open to the very next moment.

When practice is ripe, there may be no need to clutter the mind by reminding ourselves to Pause. When tension arises, there may not be a voice that says "Relax." There may be simply the conditioned movement toward releasing tension. Mutuality, impermanence, and the freedom to speak or not speak are recognized as natural. Guidelines are there if we need them, but there is no attachment to form. Underneath the noise of clinging and pain, we are paused in mindfulness. Acceptance and love arise naturally in the absence of grasping self-concern. The tight and tangled yarn of smallness, when untangled, yields a natural mind, boundless and comfortable in this extension. There is nothing other than our own grasping and the fear of contingency that keeps us from surrendering to the blossoming now. Unimpeded by hurt and by self constructs, we easily give voice to the wisdom and compassion that comprise Truth. Our hearts are unbound, our minds are unfettered; we listen to each and every raindrop that touches and soaks our soil.

~ 17 ~

THE CONTEMPLATIONS

Contemplation in Insight Dialogue

WHAT WE talk about matters. What we talk about, we think about, and what we think about forms the root of our actions and sets the tone of our lives. By talking about things that matter and considering them deeply, we open the door to transforming the existing contents of the heart-mind. The core meditation instructions of Insight Dialogue are Pause-Relax-Open, Trust Emergence, and Listen Deeply–Speak the Truth. With this practice the mind becomes sensitive and powerful. Introducing a topic into this ecosystem is like placing a seed in rich tropical soil. It quickly blossoms into a conversation laden with fruit. By choosing our topics carefully, the power of the practice is amplified. These topics are the Insight Dialogue contemplations, the rudder by which we steer on the ocean of the conditioned mind.

From a practical standpoint, a contemplation gives Insight Dialogue practitioners something to talk about. It is introduced to the group as they emerge from silent practice, just before they enter into dialogue, and provides a theme for the speaking and listening meditation. In life practice the contemplation themes exist as a background reflection available to us throughout the day, a reference point inclining the mind toward beneficial thoughts. In retreat the contemplation is usually clearly stated and continually returned to. Sometimes, though, it is offered in a general way, and its function is more suggestive than directive. When Insight Dialogue meditation is well established, beneficial practice can unfold with no contemplation theme whatsoever. But in most practice situations, the contemplations help guide us to places we would not discover when pushed by the winds of habit alone. When, over the course of a long retreat, contemplations are focused on a coherent set of teachings, they can have a powerful impact on people. They help deconstruct unwholesome patterns of thought and facilitate insight into this human experience.

After the contemplation theme is introduced, we hold it in mind as a foreground thought, seeing what images, feelings, and ideas arise in response to this thought. For example, invited to contemplate liberation, we may notice some aversion to the idea of "leaving" activities or people we love. We may or may not speak this thought. Then we may recall a story from a time when we felt imprisoned in a relationship and how liberating it was when the relationship ended. We may speak this as the truth of this moment. This may lead to memories about this or other relationships and take us off the stated topic. Noticing the mind's wandering, we Pause, and upon reentering the present moment, we once again present "liberation" to the conscious mind. If the topic of liberation stimulates a meaningful and mindful conversation, we may follow where it leads, holding "liberation" only very lightly, or even forgetting about it until it naturally emerges during a longer pause. Perhaps we discern the liberated mind manifesting right now, as the awareness not identified with any of these thoughts. In this way the topic helps orient the conversation, yet leaves room for the surprises offered by emergence.

The contemplation becomes the field where we meet as conditioned beings, where we feel heard by and hear others. It is the source of the stuff we exchange as we get to know each other as fellow humans. Contemplations form the currency, if you will, of our generous sharing. Communicating our deepest thoughts to each other, we meet time and again in what is common to us all. We all experience stress, we have all been surprised by the unexpected, and we all inhabit an aging body. On retreat in Australia, Rachel spoke poignantly to this:

> I am a middle-aged woman feeling the losses and gains that come with aging. I work in a program for people with chronic heart and/ or lung disease. Our clients die while they are still with us. My parents are elderly and increasingly frail; I treasure the time we have left together.
>
> So I came into the contemplation with enough material to talk for three days on just this. As we begin, there is so much I can say that I am mostly silent. We stop with the bell. I sit back, slow down, feel myself in my back, and breathe. Next I state my fear of aging—the losses, the unpredictability of the process. Ernest states his similar fears and I feel in company, not alone. Fear subsides.

We stop. I sink deeper into myself while staying aware of Ernest. We talk slowly. There are great pauses between the speaking. I feel more and more anchored in the present moment.

Disease holds more fear and horror than death. And just speaking and pausing means these emotions pass. By the end of the practice I feel deeply connected with Ernest in the way of all humanity being connected—living a natural process over which we have little control but through which we can live fully in action and in quiet stillness. Something has been revealed to me in experience.

I complete a session by talking about the most painfully stimulating topics current in my life, and I feel calm.

We can see in Rachel's story the release of identification that can come about when we understand that our experiences are not unique; in our pain we are simply partaking of what it is to be human. Roles, power differentials, and assumptions about each other—and all the contemplations—become obvious and thin in the raw truth of the shared human experience. At the bottom we are all biological creatures, born into a fleshy body with a tender underbelly and overactive mind. All of us share in the mystery of consciousness and a heart that is inherently awake and wise. Indeed, the extent of our commonality becomes increasingly evident as each topic reveals a new facet of our shared humanity.

The contemplation theme is a reference point. It is not manipulated by one's shifting, conditioned view. When we accept the challenge offered by the contemplations and practice with rigor, it becomes difficult to avoid the sometimes painful insights they offer. We never know where Trust Emergence will lead us; when our starting point is, say, the topic of remorse and worry, the road can be rocky. Meticulous practice counters the tricky nature of mind; it foils our endless attempts to avoid things that are strange or that hurt.

The contemplations provide an unwavering and sometimes tough reference for our excursion into truth; they help us deepen our concentration and stay focused on what matters. While contemplating aging, disease, and death, we may discover that we have little control over life's processes. This absence of control is precisely the kind of fact our minds work so hard to avoid. Sometimes meditators resent the structure of the contemplations; they feel it is artificial or constraining. I have found them helpful, or even necessary, to minimize wandering conversations and guide the mind deeper. Without this depth, the mind may simply avoid the insecurity that results from seeing things as they are, that is, as impermanent, often painful, and devoid of a stable, anchoring self.

In this sense, sticking with the contemplations is a practice of what the Buddha called *yoniso manasikhara,* or wise attention. We give attention to what matters and withdraw attention from the useless or unwholesome. From the standpoint of the Noble Eightfold Path, contemplating experience within the framework of traditional wisdom teachings constitutes a practice of Right View. This places Insight Dialogue under the wisdom element of the path. That is, these contemplations, combined with morality and tranquillity, help us see things as they actually are.

There are two general classes of contemplations: traditional and contemporary. The traditional contemplations offered in practice are largely taken from early Buddhist teachings. They include such well-established themes as aging, disease, and death; impermanence, suffering, and impersonality; desire, aversion, and delusion; the three hungers—for pleasure, for being, and for escape; the beautiful mind states of lovingkindness, compassion, altruistic joy, and equanimity; the qualities that hinder our natural kindness and clarity—lust, hatred, sleepiness and laziness, remorse and worry, and doubt; factors of the awakened mind, including mindfulness, inquiry, energy, joy, tranquillity, and so on; and many others. I sometimes introduce hybrids of traditional contemplations, such as one on the meditator's own virtues of compassion, mindfulness, and concentration. I also introduce contemplations drawn from other wisdom traditions, such as gratitude (often associated with Christianity) or the mystery of change as revealed in nature (from indigenous traditions).

Contemporary contemplations tend to be psychological and pragmatic in nature. They include such themes as: roles and identities in various aspects of our lives; judgments we form of ourselves and others; and opinions, views, assumptions, and other fabrications of the thinking mind. Such contemplations often have correlates in established religious traditions but are framed in modern terms. For example, "judgments" are based upon the basic "greed, hatred, and delusion" of Buddhist thought. Views and assumptions reveal *sankhara,* or mental constructions, an important aspect of Buddhist psychology. Still, the modern framing of these contemplations can draw forth insights with immediate and obvious relevance to our lives.

Another type of contemporary topic is the tailored contemplation. When I am teaching a specific population, for example therapists, partners, or members of a community, I will sometimes craft a contemplation theme specifically suited to the challenges of that group. I may invite therapists, for example, to focus on the role of "helper" or on the notion of being expected to have answers or to fix things. In a community I may invite consideration of the values or goals of the community. There is no expectation that meditators will arrive at conclusions or solve problems during these contemplations. Indeed, when using tailored contemplations, special care must be taken to prevent reactive identification. To support practice in this way, we strengthen the meditative core—Pause-Relax-Open—which helps reveal our reactions to the topics as mental constructs. In this way we recognize reactions in their fundamental garb of attachment and aversion. We watch as the mind clings and proliferates; we see emotions demonstrate the truth of impermanence. Even as the contemplations help us deepen our understanding of issues or emotions, the practice of Insight Dialogue re-

EXAMPLES OF CONTEMPLATIONS USED IN INSIGHT DIALOGUE

Traditional Buddhist Contemplations	Other Contemplations
Aging-disease-death	Birth: the body, gender, ethnicity
Lust-anger-worry/remorse-sleepiness/laziness-doubt	Roles: public, relational, internal
Mindfulness-inquiry-energy-joy-tranquillity-concentration-equanimity	Judgments: others, self
Impermanence-suffering-impersonality	Views/assumptions
Ignorance/constructions-feeling/craving/clinging	Community
Greed-hatred-delusion	Nature
Hungers for pleasure-being-nonbeing	Freedom: political, social, personal
Teacher-teaching-taught (Buddha-Dhamma-Sangha)	Gratitude
Preciousness of this human life	Forgiveness: society, others, self
Emptiness	Hierarchy at work, in the family, socially
Constructions, ignorance, and freedom	

mains centered on the opportunity to cultivate mindfulness and calm and to let go into change itself.

The contemplations are often presented in clusters. In one sitting a practice group may contemplate all three characteristics of impermanence, suffering, and impersonality. For example, holding "impermanence" in mind, one may consider this fact generally—in relationships, work, meditation, the physical body, nature, or society—and whatever emerges as true and meaningful at that moment may be spoken. The teacher may then move the group on to a general contemplation of suffering, and then on to the absence of a controlling self in any aspect of their lives. On the other hand, a group of meditators may focus on impermanence, but the teacher or practice facilitator may begin with a contemplation of impermanence in our work lives, move on to impermanence in our family lives, and then in our emotions. The former allows us to cover broader themes; the latter invites us to explore narrow themes with greater depth.

A single, pithy topic or a coherent set of contemplations can be used as a guiding theme for an entire retreat. While all contemplations can be viewed as falling under the theme of the shared human experience, more specific retreat themes are opportunities to deepen our knowledge and directly experience powerful truths. For example, a retreat dedicated to exploring the three hungers may include consideration of these motive forces individually and in interaction with each other; how they manifest in different facets of our public, relational, and interior lives; and how we experience and act from moments when the hungers are not operating. I have seen this kind of retreat yield refined understanding and emotional liberation, and have a lasting impact on people's ability to experience the ease of nonclinging.

Multi-themed retreats can be woven into a comprehensive insight program. For example, I have been for years teaching retreats focused on different aspects of dependent origination (*paticca samupada* in Pali). This teaching describes in subtle detail how we create suffering out of moment-to-moment ignorance, how this extends from life to life, and how freedom comes by interrupting, or reversing, this process. It is the very heart of the Buddha's teachings on ignorance, hunger, and freedom. Retreats have been offered on most of the twelve links, including on the constructing mind and its fruits (*sankhara*), the mind-body and subject-object dichotomy (*nama-rupa*), hunger (*tanha*), clinging (*upadana*), and, of course, suffering (*dukkha*). Taken together, these retreats reveal Insight Dialogue contemplations as a powerful wisdom practice, one that opens doorways between the thinking mind, emotions, and, with the support of the Insight Dialogue guidelines, direct apprehension.

Pithy topics, grounded in unbridled and mindful inquiry, challenge our safety and build trust. This is not the common trust based upon knowing we won't be attacked or deceived but that which comes from knowing we are all in the same boat. It is not uncommon for a psychologist to attend an Insight Dialogue retreat and become concerned that participants are being invited to discuss delicate issues without first developing adequate feelings of safety. Mundane notions of safety, however, are based upon the assumption that people will remain identified with their stories. By contrast, the meditative essence of this practice invites us to notice and release such identification. Supported by Pause and Relax, even most beginners are able to meet challenging contemplations and establish a strong practice. Of course, it is also the case that no one is expected to say anything he or she does not want to reveal. In this way people meet each other with honor, respect, and compassion.

Contemplations must be chosen with great care. They can have a strong impact because they are being offered as meditation objects to people increasingly sensitized by the practice of mindfulness and tranquillity. Traditional contemplations wear well. They are time-tested and proven to work as portals to deep understanding. This makes them excellent choices, less likely to lead to aloof speculation or emotional self-indulgence. In retreat, where our sensitivity to such arousal is often magnified, we may discern ever more subtle insights about the topics. This challenges the steadiness of our Pause and Relax and can make it hard to Open and Trust Emergence. With commitment and practice, though, we become able to meet these contemplations, as Gigi did while contemplating all the different roles she takes on in her life.

> As the processes went on and I had insights that I am not my stories and I am not my roles, I became confused and anxious as to who I am. However, I remembered to breathe, pause, relax, and stay with the process.

When we are committed to stay with the practice in this way, the contemplations not only help us remain in meditation but actually deepen our concentration and mindfulness.

This deepened attention, in turn, yields more subtle understanding of the contemplation—which leads to further challenge and depth. In this way the contemplations not only offer topical insights, they strengthen the meditative core of Insight Dialogue. This can deliver us to the doorstep of deep understanding, as it did for Linda.

My tears on contemplating my last breath: those were tears of joy, not sadness. This was a special place with a lot of emotion, but not being identified with it. This is, in fact, deeper contact with my experience inside than I have with my sitting meditation.

As Linda contemplated death in the revealing safety of Insight Dialogue, she offered her co-meditators her unshielded heart; she invited them into the beauty of vulnerability. She was gently teaching practice mates about the possibility of neither denying nor identifying with emotions. In another session, someone may in turn teach her about the incessancy of impermanence or the pleasures and traps of desire.

Guided by the contemplation themes, we speak about issues of substance; such an opportunity is all too rare in a rushed and guarded world. Usually everyday conversations gather around practical concerns and matters of passing importance. We long for meaning, and by directly confronting fundamental issues such as love or doubt, we gain a refreshed sense of what is possible in relationship.

Contemplation themes can also confront us with the limits of language and of the thinking mind. In ways similar to koan practice, the mind may be pushed to the edge of coherence by too much work, too much thinking, too many words. Words then seem pointless, and the cognitive mind just runs out of energy. As several meditators have said to me, "I can't think anymore." One said he felt "empty but with a feeling of well-being." Others have touched absurdity or exhaustion; they often fall silent. At these times an opening may be created in which the thinking mind becomes quiet, defeated, and insight has room to manifest.

A topic is not always necessary. When people are well established in their practice and enter dialogue with no topic of contemplation at all, Trust Emergence invites us headlong into that moment's mental constructions. We follow the Tao, as it were, and practice becomes as open-ended as life; beautiful things can happen. The rigor formerly offered by the contemplations is now provided naturally by the concentration, ease, and courage of the participants. Trust, already developed by the realization of the shared human experience, is now established on the foundation of the mind of nonclinging. There is nothing here to be hurt. Now every topic, every word, every glance, nourishes insight. We rest together in not knowing what will arise next. This, alone, is adequate. There is nothing to get and nowhere to go.

Even when practice is well established, wisely chosen contemplations can add immeasurably to the transformative power of the meditation. Meditators dwell in the paradox of the topical conditioned and the meditative absolute. Each spark that flies from the contact of idea or emotion with awareness sheds light. In this way, while contemplations illuminate the seascape, the ocean's mystery remains.

Contemplation Examples

This section presents two examples of contemplations in Insight Dialogue, one contemporary and one traditional, along with a sketch of an entire retreat based on a single Dhamma concept. While these abbreviated contemplations are teachings in their own right, they are included here to help illustrate the practice. They may also provide starting points for those inspired to try the practice themselves.

Example One: Roles

A role is a notion, an idea in the heart-mind about who I am or who you are. This contemporary contemplation—which has it roots in many traditional contemplations—covers roles, identities, personae, and self-images; in short, any mental construct related to defining ourselves or others. Our roles are one way we make sense of our lives in society. They are often necessary, as is the case with the complementary roles of parent and child. Without these schemas, it is very difficult to navigate the complex social situations that make up everyday life for most of us. We generally inhabit our roles by identifying with them—I inhabit my roles as "me"—and this determines much about how we feel, think, and act. And just as we assume roles ourselves, we project them onto others. Often we relate to others role to role rather than in a fresh and present way.

There are many kinds of identifying notions, some necessary, some problematic. We can be defined by our biological reality and all the baggage that gets associated with this: man, woman, Caucasian, Asian, African, dyslexic, paraplegic, blonde, genius, or short person. We can be defined by our functional roles: boss, employee, mother, gardener, or donor. We can be defined by our belief systems: Christian, free market capitalist, scientist, humanitarian. We can be defined by our status in relation to others: younger, smarter, sexier, poorer, stronger, or needier. Or we can be defined dynamically in our relationships: helper, enabler, fixer, burden, friend, foe, student, or guide. We may also identify ourselves in terms of broad images, individually or in relationship: spiritual one, needy one, powerful one. We have many roles in life, and many of them overlap, for example: lover, breadwinner, comedian, shopper, protector, wife; or employer, sympathizer, wise person, father figure. The possible notions and combinations are endless.

The contemplation on roles, like most others, is itself quite simple.

Roles in our functional lives:

As you begin, I invite you to sit in silence and become aware of your body and just rest, be comfortable, in that awareness. Let's begin with our public face. We will contemplate what roles you inhabit at work, in your life as a volunteer or member of a community. What titles do you hold and how deeply do you identify with them? What roles are layered in with your functional roles? For example, as a salesperson, are you also an entertainer, or a scapegoat? As you think about the things you do and the relationships you have in the world at large, how have you been cast by others? Where do you limit or inflate your capacity or function? And what roles do you impose on other people? Do you see people in a fresh way, or do you see them primarily as they feed into the roles you play? As you speak, notice the tendency to inhabit the story you have made for yourself, and the one others have made for you. What is it like, now, to step out of that story in the Pause, accept whatever tension you find as you Relax and Open beyond your self center—to not be in that role in this moment?

Roles in our relational lives:

Now let's extend this contemplation to your personal, relational life. Simply being born, we have roles in relation to other people. I invite you to contemplate what roles you take on in your family: brother, mother, peacemaker, "the practical one." What roles do you assume in your friendships: talker, listener, giver, steady or erratic one? How does it feel to live in the many roles you assume in your intimate relationships: the sympathetic one, the wise one, the joker, the angry one? Perhaps the helper or the peacemaker? Is there any relationship outside of those roles? Take the time to pause out of the stories, the bodily feelings, and tensions associated with these roles. Even pause out of the joy. Just see how you enter into and relate from a persona, perhaps just the subtle and intimate persona of "the male" or "the female" in relationship. You might also explore whether there is choice that might exist behind that.

The role of self:

Now we come to the role behind all roles: the role of self. In this moment of meditation practice you have the opportunity to observe yourself as you begin to speak. What self is speaking? At what point do you inhabit the role of "me"? What is it like to be that "me"? As you listen, are you listening through a filter of conditioning? Is that a self? I invite you to take the time in your practice to speak from silence and to listen deeply. What remains when you step out of roles, even for an instant? As the mind tumbles forward in the Pause, does it have to land in an identity in order to relate to your meditation partner or partners? In the changing moment of Trust Emergence, is there any role or anyone to believe in it?

As this last contemplation makes clear, the ultimate identity, the role behind all roles, is the self. This self appears to generate our wandering thoughts or be the beneficiary of our insights; it sparks to life when we are with another. Can we exist without this identity? Can we exist in relation to another without this identity? Can we communicate with another without it? The persona is the form, the substance, of the individual in the world. In individual meditation practice, the self is the keystone construct: it upholds the arch of identification. In interpersonal meditation, persona is self in relation to other, and this is the keystone construct, the one that enables identified relationship. This form, the persona who relates, is empty; it is just a construct. But without it, who relates, and is relationship even possible? Who speaks? If form, or persona, is empty, but there is still speaking, then emptiness must also be form, form in relation. What is the difference? We can take liberty with the *Heart Sutra,* which says that "form is emptiness and the very emptiness is form"[1] and say, from experience, that "persona is emptiness, emptiness is persona."

Example Two: Already-Arisen Virtues—
Compassion, Mindfulness, and Calm

Giving attention to qualities that have already arisen in the mind tends to increase those qualities. This is true for difficult qualities like agitation and doubt, and it is true for wholesome qualities like kindness and concentration. In addition to teaching that specific qualities, such as concentration, increase when we attend to them, the Buddha also counseled paying attention to our virtues in general.

> There is the case where you recollect your own virtues: "[They are] untorn, unbroken . . . At any time when a disciple of the noble ones is recollecting virtue, his mind is not overcome with passion . . . aversion [or] delusion. His mind heads straight, based on virtue. And the disciple of the noble ones gains a sense of the goal, gains a sense of the Dhamma, gains joy . . . [and] the mind becomes concentrated."[2]

The contemplation itself is quite simple. I offer here a hybrid contemplation of compassion, mindfulness, and concentration. In formal Buddhist terms, compassion is one of the "divine abidings," or "illimitables," so called because they are extended without limit to all beings. Mindfulness and concentration are two of the "enlightenment factors" as well as factors of the Noble Eightfold Path. In short, all three components of this contemplation are central and highly valued qualities in all schools of Buddhism.

Compassion:

> As you sit in silence, aware of your body, I invite you to begin by simply relaxing in that awareness. So just come home to the moment. I'd like to invite you to contemplate the already arisen virtue of compassion. Consider where in your life care for others manifests naturally. Does your heart vibrate when you see an elderly

person having trouble stepping down from a curb? Do you feel sympathetic to the pain of malnourished children, in Africa or across the street? Do you feel compassion for the physical pain of your parents or the emotional pain of your brother or sister? Mindfully speak this truth.

Many of us are reluctant to acknowledge our virtues. In this practice, please don't look away from your goodness, your caring heart. This compassion is already there. You may find it in how you interact with animals or in the sadness you feel when watching the evening news. You may feel this compassion now, simply looking at the people you are with or thinking of a family member in crisis. Identify and acknowledge the tenderness and availability of your heart. When you Pause, find the truth of the moment. Speak the Truth of this compassion. Speak the Truth that reveals itself in your body. Also, as a gift to your partners in practice, reflect back to them the compassion you observe manifesting in them. Observe and honor their compassion, and as you do so, notice the care that arises in your heart.

Mindfulness:

Before we continue this contemplation, let's take the time to recenter in silence. There is no rush. As you sit quietly, do you notice how you can easily be mindful of your body sitting there? Can you easily feel your hands touching? I invite you to notice when you are mindful. This is very simple. Don't look for some penetrating awareness, just the simplicity of mindfulness. Do you notice sensations now? Do you notice your thoughts or moods? What is that like? What does mindfulness feel like? What qualities of mind are associated with mindfulness? Lightness? Clarity? Flexibility? Give some attention to those qualities. Notice how it feels to be aware of awareness. Your thoughts are not enemies, they are merely naturally arising traces of being alive. There is no holding to any of them; they just rise and fall. How is it simply to know this arising and passing?

As you enter into the dialogue, notice this quality of mindfulness in the moment: stable, light, and wakeful. Give voice to what you perceive. If the mind goes off into habitual thought, and then, in the

Pause, you come back and notice that you were off, notice the noticing. Speak the truth about this noticing. This becomes a gift to your meditation partners. You are pointing to your own mindfulness, and this reminds them to observe their own mindfulness. And, importantly, when one of your partners makes an observation born of mindfulness, acknowledge his or her mindfulness, reflect it back to the person. Listen Deeply, too, and notice that this is your mindfulness at work. Let there be a virtuous cycle of attending to and increasing the already arisen, the naturally manifesting quality of mindfulness.

Concentration:

Most of us recognize the busyness of our minds and don't think of ourselves as being concentrated. In this contemplation I would like to invite you to attend specifically and intentionally to the signs of the already-concentrated mind. Ask yourself, "Is my body relaxed?" Don't attend to the parts of the body that may be tense; specifically explore and contemplate the ease you find in the body-mind. Perhaps you are attending to only one thing right now, for example, some words or sensations. Notice the gentle concentration inherent in this. Dropping all assumptions about your level of calm, all criticisms of your mind state, I invite you to attend to the ease and steadiness manifesting right now. This is what we speak of, what we give voice to in the moment of experience. Notice how, when someone speaks, you attend to what the person is saying. This is the centered mind, remaining alert to these words, this person. Notice that stability. Notice the ease that reveals itself when you relax into the Pause. This is the manifestation of tranquillity that you have already cultivated.

This particular contemplation tends to yield a dialogue with many silent gaps. Notice the ease with which you accept and rest in these gaps. Notice this in your partners, too. Observe and give voice to the feelings associated with the body that is calm, steady. As you do so, let the calm be unbroken. Notice how concentration increases as you attend to it. Generously offer to your partners the gift of words spoken from the still center. Let the silences ring with quietude. Awareness becomes naturally unified.

These contemplations on wholesome qualities function on many levels. As the Buddha taught, wholesome factors increase based upon giving attention to them. This basic dynamic is then amplified by the power of group practice as people help each other stay with the topic, notice when nuances shift, and offer mutual encouragement. When people offer each other basic kindness and appreciation, feelings of affiliation and intimacy grow. Meditators become able to leave behind habitual self-criticism and to offer themselves goodwill, confidence, and encouragement. Dialogic contemplation of already-arisen wholesome states builds into a powerful practice, one full of joy.

The Thematic Retreat
Sankhara — *Constructions*

Contemplations are not only used independently of each other; an entire retreat can be given over to an in-depth exploration of some aspect of the human experience. For example, over the course of a weeklong Insight Dialogue retreat, a sequence of topics based on the idea of *sankhara*—constructions—may be introduced. To prevent an intellectualized or disembodied practice, special care is taken at these retreats to invite meditators to recenter in the body and sensations and to Speak the Truth of presently alive experience.

The body and mind are constantly blossoming into the moment, built upon what came before. *Sankhara* refers to this moment-to-moment building process and also to the accumulated life tone, or karmic edifice, that results from the constructing process: the personality, memories, and so forth. Contemplation of *sankhara,* undertaken with the keen eye of meditation and aided by the power of mutual inquiry, starkly reveals both the process and the results of this building process. We begin with the body and move on to various aspects of self concept and self in society, and then to qualities of the constructing and constructed heart-mind.

For example, a retreat might begin with contemplations on how the body is constructed of genes and food, and conditioned by actions taken. From those realizations the group might go on to consider how the lived experience of gender is constructed on top of biological sex, how one's body image is constructed from the raw materials of body type, and how ethnicity is fabricated from race and culture. A further exploration of the constructed self might include many of the same reflections undertaken under the heading of roles: the meditator's experience of the constructed persona at work, in the family, and in intimate relationships. Our constructed personality, character, and views are then also considered in the light of education, religion, and wealth.

The retreat might move on to other thematic clusters related to *sankhara,* including the personal experience of living with the intentional constructs of society, such as brand names, celebrities, patriotism, and religious communities and beliefs. We might also consider how cosmetics, fashion, and other consumer products accrete to this fabricated self. All the while, we are also observing the constructing mind at work and the clear awareness balanced amid that process.

From here a group might contemplate how a lifestyle that locks these patterns into place is built or how a lifestyle that tends toward liberation can also be built. We also contemplate our built-up notions of the Teacher —whether here on retreat or in historical figures such as the Buddha or Jesus—the teachings and views we guide our lives by, and the path we perceive ourselves to be on.

As the mind settles in practice, meditators are invited to consider constructs associated with their fears and those associated with the traditional Buddhist hindrances of lust, anger, worry and remorse, torpor, and doubt. Likewise, we might meet the constructs associated with the three hungers. This can reveal how hungers drive this constructing mind and how a personality is built around managing hungers. Throughout the retreat we see how each moment of thought builds and dissolves, leaving traces on our mood and, ultimately, our character. A lifestyle can be built that locks these patterns into place or that is liberating.

Such a retreat may lead us to an exploration of how we can, and do, construct the wholesome as well as the unwholesome. We form mental images and personality characteristics associated with kindness and generosity, and we develop habits that support mindfulness and tranquillity, whether it is meditation or walks in the park. We explore these already-arisen wholesome qualities and the ways we support their increase. Ultimately we contemplate three wholesome ways we relate to the fact of this constructing body-mind: we build wholesome constructs, we deconstruct by way of contemplation and meditation, and we simply become aware of the process of and products of our fabrications and meet them with acceptance. Over time, loving mindfulness, without any pushing or aversion, melts old constructs, disentangles the heart. It can be a slow process, but it is steady. It works.

By the close of a weeklong retreat, most participants have gained some direct experience and understanding of this central teaching of the Buddha. More than this, they will have recognized and released many unwholesome constructs, recognized the fundamentally fabricating nature of the body-mind, and in some way opened their hearts to moments of the unconstructed.

— 18 —

FORMS OF PRACTICE

Four Forms of Practice,
One Set of Instructions

The meditation instructions and the contemplations of Insight Dialogue can be used to support retreat practice, group practice within our ordinary schedules, and online meditation practice. The same instructions and contemplations can also be called to mind during our everyday lives, helping us to be more awake, peaceful, and kind as we engage with others. The meditation instructions are the same for these four forms of the practice. Most people find it helpful to remind themselves of the instructions and contemplations when they are learning the practice or reorienting themselves to it.

At first such conscious recollection of the meditation instructions can feel awkward while engaged with people. A contemplation theme, added to mindfulness of the body and of our meditation partners, might seem to add to the confusion, but facility and ease come with practice. The guidelines become wordless. Rather than thinking "Open," we simply expand our awareness; rather than thinking "Trust Emergence," we let go into the actual experience of impermanence and contingency. The contemplation theme sets the tone and direction of our collective inquiry, and little cognition is required to sustain it.

Like all things, the practice is changeable: sometimes it will be easy and natural; at other times we may need to recall a meditation instruction to refresh or deepen our practice. Over time our individual practice deepens. The guidelines and contemplations work together. The growing commitment and skill of the community of practitioners draws everyone deeper—like a pod of whales sounding.

The four forms of practice—retreats, regular groups, online practice, and practice in life—are mutually reinforcing. Insight Dialogue practice embedded in life helps us come to groups and retreats more calm and awake as well as more facile with the guidelines. Regular groups, online or in person, rejuvenate our in-life practice and provide opportunities to deepen understanding of the nuances of practice. Retreat practice, where we have the opportunity for extended and uninterrupted meditation, reveals possibilities for living. Together these practice forms point the way toward a life of increasing clarity and care.

The Insight Dialogue Retreat

An Insight Dialogue meditation retreat has much in common with other forms of retreat. A retreat can last anywhere from one day to more than a week. Participants are asked to leave behind their work, mobile phones, and books and are invited to "set aside covetousness and grief for the world."[1]

Insight Dialogue retreats are somewhat like an inverse of life: we are always in silence except when we are meditating. Meals and rest times are in silence, and there is traditional silent meditation following each meal and rest break. The silence is essential for many reasons. Random social interactions are a petri dish for habitual speech patterns, which we are learning to abandon in Insight Dialogue. Silence also helps foster a calm and concentrated mind. Because the meditation is interactive, mindless talking and other distractions at an interpersonal meditation retreat will impact other meditators. This is a truly shared practice, and we maintain mindfulness and tranquillity for the support and benefit of everyone.

Practice at Insight Dialogue retreats is virtually continuous, another similarity with traditional retreats. From the early-morning silent practice through morning, afternoon, and evening sessions of relational meditation, the day is spent cultivating uninterrupted mindfulness. We orient our hearts toward calming down; the retreat center environment and our meditating colleagues support us in this. The retreat days are long and immersive. The evenings close with lovingkindness meditation before each participant walks silently off to a good night's sleep. With such care, practice ripens well.

Most Insight Dialogue meditation sessions begin with individual silent meditation, usually with bodily awareness as a foundation. Then instructions are offered, and people are invited to self-select into groups. Early in the retreat, most groups are dyads—pairs. This may expand over the course of the retreat to groups of three or four, or the entire assembly. Even the self-selecting into groups can be revealing. Meditators often wonder, "Do I choose someone or wait to be chosen? What if someone says no when I choose them?"

As the retreat continues, the groupings change with nearly every session. This can offer other challenges, such as the discomfort of developing trust with different people and then releasing those relationships. Frequent group changes at the beginning offer precious opportunities to recognize the hungers behind our discomforts and witness the heart constructing what we call familiarity. In the absence of familiarity, we are invited into clear awareness of our social conditioning. Katherine, on retreat in New Zealand, found this demanding.

> Small group contemplations were difficult for me, as I wasn't completely easy about when to speak up or if I should initiate the conversation at the beginning. I found myself hating awkwardness; it brought back stuff from my childhood where us kids were never free to talk when adults were present.

Katherine felt awkward, but Bjorn's experience with people he didn't know had a different ring to it.

> It was easier being with strangers because there was no mental or emotional or historical structure to hear and see from. My partner was able to be fully present with exactly what I was expressing. I could be likewise present for him.

Early in retreats I try to take advantage of this lack of "historical structure." I advise meditators to practice with people they don't know, specifically so they can benefit from the freshness Bjorn mentioned. To know someone is, after all, to have mental constructions about the person. In most cases it is actually easier to establish meditative practice with people we do not know.

This freedom from historical structures extends to the historical structure we call the self. This becomes clear whenever we step into the Pause and watch the habit-mind struggle to maintain its persona. The mind is called to adapt, to open wider. Different group sizes are a moving target, making it more difficult to readjust and reestablish the constructions of self. Changing group size helps us let go of these constructions and so provide an avenue for growth. It is not always easy, as one meditator points out: "I can practice Open and feel intimate with one person but not with a larger group. It's the eye contact. I can't have eye contact with all of these people."

Some people find one-on-one meditation easy or even relish the opportunity to meet outside the estranged norms of our privatized society. Other people experience particular difficulty being calm and highly aware with one other person. It feels too intimate. But the questions still come up: Who do I look at? Where do I place attention?

The question about how to practice with more than one person, about where to look, are answered by Open. With this guideline we extend our attention beyond a narrow focus. We effectively have eyes all over our bodies. Our glance may be in one direction, but our awareness is wide. This open awareness with others is learned over the course of the retreat as the size of the groups is gradually increased. The energy and clarity of practice in small groups is, as one meditator noted, "stretched out" to the larger group.

Larger groups can sometimes evoke habit patterns that are not so likely to emerge in small groups. People who hunger to be seen typically feel pulled to speak and to be heard by this larger audience. Those who hunger for invisibility often feel their habitual shrinking even more strongly in larger groups—they are scared to speak.

It is nevertheless easier to hide in a larger group and to coast on the energy of the whole. While this can be beneficial, it can also yield laziness, as it did for Shawn.

> I felt such a dichotomy between my dyad dialogue and the large group. In the dyad my commitment to the process was strong, and so was the connection with others. But in the big group I was satisfied to let the "teacher" do the work, and I could indulge in my agitated mind, which separated me from everyone.

On retreat, though, the designated teacher is only one source of learning. The practice is also carried by the traditional teachings, the other meditators, and the teacher within ourselves. We are challenged to meet and honor this capacity in ourselves.

> You said something like, "So now you're waiting for me to tell you what to do, right?" I felt all of my assumptions and expectations of teachers arise. You were trying to tell me something I didn't want to

hear, that each one of us is our own teacher, responsible for whatever is happening.

Insight Dialogue radically alters the usual flow of meditation teaching and learning. In the process, it challenges us to expand our notion of the student-teacher relationship and turns us back to ourselves and to each other as rich sources of wisdom. In the classical student-teacher or master-disciple relationship, knowledge is dispensed. This sage-on-a-stage model is common in many spiritual traditions. Insight Dialogue injects peer-to-peer learning into a vast system of traditional, primarily Buddhist, wisdom.

Learning unfolds during retreats not only from Dhamma talks and internal experience but also from every encounter wakefully met. The number of teachable moments expands as we see suffering in others as well as ourselves and as we experience the contingency of our moods and identities. Other meditators teach us by their behavior, modeling stillness when we are agitated, mindfulness when we are self-absorbed. Our brains seem to be equipped with so-called mirror neurons that make this kind of learning faster and easier than the cognitive learning of being told or figuring out something. The meditation groups and the teacher also invite and induce us directly into wakefulness, because we are in active, meditative relationship with them.

Still, the support of a teacher or facilitator is one of the benefits of formal practice. Teachings are offered by way of the contemplations, where even a two-minute talk can stimulate new understanding in the subsequent dialogue. Also, breaks between groups frequently become interludes for questioning the teacher and for mindful discussion of the practice.

Along with sharing the guidelines and introducing the contemplations, the teacher also helps participants sustain their practice. During retreat I typically ring a bell several times during a contemplation, calling the meditators to silence. This outwardly supported Pause often offers relief, especially when people are just learning the practice and need time to reestablish serenity. It can be an opportunity to see where the face is tense or where habits have taken over. On the other hand, the bell can be perceived as an interruption of a cherished emotion. It can arouse grasping and a sense of loss about what is left unsaid. If the group changes after the bell, there may be a feeling of loss about the group itself. In this way the bell is the trickster, interrupting the normal mind and creating an opening to change.

Over time people become more adaptable; they grasp less at their desires and fears. They find that the mind states cultivated in practice—for example, tranquillity, or nonclinging—are sustained even when groups change. So it was for Claude.

> Early in the retreat, your talk about how the mind grasps, resulting in tension, helped me to observe the nature of my own thought process. I was especially grasping at thoughts about our group—but the groups kept changing. As thought arose and I practiced pausing and relaxing, a lot of my reactivity subsided. The silence after each bell invited me to let go, to release whatever selfing was occurring, and to trust emergence. It was a much more fluid experience of life, one that innately felt happier and less defended.

The centering and recentering that Claude mentions constitutes a practice of mindfulness and concentration.

In personal, silent retreat we are on our own, but in interpersonal practice we remind each other to be present. In Insight Dialogue in particular, we also have the teacher reminding us, and this can greatly enhance the quality of our practice, as it did for Bruce.

> Toward the end of our three-day retreat, I achieved a stillness that I don't believe I'd ever experienced before. I think the depth of stability and tranquillity was due to your constant and clear instruction that enabled our focus and intention to stay strong. In prior retreats the teacher has set a tone and a container for our individual experience, but the rest was up to us; we could lapse into "mindlessness." This certainly cannot happen in Insight Dialogue, in which we were continually challenged to go deeper.

The bell calls us not only to mindfulness but to Trust Emergence and to remember the contemplations. Seth's experience of a deep truth flowed out of this structured practice environment.

> Because I referenced the Dharma to speak, my understanding of "who" spoke clarified. The words were unrehearsed and present, and the contemplations on the path itself created peace; moments arose from the unbound, from the enlightened place. Words fail me.

When an entire retreat is focused on a single contemplation theme, understandings branching from that theme unfold as practice deepens. Contemplating death for several days may evoke and help resolve long-held fears. Exploring the many facets of sensory contact and reaction can help reveal the extent to which we are dominated by our desires and aversions. Complex points of Dhamma, such as the self constructs by which we limit our lives and cause ourselves great pain, can dissolve in the on-going light of investigation and acceptance. Celia, the mother of a two-year-old girl, shared, "Seven days of contemplating mental constructions showed me that I doubted that I could fully love my husband. It also showed me that this was an empty fabrication. One more painful mass of my self-notion vanished." Celia's relaxed smile after retreat was a joy to see.

Practice is not always easy, however. Meditation on retreat brings us up against inertia and habit—the concrete bunkers of defense. We may experience mood swings and sleepiness, in both personal and interpersonal retreat. Sometimes the structure, and the invitation to release limiting habits, can evoke anger and resentment. This is all part of the resistance to letting go. The body can feel sore. Attending to new guidelines can become confusing or tiring. And sometimes facing our conditioning is just taxing.

It is true that practice can be intense. It can also be elucidating and liberating. With all of these changes, we would do well to remember to laugh with each other at the folly of our painful attachments. As one meditator said, "Humor is a clear indication of the health of the process: when playfulness and joy are at the heart of it." Just as humor lightens the mind, retreats have times for movement to lighten the body and help us feel grounded. The nature of the body practices changes with the needs of the moment and can range from slow and calm to fast and energetic. Also leavening the practice are times in nature, sometimes with practice in pairs, sometimes alone.

All of these elements create the conditions for change: silence, personal practice, lovingkindness meditation, and the support of other meditators; the teacher's support offered in discussion, formal teachings, and the structure offered by bells; the continued emphasis on relaxation; varying group sizes, movement, time spent in nature; and the core meditation practice and the contemplations. As Peter put it:

By the end of the first full day of the retreat I felt I'd been there for nearly a week. It's not that the day seemed long at all. Rather it was that so much had happened within me. My state of being had already shifted to a heightened state of attentiveness and calm. I have done a lot of meditation, and it seemed odd to feel that different in such a short time.

In fact it is quite common for the end of the first day—or even the first evening—to find the meditation hall ringing with awareness, pervaded by blissful feelings. It almost seems like beginner's luck, except it happens fairly often.

It also happens often that two or three days into retreat, many meditators experience resistance, fatigue, frustration, or a desire to leave the retreat. Strong practice offers benefits, but on the way to such depth we can expect to encounter many ups and downs, individually and in the whole group. As Denise found, something sweet may linger beyond the veil of resistance.

I had been feeling extremely tired, with a heavy, uncomfortable body fraught with resistance and an active, agitated mind. Then people began to speak about the freedom that comes with acceptance and relaxation, and about accepting things in others with no expectations. It poured over me; my resistance melted. I almost never encounter this kind of peace. Instead of volition, requirements, and conditions, I feel relief at being able to just be. Tears came to my eyes, tears of joy and relief. I felt such closeness, then, and presence with the others—just sitting, being. My body was supported; I was out of pain.

A primary benefit of extended retreat is the opportunity to develop the high degree of clarity, tranquillity, and depth of concentration that is a hallmark of extraordinary practice. Such states have a clear purpose: they support seeing things clearly. Attachments and fears, doubts, and desires can be known, and only then can they be released. We relax out of our entanglements in ways that rational explanation cannot reach.

We see here a very powerful truth, one that invites us outward from our thousand-island lives: the capacity for mystical experience is common to all of us. Whether we think of God, essential goodness, ever-changing emptiness, or the immensity of compassion, this spark, like the knife of suffering, is our common inheritance. Yes, we hurt. Yes, meditative intimacy opens onto our common vulnerability. It also opens onto our common vastness. Such insights can buoy us, and we welcome them.

On Insight Dialogue retreats the energy generated in meditation practice—experienced as both bodily vitality and mental alertness—is amplified in the group system. These forms of energy are also generated in personal meditation retreats. But when this energy (*viriya* in Pali) is reflected between two or more people who do not fear or grasp at pleasant or unusual experiences, the energy grows to reveal a usually hidden interdependence among people. It points to something mysterious. At the same time, this energy is meditatively effective: when we are energized and awake, impermanence, suffering, and nonself become starkly evident.

Altered states, however, are temporary: they pass. We yield again to impermanence. Experiencing such highs and lows can in itself foster change and acceptance. We are coming to understand that our moods are impermanent and not to be clung to. More to the point, deep mindfulness and concentration can yield insight into how things actually are, within and around us. And insight is freeing.

Perhaps it is true, as a seasoned meditator named John said of Insight Dialogue practice, that "this is the real deal, even though it is not typical Buddhist meditation." If so, we can expect highs and lows, insights and dullness, fear and release. We can also expect practice to deepen from one retreat to the next as the simplicity of meditative practice yields ever more subtle fruits—both in retreat and pouring naturally into other forms of practice, including our everyday lives.

Weekly Groups

The form of nonretreat Insight Dialogue groups varies, but a typical group comprises from five to fifteen people who meet every week or every other week for about two hours. The group may have a facilitator or teacher, who may have modest or extensive training in Insight Dialogue. Some groups begin with a check-in, where everybody says their hellos, with perhaps a brief reporting of their personal practice since the last meeting. Then they practice silent meditation for half an hour. Some groups simply begin with silent practice. In the spirit of the guideline Trust Emergence, there need be no hard-and-fast agenda. Rather, groups endeavor to remain pliable but focused on the meditative intent of their gathering.

Following silent meditation, the facilitator—a peer practitioner who may remain constant or change from week to week—offers a reflection on some aspect of the practice, typically one of the guidelines. The group then moves into dialogue practice, usually with a contemplation theme. Some groups always practice as a whole, some only in pairs, and some vary the practice groupings. Some groups will have the facilitator interrupt their practice with a mindfulness bell; others feel the discipline of the Pause offers all the support they need. Groups continue for varying lengths of time. I have known of groups that met for only a few sessions and others that have lasted for years.

In weekly groups people alternate between their ordinary lives and these two hours set aside for extraordinary practice. Because weekly groups do not have the support of the unbroken practice offered in retreat, practitioners are less likely to develop acute mindfulness or deep calm. On the other hand, movement between everyday encounters and relational meditation can help them integrate the practice more fully with their daily lives. Each time a meditator enters into the practice group and then returns to everyday relationships, there is an opportunity to carry the insights of set-aside practice into ordinary life circumstances. Group members join together with the shared intention to become more awake and compassionate, and they are supported in this intention by the specificity of the format and the scaffolding offered by the Insight Dialogue meditation guidelines. As one meditator points out, this can yield a strong sense of affiliation.

> This group became a sangha [community] very quickly, and I credit Insight Dialogue for most of that.

Going directly into relational meditation from our typically distracted and demanding lives can seem awkward at first. The Insight Dialogue group initially looks like a normal social situation—people sitting and talking with other people about "personal" matters. But in co-meditation, we are invited time and again to let go of topics and reactions and to find the bare moment together. This quality of intention falls outside most social norms, as Doris found.

> I felt confused, because my usual way of being with people is to be very responsive to what they are saying. This nonclinging way of being with others rubbed against my expectation that I should be responsive to others and that this looked a certain way.

Doris carried into the meditation an expectation of herself: to be the same kind of "good listener" she normally is. Such a listener holds on to and pursues emotional reactions and continually offers supportive feedback. As her understanding of the practice matured and she grew comfortable with it, she became appreciative of a kind of listening that was both empathic and unattached.

The personal commitment of group members has a direct impact on the benefits people enjoy from their practice. Commitment affects the depth of the practice and insights of a group as well as its longevity. This is no different from the role of commitment in personal or retreat practice. In some groups commitment is established because the group members have all attended an Insight Dialogue retreat. They have already had first-hand experience of the benefits of practice; no abstract belief is necessary. Commitment can also be supported by initial agreements among group members, for example by participants agreeing to attend regularly for, say, the first three months.

Commitment to attend regularly is especially important at the beginning because the practice can take a while to gel. A feeling of affiliation may arise quickly enough, but a sense of truly shared practice can take longer to ripen. The practice is likely to begin on shaky fawn's legs, with awkwardness in the silences, confusion about how to practice, and a tentative approach to the more challenging contemplation topics. After a group has had a number of practice sessions, however, much of the initial clumsiness or strangeness is likely to abate.

As clumsiness fades, the more insidious problem of laziness can set in. Commitment is not simply a matter of attending the groups but of bringing full energetic presence to the practice. This can be difficult because when our everyday lives are full of stress and disconnection, simply sitting in comfortable silence can be alluring. The challenge for more mature groups becomes the challenge of our whole path of awakening: Do we fully commit in each moment? Do we extend and open awareness even when habits draw us inward? Do we meet the invitation to deep inquiry with energy and courage? Can I be deeply relaxed and still clearly aware?

In weekly practice, contemplation themes can be especially valuable in helping sustain the inquiry. Some topics, whether introduced or emergent, may even unfold from one week to the next. This was the case in a group at a spiritual community in India.

I've noticed that there are some dialogues that are completed in one sitting and others that are quite spread out in time. In a way it is as if we have an ongoing dialogue about consciousness.

In weekly groups without a contemplation theme, the challenge arises of meeting in the open space defined by Trust Emergence. This same group in India noted the nature of meeting without the support of a contemplation topic.

> It's interesting to me that the question that arises over and over again is, "What are we doing?" or "Why are we here?" We have answered it in many ways for each other, but that doesn't seem to set it to rest. It is difficult for people to accept a gathering without a clearly defined agenda/topic/goal, and saying that we are exploring consciousness doesn't suffice for everyone.

Even without a guiding topic, the good feelings of meeting with people in a calm, attentive, and spiritually inclined context can be quite attractive. But without a doubt, interpersonal dynamics are likely to arise. This is another good reason to be clear about the intentions and commitment of group members. As occurs in many group situations, people may fall into unwholesome patterns of seeking validation or control. Habits of unkindness or dishonesty may manifest.

Conflict can be transformed into harmony if the container of the group is strong. If conflict arises while the group is too new, however, or perhaps not sufficiently established in meditation, it may be necessary to restructure the group or to engage in a conflict-resolution process. Strong feelings, positive or negative, can mire the group and even carry over from one week to the next. Marcus observed:

> We got quite attached to the good vibes that were being generated in our dialogue and had some minor difficulties when we had two sessions where we ended on a note of doubt or uncertainty. The third meeting finally completed that particular process, and we were again able to attain a level of harmony that satisfied the group expectation. It is so much easier to inquire when we are suffering and to let things slide into unawareness when we are pleased.

Weekly group practice supports the integration of extraordinary practice with daily living—our family, work, and social lives. The significance of this comes into perspective when we consider our motivation to practice. We are meeting to discover what is real and true in this shared human existence and to let these realizations affect how we meet the world. The weekly Insight Dialogue group is valuable if only because it helps us maintain our focus as to life's direction.

Weekly group practice is midway between retreat practice and practice embedded in life. It has the set-aside intentionality of retreat, if not the depth. This gives it a clarity of form that helps it migrate easily into our lives. Weekly groups find us weaving into and out of ignorance and clear awareness, as we do in life, but perhaps not so quickly or jaggedly. A week at a time, the sweetness of tranquillity and interpersonal mindfulness can be cultured within us.

Online Insight Dialogue

Insight Dialogue can be practiced effectively over communications networks. It is different from in-person practice—perhaps not as warm or immediately engaging—but online practice has many strengths. It can be calm, concentrated, energetic, and transformative. Most of the basic elements are the same as in-person practice: a small group of people gathered with the intention to release grasping and become more calm and awake; meditation instructions and contemplation themes that support these intentions; and the possibility for people to encounter each other and so support each other's mindfulness, tranquillity, and compassion. Many people who have practiced online Insight Dialogue report feeling alert and relaxed as a result. Some talk about experiences of shared presence and subtle mindfulness even when meditating in spartan, text-only environments.

Online Insight Dialogue can take place via text-only interfaces (chat or bulletin board sessions) or by audio or video conferencing. The audio- and video-based practices are essentially identical to in-person practice, with the notable exception of the absence of bodily proximity. The unique features and challenges of this practice, then, will be revealed most clearly as we look at text-only practice, the variant most different from eye-to-eye, in-the-flesh Insight Dialogue.

Online Insight Dialogue got its start in 1995 using dedicated text-only chat rooms and bulletin boards.[2] Since then it has continued to be a viable and effective meditation practice. Using the Insight Dialogue guidelines during other online meetings—an increasingly common aspect of daily life—helps people manifest greater mindfulness and calm in those encounters. Such practice can help temper the emotional outbursts, or flaming, that can arise online in the absence of aural and visual cues. Text-based practice centers around the simple fact that the words shared in meditation remain visible on the screen long after they are "spoken." This has the effect of stretching the moment, enabling meditators to notice thoughts and feelings as they arise and to continue the reflection while the text lingers. One is uniquely empowered to reread one's own words and to inquire whether they arouse a reaction in oneself. In this way hunger and clinging can be revealed and released. Ignorance can be recognized and dispersed. Sparks of insight can be acknowledged.

There are two main forums for online practice: synchronous meeting venues such as chat rooms and asynchronous forums such as bulletin boards. The practice guidelines translate easily into both contexts. Pause still functions as a reminder to release identification with our reactions and step into mindfulness. This may mean stopping midsentence while reading what someone has posted or pausing while writing to turn awareness inward and sense the body. Relax is still a reminder to calm down and accept whatever thoughts and feelings arise internally or in others. Without the tension that often arises in the physical presence of others, online practice can become quite serene. Open still implies an extended awareness, but without the physical presence of other people, this guideline can be challenging. It may mean something as private as opening awareness to one's entire body, or possibly to the words on the screen, or opening to something as vast as practitioners on the other side of the country. One can further open imaginally to the breadth of the entire Internet, which covers most of the planet.

Trust Emergence remains an invitation to observe impermanence and to enter each moment with no attachment to outcome. Online, however, emergence involves "What text will arrive next in the chat?" or "What will unfold when I open this message?" One is poised in a sparse and specific environment; practice can become quite focused. Listen Deeply involves attention to the multiple levels of nuance in text: from meaning to emotion and on to the presence conveyed "between the lines." Words spoken in person carry far more information than text on a screen—the tone of voice and facial expressions offer the listener access to the speaker's heart. However, while spoken words disappear as soon as they are uttered, words printed on a computer screen endure. As someone's statement lingers in awareness, deep listening can unfold. Layers of meaning and subtle reactions can be discerned. Likewise, working with Speak the Truth, one can explore the arising of words in one's mind, noticing how they resonate when they are typed or dictated on-screen—and perhaps most significantly, one can reflect on these words before and after posting them. This enables a reflective quality of practice not available in video conferencing or in-person practice and can be reason enough to opt for text-based practice.

In both synchronous (chat) and asynchronous (bulletin board) sessions, meditators typically agree they will meet for some number of weeks or months, committing to show up and participate in the spirit of the meditation guidelines. It is best when people enter the practice environment mindfully and with the same sense of respect they would bring to beginning personal meditation practice. It is helpful to establish mindfulness of the body, for example feeling one's body on the chair or fingers on the keyboard. One may even settle the mind on the rising and falling breath. Body-centered practice is especially important to counterbalance any tendency toward intellectuality that may arise as a result of a practice so dependent upon words. The online meditation session is a time to calm down and let go of habitual modes of engagement. There may be a teacher or peer facilitator who begins and ends the sessions and introduces the week's contemplation theme.

Synchronous and asynchronous online meditation sessions are structurally different, and this is reflected in the duration and frequency of the sessions. A typical chat session involves everyone's meeting at the same time, lasts about an hour, and is typically a once-a-week affair. An individual's typical bulletin board session may last anywhere from five to fifteen minutes, although one may show up and, after mindful consideration, just post, "Here and listening," then sign off. Everyone participates in a single thread at times of his or her choosing, and people may log on anywhere from once a week to more than once a day.

Using the Insight Dialogue guidelines in other online interactions—unilaterally and outside of formal groups—can create random opportunities for "practice" that are only a couple of minutes long. We may simply approach reading or writing an e-mail with an intention to be clearly aware.

As a result of these differences, the tone and impact of these practice forms differ. Chat room sessions, being longer, tend to be more concentrated than bulletin board practice. Everyone shows up at the same time, and the sense of the shared moment can be quite strong. However, there may be no further practice until the following week. Bulletin board practice sessions are shorter, and therefore people generally do not settle down as deeply. People can check in to the practice space as frequently as they like, however, so the sense of meditative practice can easily be reinforced throughout the week. Also, the contemplation theme can be deeply explored in practitioners' daily activities. There is no simultaneously shared moment in bulletin board practice. The present moment of shared practice is created whenever anyone checks in to the forum. This generally requires a high degree of personal commitment, and this effort often migrates into our everyday experience of computer use.

Actual meditative practice is rare in communications networks. The Internet is widely used as a medium for religious communication and outreach, but agitated social norms have dominated the medium. Text-based chat rooms and bulletin boards have been associated with mindless social chatter, efficient business communications, or bare information exchange among interest groups. Emotional outbursts, stress, and confusion are not uncommon in online communications. Meanwhile, audio- and videoconferencing have been employed primarily as a substitute for in-person meetings, and have been geared to accomplish particular tasks. The oldest and most familiar networked technology, the telephone, offers the emotional contact of "touching base" with friends and family and sharing our day-to-day stories. In short, interpersonal contact on networks reflects the quality of most interpersonal contacts in life: stressful, identified, hungry, and occasionally warm.

Despite the fact that the Internet has not usually been seen as a context for loving awareness, there are substantial benefits to online practice. People can participate from anywhere in the world. This has powerful implications for people who are disabled or located in remote regions or who otherwise lack communities of practice. This global reach opens the door to contemplative cross-cultural dialogue and broadly distributed communities of practice. Asynchronous practice also has the advantage of being accessible at any time. This means one can set one's own schedule and even briefly check in to a meditative environment and refresh one's practice as an interlude during work or family life. Collaborative endeavors of many kinds can be deepened and refined as the result of applying the Insight Dialogue guidelines. Communities can be formed across time and space that are built on the shared values of clear awareness and compassion.

Online meditation can help us humanize networked communications environments and may help us understand their true potential. The refined awareness cultivated in meditation can shed light on the assets and liabilities of various modalities of interpersonal contact. Which media are sensitive in the ways that are most appropriate for which tasks? Is more sensory "bandwidth" always better than less? What kinds of networked environments can be designed to match or even enhance mindfulness? What enhances serenity? What qualities contribute to a felt sense of presence? There is no more sensitive instrument for exploring such questions than the meditative mind.

Online Insight Dialogue challenges our usual notions of meditation. It is not difficult to understand that one can cultivate clear awareness while engaged with others over a communications network. But to understand how this is truly meditation practice, we must revisit the essential nature of practice. The intention in meditation, formal or informal, is to see things clearly and become free of suffering. This means we practice to diminish greed, hatred, and delusion and to let hunger and ignorance fade as forces in our lives. We practice to recognize the inherent luminosity of awareness. Any online encounter can do this if we enter it with wise understanding, supported by effort and mindfulness. This sounds familiar because it is the same process we have been speaking about all along. At first it may seem a quixotic task to sacralize the Internet. Then we see that this is just a neglected component of our lives, as potentially supportive to awakening as a meditation hall, a living room, or a picnic table under the trees. With the support of the Insight Dialogue guidelines, letting go can happen anywhere.

Practice in Life

Living every day with high standards of relationship and clear meditative principles is a supreme challenge. Very little of our time is actually spent in retreats or practice groups, where intentional practices can get the attention they need to become established. On the contrary, nearly all of our encounters with other people occur in the throes of getting things done and encountering the spectrum of emotions that we humans are so adept at breeding. Life is a process of *being* who we are, not *doing* special practices. Doing practices, such as using meditation guidelines as we go about our everyday affairs, can seem unnatural and awkward. It is preferable when the benefits of interpersonal meditation present themselves naturally in our lives. But this natural unfolding can sometimes use some help. How can we develop the qualities indicated by the Insight Dialogue guidelines in everyday life? How do we transform the ordinary into the extraordinary?

Nearly everyone wishes for some positive transformation in his or her relational life. A more specific vision of what this could mean may have awakened as a result of experience of relational mindfulness, ease, or compassion during an Insight Dialogue retreat or group. Or maybe this universal hope became a more focused vision as you read this book. The simple act of paying sustained attention to the possibility of a more awake interpersonal life will have an effect on our relational habits. But without ongoing support, too much will be lost. Given the strength of emotional habits, intentional practice is essential.

Life practice is certainly the most challenging. It is the best place to see the dynamics and persistence of the deluded and grasping mind. It is the best place to see suffering and to feel the hurting urge of hunger. Life is also the place where we can see compassion in action, and the dynamic force of equanimity. In our engaged lives we harm others or do them good. Here we do not have the luxury of discounting anything as a distraction; it is all just life: what we have to work with. Here the stakes are highest: our words and actions impact others with the full force of reality; there is nowhere to hide. Realizing this, we are motivated to do our best to be as kind, truthful, and wise as we are able.

Most of this book deals with mutual interpersonal practice—that is, practice with others who participate actively with us, use the guidelines together, and support each other. Whether in groups or at a retreat, this happens at a set-aside time and with shared intent. But retreats can be expensive, in both time and money, and groups may not be accessible to us or appropriate to our circumstances. Mutual interpersonal practice is very, very helpful, but fortunately it is not the only avenue for transforming our relational lives.

Unless we live in a community dedicated to mindful relationships and to diminishing hunger and grasping, most of our encounters with other people—and most of our opportunities to engage the interpersonal path—will be undertaken unilaterally. That is, we may decide to Pause and Relax, but the people we are with may not be similarly inclined. We can still do good and important work. Whenever we remember one of the guidelines in the course of our everyday interactions or spontaneously experience one of the mental qualities the guidelines point to, and we notice or nurture it, then we are engaging in unilateral interpersonal practice. And since many of the same habit patterns come up when we merely think of other people, it is possible to Pause out of those reactions and engage the practice in an intentional way, even when we are alone. It is comforting to know there are many ways to support the interpersonal path, ways rooted in our daily lives.

But we do need support! Our lifestyles are conformed to strong mental habits; we live as we think and think as we live.

There are some basic practices we can do to establish a good foundation for Insight Dialogue and for the release of interpersonal hunger. Interpersonal practice is based upon mindfulness and tranquillity; cultivating these qualities individually will improve our relational practice. One of the best ways to begin improving the quality of our interpersonal lives is by developing a practice of traditional, personal silent meditation. In personal practice we learn what it is like to be calm and mindful and then begin to establish these qualities.

A simple practice is best. I recommend beginning with short sessions, ten minutes or so, just sitting and calming down. When first sitting, it is good to notice the posture of the body; note where any discomforts or tensions manifest, and invite ease. If tension remains, meet the sensations with acceptance. Meditation can be done once or several times daily and lengthened as one sees fit. As the body calms down, we might begin to notice that the body is breathing. Each time we breathe out, the diaphragm relaxes. We notice this and invite the rest of the body, and the mind, to relax further. Thoughts come and go; this is not a problem if, just for now, we don't pursue them. These thoughts, however important they may seem, are mostly the results of residual brain activity springing from habitual tension. When a thought arises, let go of the thought itself and gently shift attention to any associated tension in the body. Meet this with acceptance. What is important at first is to simply notice what tension feels like, and what ease feels like. We learn to discern the difference between the two, in ourselves and in others, to accept the pain, and allow the ease. We learn to recognize the capacity to let go. Along with these understandings, mindfulness begins to arise. Even as thoughts or emotions persist, we can allow them to come and go, knowing but not identifying with them.

Silent, solitary meditation is a good basis for interpersonal practice, both mutual and unilateral. By establishing some tranquillity, we will become less reactive when we are with other people. We interrupt cycles of wanting and aversion, and our minds begin to clear. In the moment of experience, we perceive our emotions more clearly, and with them the emotions of others. We perceive the results of these emotions. We become more present to things as they are. With this basis in individual meditation, it becomes easier to bring a meditative approach into our relationships, whether in the explicit interpersonal practice of Insight Dialogue or in everyday encounters with others.

Contemplation of the interpersonal Dhamma can also be engaged in solitary practice. We might call to mind the ubiquitous hunger for pleasure, and this may help us be more present and compassionate. Likewise, we might contemplate interpersonal stress, or suffering, and notice its cessation in any given moment. Like the guidelines, these contemplations can help us become more awake, adept, and appropriate.

The guidelines of Insight Dialogue can support unilateral practice. They will be easier to use if we set a clear intention and choose our method of practice skillfully. We might begin with a focus on just one guideline. Pause is probably the one guideline people most frequently recall. It is concrete; in our hyperquick culture, it is nearly always applicable. We could work with Pause for a day, week, or month. We could experiment with using the word *pause* as a cue to practice, or we could practice without the support of a verbal cue, just dropping delusion and stepping mindfully into the moment. We could work intensively on some days and lightly on others, finding a rhythm and style that suits us. The same approaches work with the other guidelines. We might rotate from one guideline to the next, spending a day on each one, or perhaps giving more time to one that needs more attention. If stress is a major issue, we might stay with Relax/accept for a long time. If we find ourselves obsessed with worry, we might find daily support in Trust Emergence. A dedicated focus on each guideline will offer its own gifts. If we are drawn to hold a general intention to incorporate the guidelines into our lives, then we might just recall any guideline or combination of guidelines as needed. We will know what works by how we feel and behave. We can ask, "Am I more aware?" "Am I more kind?" "Do I see things more clearly when I live this way?"

Skillful practice also includes choosing how, when, and with whom we engage the path. Another approach to using the guidelines explicitly is to practice with a single guideline in a situation with a clear beginning and ending. This is less daunting than open-ended practice. We don't take on too much and just set an intention for specific episodes. This approach is particularly effective when we choose a guideline that addresses the needs of the situation. For one specific encounter with our children, for example, we might think, time and again, "Relax, accept, love." This may help to heighten the love we already feel and invite greater ease into a relationship where we may have grasping or anxiety. Working so explicitly with one person and one guideline may at first seem awkward or even false, but this will pass. The body memory associated with acceptance and love will establish itself—and, by the magic of neural patterning, make itself available in the future. Likewise, we might enter a particular business meeting with the intention to Trust Emergence. As we habitually grasp at accomplishment and plans, we remind ourselves to let go, to drop again and again into the contingency of the moment.

We can also practice in everyday situations by noticing how we engage with people who are more or less difficult. We tend to be comfortable with certain people—and then, well, there is everybody else: the taxing, the admired, the feared, the envied, and the simply unknown. Beginning with a person we are comfortable with, we might explore Speak the Truth. Recalling that this refers to subjective truth that is known by mindfulness, we may simply notice how "Good morning" arises and how it is spoken with sincerity and presence. We might explore Listen Deeply, receiving the words of our child or spouse with exceptional receptivity and noting how they impact the body and mind. When we are moved to extend practice to a more challenging arena, we might engage the Insight Dialogue guidelines while relating with someone with whom we feel stress. We might begin with Relax, not only to calm our bodily reactions but also to meet the other person with acceptance. We might engage them with the compassion of Listen Deeply or the careful integrity of Speak the Truth. Or, remembering that all the guidelines work together and even coarise, we may experiment by encountering a difficult person with a commitment to clear and loving awareness, recalling the guidelines as needed to support this. If the person attacks us, we relax—that is, let go of stress and cultivate ease; if he or she launches into an adversarial tirade, we Trust Emergence and notice the stressful flux of this human moment. We recognize the shared human predicament and cultivate compassion.

Another way to invite skillful practice is to notice the emotional tenor of a situation and adapt accordingly. Sometimes we are with many people, sometimes with few, and this can affect our practice. Some social situations are relatively relaxed, like dinner at a friend's house. There, nested in the freedom of acceptance, we might drop into very deep listening, then turn our attention to the impermanent rise and fall of voices, facts, and emotions in this very common, human meeting. But at a family gathering simmering with tension, we might engage in many little pauses, using each interlude of clarity to observe how our mind is recalling, believing, and reacting to multiple generations of constructs: "Oh, there is Uncle John; he's probably still angry at my father." Or "How did

I get into this family, anyway?" Each time we recognize a construct—which can take place in the Pause—we have the opportunity to release it, using Relax and Trust Emergence. Perhaps we will also notice the unsullied awareness that illuminates and surrounds these constructs. These are all little movements toward freedom.

Integrating Insight Dialogue into our lives can also be more or less difficult—at least different—based upon whether people are trying to accomplish a task together or not. Again, skillful practice means adapting our practice accordingly. If our work group is intensely focused on a strategy meeting, it may be all we can do to occasionally relax the body and reopen to the flow of people and ideas. If we are with some friends and deciding where to go for dinner, we might play with the situation, perhaps noticing the impermanence in their animated faces—Trust Emergence. Or we might Pause from debating the merits of pizza or stir-fry and notice quiet feelings of fondness, both internally and as expressed in others' voices and eyes. Or if we are just sitting with our child, perhaps with nothing special to do, nowhere in particular to go, we may drop any use of guidelines. Practice as such may not be necessary, as clear awareness arises naturally: a pause has no beginning or end, there is just mindfulness; we find Open naturally unfolds while we are at ease with someone who has a home in our heart. If there is any practice, it consists of simply noticing the relaxed, awake mind.

We can also benefit from the mindfulness and care inherent in the guidelines when we are alone, thinking of encounters with other people. Athletes are trained not only by physically practicing their game but by mentally rehearsing its critical movements. A tennis player who mentally rehearsed all the things wrong with her serve would actually damage her skill. Whenever we think of other people, reactions arise, thoughts proliferate, and emotions are aroused. The way we meet those reactions—whether we reinforce them or release them, whether we are mindful or deluded—helps shape the habits that manifest when we interact with others, for good or for ill.

Fortunately, the attitudes and responses that support wakeful encounter can be cultivated when we are alone. We can practice releasing the automatic thoughts and emotions that are triggered by specific people in our lives or by certain kinds of situations. Away from the pressures of interaction, we can take the time to notice the character of these thoughts; we can pause for a while when the imagined situation becomes too stimulating and calm down before continuing. This practice must be disciplined to be fruitful; it is easy to drift into mindlessly rehashing the past or planning the future. Such habitual thought reinforces identification and obscures clear awareness. When we integrate the guidelines into our thinking, they can help support a clear, strong intentionality. As we practice transformed thoughts and reactions, these become a basis for transformed emotions and behavior.

Before getting together with a good friend, we might ask ourselves how we can release an old habit of sharing complaints and begin to speak a gentler truth. Before a holiday gathering, we might call to mind one of our parents and consider how it might be to Pause the next time he or she is disrespectful of our lifestyle choices. We might consider if we crave safety or shrink from intimacy. At those moments—alone but thinking of other people—we can learn to release judgment and to nurture acceptance and patience toward ourselves and others. This internal and solitary form of practice can lead to more skillful and harmonious encounters. Peace and kindness infiltrate our lives and become part of the path of unbinding.

Another way to integrate the interpersonal path of awakening into our lives is with a focus on Right View, Right Effort, and Right Mindfulness. Whenever these qualities are intensified—whether in mutual or unilateral practice—the ordinary becomes extraordinary.

The entire path turns around Right View, or Wise Understanding. Unless there is a sense of direction—a felt sense of what we are doing and why—it can be frustrating to try to "be mindful" or to recall guidelines. Hunger and ignorance do not respond well to brute force; we need the strength of emotional conviction and clear understanding. We are learning to let go into freedom, not to contrive happiness. A motivating sense of direction is nurtured when we understand the four interpersonal truths—of suffering, hunger, cessation, and the path to freedom—and contemplate them in ourselves and others. It is nurtured when we seek to recognize interpersonal suffering. In our everyday encounters, we can notice tension and fear, desire and its results. One of the first teachings Anagarika offered me, after basic meditation instruction, was to notice pleasant and unpleasant experiences in my daily life. I didn't think about Right View, but this is what I was practicing; the endlessly flickering reactivity I saw surprised and motivated me. Similarly, we can notice the manifestation of the three hungers in ourselves and others during everyday interactions. When we do, our compassion grows. We can notice our own reactivity to others when they are not present, too. Do we replay an encounter at work as we wait for the train, mutter through a past conversation while vacuuming? Does a conflict that arose hours—or decades—ago disrupt our individual meditation? We can contemplate these reactions with compassion. We can experiment with feeding and releasing hungers, testing these strategies for happiness and observing their results. We come to know experientially that the hungers can never be lastingly satisfied. If we find that letting go results in the most happiness, then relinquishment becomes the direction of our lives. This is the practice of Right View.

These opportunities to nurture wise understanding begin with thinking but lead to a deeply felt change in our sense of the world. A vision of higher happiness turns the mind and emotions. This turning sets the direction and intention of our lives. The turning is not just cognitive; it is also emotional. Energy is aroused for awakening, and we begin to practice careful attention and make wise choices. This energy is the beginning of Right Effort.

Right Effort means bringing energy and commitment to each moment of experience. We can apply Right Effort in our daily lives. Guided by Right View and made practical by Right Mindfulness, this energy wakes us up, brings attention to how things actually are in this moment, and calls us to action. The nature of the action, of our practice, is described in the four facets to Right Effort: prevention, abandonment, cultivation, and maintenance and increase.[3] These wise efforts are a skillful response to the simple fact that in life we are embedded in a system that is basically out of control. Our culture, many of our acquaintances, and our own habits do not usually support awakening. In this melee, our four efforts begin with making good choices.

The Right Effort of prevention includes acknowledging that some interpersonal situations are more complicated and difficult than others. Wise attention and skill mean choosing which thoughts or situations to engage in and which to let pass or withdraw from. We may decide that certain circumstances or relationships are too stimulating, too toxic, or otherwise too challenging and elect not to enter these situations. We don't always have this option, however; when we don't, prevention may lead us to a modest form of engagement: we sit back, relax, and observe. Patience is essential.

The next two elements of Right Effort are abandoning unwholesome thoughts and emotions and cultivating wholesome ones. These two actions are reciprocal, so we will examine them together. Abandoning anger toward someone, for example, may be accomplished by intentionally shifting our attention to other things. Sometimes turning away is necessary because we may not always be able to meet our anger head on, with awareness and love. Release from anger may also come from cultivating kind thoughts in place of resentful ones. Similarly, releasing selfish desire in a relationship may take the form of abandoning our self-obsessed thoughts; it can also be accomplished by cultivating generosity and nurturing kind thoughts and actions. These shifts can be aided by the Pause, which allows mindfulness to reveal the nature of our reactions: the pain of rage, for example, or the isolating shell of self-fixation. All of the guidelines have something to contribute here. For example, Open helps us extend the heart in compassion, while Listen Deeply invites generosity and sensitivity to others. Speak the Truth is a global invitation to release hurtful speech habits and reorient our attention toward truth and kindness. Each of the Insight Dialogue guidelines can be understood as an invitation to abandon unwholesome tendencies and cultivate corresponding wholesome ones.

A powerful form of Right Effort is found in the type of practice described earlier in this chapter, in which we practice alone but call to mind other people in order to nurture wholesome mind states. Formally speaking, these are extraordinary practices. There are examples of these cultivating practices from many religious traditions. The set of Buddhist practices called the Brahma Viharas, or divine abidings, involves opening the mind wide in kindness and perhaps bringing to mind different people who are beloved, neutral, or difficult, or people who may be ill, in pain, or experiencing good fortune. Thoughts of kindness, compassion, sympathetic joy, equanimity toward these people are cultivated. By developing these qualities during meditation, we are literally practicing—rehearsing—how we might respond to these people in person. More than this, we are cultivating the heart and inclining the mind toward these elevated states of goodwill and care, and actually reconfiguring our gray matter. In other traditions, prayer, healing visualizations, and aspirations to world peace are central to wholesome practices and lifestyles. All of these practices are mental acts of cultivation and are part of the engaged interpersonal path.

The fourth facet of Right Effort is to maintain and increase the wholesome qualities of our practice. Wise effort here refers to discerning those wholesome qualities that have already arisen, in any given moment, and nurturing and protecting them. Do we observe the ease of lovingkindness as we speak to our parents on the phone? We can notice this and relax more fully into this nonaversive, loving state. Do we discern rays of mindfulness shedding light on our encounter with the hair stylist or auto mechanic? We can smile internally as this natural clarity is sustained and nurtured simply because we noticed it. Do we notice more equanimity in our relational lives? We allow the joy of the balanced heart to arise and encourage us.

Mindfulness, the third quality that catalyzes the extraordinary from the ordinary, runs through all of these efforts of prevention, abandonment, cultivation, and increase. They are only possible with the support of Right Mindfulness. Right Mindfulness keeps our efforts on track. If we are mindful internally of when we are tense, we can cultivate ease. If we are mindful externally of others' tensions, we can perceive the need for additional generosity and compassion. Without Right Mindfulness our practice will not mature. Mental constructs and emotional reactions will dominate the moment, replacing reality; even our finest intentions will vanish like stars behind a rolling fog. Right Mindfulness dissipates the fog and returns us to actuality. Taken together, Right View, Effort, and Mindfulness form an exceptionally effective path for awakening in our relational and social lives. Our efforts in this direction will be lushly rewarded.

One of the first things we will notice as we walk this interpersonal path of awakening is the strength of our relational habits. Practice in life begins just like silent meditation begins: awkward and jumpy. When we begin practicing traditional meditation, we often experience sore knees and a mind crammed full of thoughts. It is not a lovely sight, but over time it changes. When we invite Insight Dialogue into our lives, we should be prepared for a similarly inelegant beginning. The usual array of distractions, uneven effort, tension, and identification will likely be our starting point.

As we begin to work with the Insight Dialogue guidelines and contemplations, the mind will jump between idle thoughts, worries about our appearance, lusts, and fears, but these things will be interleaved with occasional moments when we Relax or Trust Emergence. The mind may still be jumpy, but our practice is set in motion as we bring intention into the picture. We engage with patience, with compassion for our own stumbles, and the moments of clarity increase.

Our aspiration on this path is not simply to achieve certain mind states, even keen mindfulness, but to grow in understanding and compassion, see things as they actually are, and so to be free and able to act with natural kindness and wisdom. The forces of the habit mind are great, however; guidelines will be of little help in this process if we do not commit ourselves to using them. As the Buddha pointed out, diligence is the key.

Just as the footprints of all living beings that walk fit into the footprint of the elephant, and the elephant's footprint is declared to be their chief by reason of its size, so diligence is the one thing which secures both kinds of good, the good pertaining to the present life and that pertaining to the future life.[4]

Our everyday relational life is the most difficult place to practice—and the most fruitful. Because of the difficulty of practice in life, and the consequences, we must be patient with ourselves and with others.

We must also be adaptable. We try to choose the best approach, to pace ourselves, and always, endlessly, to be patient with ourselves. Sometimes we will even forget this noble endeavor; we need not make that a problem. Time and again we are humbled by our conditioning. We relax, drop back, and let go. During these times we may be able to refrain from hurtful thoughts, speech, and actions. But even if we don't try, or if we try but don't succeed, if we hurt others, we can meet our frailty with compassion and patience. Always, we rest in kindness to ourselves.

Practice embedded in life is the form most available to us. It does not require that we go anywhere special, be with a teacher, or take time away from our work and families. Retreat, group, and in-life practice all support each other. Just as the Insight Dialogue guidelines are the same for all of these forms, the intentions behind them are also the same. This is practice in action. Our job is to choose the approaches that work for us now—and to live gently, wisely, at the intersection of diligence and ease.

In truth there is no such thing as unilateral practice, just as there is no practice separate from life: it is all life, is it not? Everything we do affects those around us. Our diligence spreads wholesome results outward from our center of simple awareness. Personal change brings about relational change, and wakeful, peaceful relationships become the basis for grassroots social change. When we slow down, when we relate with mindfulness and care, we evoke similar behavior from others. When we are able to be calm, others begin to calm down. When they are calm, their calmness supports us in our efforts, without any explicitly shared practice. Qualities like serenity, wisdom, and kindness are contagious. In "unilateral" practice, we share our practice with others through induction, or resonance, and they are naturally invited into their own greater capacity. This may not happen immediately or in obvious ways; stress may obscure the sprouting of the seed that has been planted. But a transmission does surely happen; our practice quietly changes from unilateral to mutual. When we recognize our own inherent wisdom, others around us are invited to do the same. In this way relationships change. I have seen it in my own life, and I regularly hear back from meditators how their family, work, and other relationships have changed. Life relationships do not offer the same definite, mutual support as relationships built around explicit practice, but they share something that the fabricated nature of retreat or group relationships cannot touch: awakening to the true nature of the lived relational life, replete with its constructions, challenges, and embedded moments of freedom. As the Buddha instructed, we can see things as they actually are, right now, in the midst of life. And we can respond from a fully natural wisdom and compassion.

~ 19 ~

DIVERSIONS
IN PRACTICE

INSIGHT DIALOGUE meditation brings into being a plain canvas upon which are painted the conditioned habits we bring to the practice. Different groups at different times will reflect higher and lower capacities; sometimes groups will get derailed. In groups of all sizes, patterns can manifest that keep meditators from letting go of grasping and realizing the clarity and ease available to them. Sometimes individual comeditators get bogged down in habit for a single session. Sometimes whole groups enter sustained, unproductive holding patterns.

It is not always obvious when we are stuck. Just as indifference bears some similarities to equanimity, skillful and unskillful practice share certain characteristics. But good practice moves us steadily toward understanding and selfless concern for others, while bad practice keeps us lost in patterns of selfishness and confusion.

I will talk about six common stuck places: identification with emotions (the sharing group); avoidance of discomfort and attachment to superficial pleasantries; attachment to ideas and identification with the intellect (the discussion group); preaching, counseling, or advice giving that gives rise to formulaic teacher/student roles; drooping into practice that is primarily silent and individual; and gazing or trance modes driven by a greed for fancy experiences. Some of these patterns arise as part of the natural maturation of a group. Every one of them emerges from a quality that—skillfully handled—is also a strength. Even so, each trap must be left behind for further spiritual maturation to unfold. Often, just identifying these dysfunctions is enough to free us from their grip.

Identifying with Emotions
The Sharing Circle

During meditation our hearts become highly sensitized. We feel emotions acutely: both our own internal emotions and the emotions expressed by others. Likewise, delicate emotional matters can come up as we relax out of some defenses. It is as if our words were spoken into a reverberant church: each expression echoes in a hall of hearts. This can challenge our equanimity. For one thing, we don't usually have a window into other people's emotions, and it can be compelling to hear about people's inner lives. But our emotional reactions to what people say, and specifically our grasping at those reactions, can undermine our practice. It is the same in daily life or in retreat. We grasp at good feelings, hoping they last. We grasp at painful feelings, internal and external, recycling them in the group or in our own hearts.

Edith bluntly described her experience of being stuck in identification with emotions:

> We were six people in the morning group. As we started talking, the topic that took shape was fear and being invisible in a group. The person who brought up the fear was concerned about not being approved of by the group. This brought up my own fears. He got over it and started talking freely, while I was getting wound up and didn't even know it. A woman said she just had to talk, because if she didn't, she'd be invisible. We shared her concern, just as we did for the guy with the fear. The whole process was so intense that I did not realize I was totally caught up in it, that is, until the Pause bell rang. I had to go for a long walk to unwind and soften my body. It sure made me treasure the Pause.

Edith found a way out of identification—the Pause—but not until the group ended and she could get some perspective. Until then her practice was heavy with tension as she took on the emotional challenges of her partners. Her body became tense as she inhabited and held on to these emotions. When our speaking and listening are rooted in emotional identification, we perpetuate and even strengthen old patterns.

When habit patterns are reciprocated by other group members, meditative clarity wanes. Another meditator, Gerda, sensed people's insecurities and dropped into judgment rather than compassion. This probably perpetuated her partners' concerns.

> All weekend I encountered people stewing in their insecurities. Maybe this practice reveals silly head trips? Are we all, always, insecure? Maybe I heard so much of this because I bring it out in people. I don't know. In my dyad with Donald, which lasted maybe ten minutes, he said he felt rejected by me at least three times. It's like he was listening for just the information he expected to hear—you love me, you hate me, you think I'm stupid. It didn't endear people to me.

When Gerda experienced reactive judgment and her partners experienced insecurity, there appeared to be little clear awareness of emotions as they arose. The insecurities felt real to the people experiencing them; the aversion felt real to Gerda. Locked in like this, practice was stuck. There were no insights by the meditators into the painful nature of grasping. There was no experience of impermanence, no sense of the impersonal and automatic ways these patterns were unfolding.

We may come to the Insight Dialogue group seeking fodder for the emotional animal. We may desire and value emotionality. We may seek to soothe our loneliness with human contact rather than know the hungers that gnaw at our bellies. There are plenty of precedents for this expectation. Sharing or support groups exist with all kinds of convening themes—psychological healing, spiritual or religious commonalities, and other shared interests or needs. Such groups temporarily feed a need for connection as well as provide practical benefits. There is value in this, and Insight Dialogue can also offer commonality and companionship. But the emphasis in Insight Dialogue groups is on meditation and all that this implies. When participants seek only soothing or validation of their emotions, they may find something different from their expectations. Ella commented, after her retreat, "This is the only retreat of any kind where we never held hands." The point is not that holding hands is not part of an Insight Dialogue retreat or weekly group. What matters is clarity of intent: we are here to recognize, accept, and release underlying hungers, not to feed them. Without this, individuals or groups can get stuck in emotional habits.

When we try to bring the Insight Dialogue guidelines into our everyday interactions, the intention is the same as in group practice, and so is the challenge. We may want to Listen Deeply, but the upsurge of emotion that comes with such a practice finds us swimming in reaction to what we hear. We may have the overall intention to Relax, but our emotional habits—for example, to get excited by someone's troubling news—cause us to grasp and become tense. When we are lost in identification with emotions, our practice weakens. Awareness of this trap is already a big step toward a stronger practice, and we can easily explore this in everyday life. When with a close friend, we can notice and reflect on how we share, repeat, and live in our concerns, complaints, and victories. We might ask ourselves if we can be with this person outside those stories, just in the simplicity of what is around us.

In groups, one person's reaction can trigger another's, creating the negative cycle I call interreactivity. This can spiral into a noisy and decidedly nonmeditative quality of interaction. Even in explicit retreat practice, the benefits can be limited when there is a wrong view of what it can offer. During the retreat we may find respite from festering loneliness, but is this the only gift? Is there nothing of lasting value? Perhaps not, if we see respite as the primary goal of retreat, rather than the diminishing of fundamental hungers.

Undeniably, emotions are significant in Insight Dialogue. Emotions constitute a large part of the shared human experience; they help us know each other and feel compassion. The emotional sensitivity that causes us to get stuck can also be a gift to our practice. The turning point is simple: Does emotional sensitivity result in heightened awareness or in grasping? Heightened awareness is a doorway to wisdom and even deeper compassion. Grasping is a doorway to wallowing and pain; it sustains delusion.

When we find ourselves, or our entire group, stuck in identification with emotions, it can be helpful to remind ourselves of the purpose and nature of practice. We tell ourselves—or remind the entire group—that this is an extraordinary practice, a time set aside to see things clearly. If we are practicing without a group, we remember the value of releasing emotional habits. Practicing Insight Dialogue is not a time to indulge and reinforce patterns of identification but to awaken with love and nonclinging. Many practices can serve as antidotes, helping us renew and sustain our commitment. Here are three.

1. *Emphasize the Pause.* As emotions feed on themselves, we tend to speed up our speech and react quickly. This is true whether our speaking is motivated by anger or by sympathy. When we remember to Pause, we slow down habitual reactions and open up new possibilities for clarity and letting go.

2. *Attend to the body simply as a body.* Return to feeling the body sitting; just know the basic form of the body. Let this practice be clear, natural, and very basic. It can bring us back to simplicity and peace when inner or outer storms are raging.

3. *Contemplate the impersonal nature of emotions.* Consider their causes and effects—someone says something, a reaction arises; there is no self that decides to react. See the automatic nature of emotional reaction.

By recognizing when we are caught in the limitations of sharing groups and sharing routines, emotional sensitivity can be turned from a glue binding us to old habits into a source of energy and compassion.

Hypersweet
Mired in Superficial Niceties

Sometimes, early in their development, Insight Dialogue groups fall into a pattern of superficial sweetness. Such groups exhibit low energy and a distinct avoidance of anything challenging or overtly expressive. There are two easy explanations of why such groups avoid challenge and douse fires. Often the members of such a group have a distorted image of what constitutes transformative spiritual practice. They figure that if this is meditation, then everything must be soft and quiet. They imagine that strong feelings are not spiritual, that stress and anger are bad, and that meditation is a fragile thing. Internal emotions are suppressed. External displays of emotion are feared; they are met with soothing and fixing, or even condemned.

The peace such a group cultivates really is fragile! The mindfulness is narrow and shrunken. There is little authenticity. People don't act as they do in the real world because they are afraid something nonspiritual may slip out. The way to impress people in such a group is to show how spiritual we are. Informed by spiritual stereotypes, we talk softly, smile a soft and knowing smile, and say delicate, wise, and sometimes obscure things, always with our eyes aglow with fluffy love.

Such shallow and fearful assumptions about the nature of the spiritual path can be suffocating. Learning is inherently risky, and this can be scary. This points to a key dynamic of the hypersweet group: fear of discomfort. Because they fear discomfort, participants avoid risk and avoid speaking the truth. Group norms develop that favor safety over realization. In such a sterile climate, love does not grow. Honest expression that might elicit and test the acceptance of true lovingkindness is not allowed. The sometimes rough grit of life is smeared with a protective gel of platitudes.

This behavior manifests during in-life practice as spiritual posturing and avoidance of conflict. We may not trust our capacity to Speak the Truth and still be kind. Or we may feel that the only way to Relax and accept with others is to be limp. We may "make nice" with a family member or roommate, pulling away from the grittiness of everyday life. Inhabiting a spiritual persona makes us unavailable to others in any authentic way and keeps repressed the emotions we most fear. Noticing life's messiness as a challenge to be met with energy, even joy, opens a path of greater integrity in life.

Interestingly, this fearful, shallow, sweet, stereotyping group, or individual, is a subset of the one that is stuck in identification with emotions. While the sharing group reacts to emotions with attachment and identification—spinning into rapid talk and effusiveness—the hypersweet group reacts with avoidance. But the avoidance comes up because, underneath, participants identify with these emotions; they fear them because they believe in the reality of that which would be hurt: their self constructs. Based on this belief, the entire path of meditative development—including Insight Dialogue—is reconstructed to maintain safety and avoid pain.

If we are brave and move beyond the comfort zone, our risks are likely to be rewarded by a practice charged with truth and energy. As Amanda put it, chaos can lead to high function.

> There was a tremendous chaos in the group last night. I won't go into depth, but one person spun into a rush of fear, another reacted with judgment, a third expressed discomfort, and many of us felt confused. There were some very long and charged silences, where we stewed in stress, but there was also wakefulness to meet that stress. I joined you as you contained and tolerated the anger and pointed to the potential for growth or despair. It was an invitation to see what would emerge. In the subsequent dialogue, the chaos led to higher functioning, which emerged expansive and joyful, even in the pain and suffering that was shared.

What Amanda referred to as expansive is the quality of mindfulness that is flexible, tolerant, alive with things as they are, and thus courageous. Such a state has great potential for joy because it is free from the stress of denial and fear; in this state group members are connected in the human experience. In the well-functioning Insight Dialogue group, conflict is not avoided; it is met with mindfulness, kind intentions, and the invitation to meet pain with acceptance.

Such an experience points to ways we might help ourselves and our practice group rise out of the stuck place of superficial niceties.

1. *Focus practice on Speak the Truth.* Consider deeply what it means to offer the gift of truth. Consider the energy and mindfulness required to discern the truth. Consider the generosity of offering it to others. Consider the courage required and feel that courage in your body.

2. *Contemplate suffering.* It can be helpful here to consider the shared heritage of stress in our society, the pain inherent in having a body, and the challenge of meeting each other authentically in Insight Dialogue.

3. *Explore assumptions about the nature of the spiritual path.* Set aside all reticence and inquire: What is meditative growth? What is the purpose of extraordinary practice? What do evolution and maturity look like? Exploring assumptions like this will be hard work. Dig in, fearlessly. Goad your own sacred cows.

4. *Exercise physically.* Spiritual syrup thickens when the body is placid. Physical exercise can help, especially exercises that emphasize the *hara,* the belly, where we connect with the fires of being human.

Genuine kindness and good intentions are wholesome qualities that tend to be strong in individuals and groups that fall into superficial niceties. With reinvigoration, strong inquiry, and a commitment to energetic practice, the flabbiness of such groups can be avoided, and their good-heartedness can yield a practice abundant in safety, affinity, subtlety, and patience.

Identifying with Thought
The Discussion Group

Meditative alertness reveals a constant flood of thoughts. Moved by habit, generosity, or longings for recognition, we pluck certain fabrications out of the stream and voice them. Concepts proliferate. Intellectual stimulation feels good; ideas entertain us and offer our attention something interesting. When meditative immersion clears the mind, creativity is enhanced, and our ideas become even more seductive. This good feeling is experienced as intrigue. When others become intrigued, too, and our individual proliferation of ideas is joined by proliferation in the group, our meditation group becomes a discussion group: wrapped up in ideas, barely touching the terra firma of the present moment.

The diversion into a discussion group often manifests as fast and personally distanced talk. We may talk about meditative dialogue as an abstraction, not pausing to appreciate the irony that such talk removes us from the experience of it. We may talk about the Dhamma or about other philosophies. We may talk about feelings, analyzing them in the hope of obtaining deeper understanding. We may discuss current events, exploring the complexities of the world with passion and commitment. Such conversations generally lack the mindfulness and attention to emergence of truly meditative inquiry.

In such discussion groups, there are few references to experience of the moment. There is little attention given internally to mindfulness of the body. Likewise, very little is said in the group about bodily awareness. Participants make few references to sensory experiences or to mind states experienced in the present. We can notice, when we find ourselves in such a conversation, whether these thoughts bring us closer to the suchness of life or are a shield between us and the truth.

Sam described the subtle shift into identification with the analytical mind:

> We were discussing "neutral people," and the dialogue had taken a warm and loving tone as we discussed our desires to be loved. Then, speaking more from intellect than from Trust Emergence, I made the comment: "We need to discriminate to protect ourselves." As I said this it sounded false, and I felt my heart contract.

When the shift to identification with thought takes hold, we no longer perceive these small movements of contraction. They blend into the discursive background noise, another ripple in an already-turbulent river.

Sam saw his movement into intellectual self-protection in contrast with the expansiveness of Trust Emergence. More typically, intellect is contrasted with emotion, setting up a dichotomy between head and heart. We see this in Evelyn's dialogue experience.

> We were a group of two men and two women. The women began sharing from a "feeling point of view." As a woman, I felt that I was speaking from my heart. Then one of the men questioned the semantics of a word, and the discussion tumbled into intellectual, dis-

cursive stuff. This pattern repeated itself when our group of four joined others to make a group of about fifteen people. The discussion turned to the intellect, which was followed by women, including me, supporting each other's sufferings in a heartfelt way . . . then back to the intellect, where the same guy was challenged by his friend: "Why do you always have to be so intellectual?" Another male looked at me, saying it seemed the group was leaning toward a support group. I got so angry. I'm mainly an affirming, supportive, sensitive-to-the-point-of-tears woman, and I just got unplugged.

Whether or not Evelyn was identified with her emotional reactions, her story illustrates one way groups get locked into identification with thought. Fearful of emotions, seeking comfort by distancing ourselves, seduced by language, and curious about this or that concept, we follow a thought into a whirlpool of intrigue.

In Insight Dialogue sustained identification either with our thoughts or with our emotions is seen as a diversion from the ongoing process of letting go. There is constriction and disconnection, as we saw in Sam's experience, as ideas keep emotions at arm's length. But we are protecting ourselves from more than emotional vulnerability. Identifying with our thoughts is also a defense against threats to our self system. Conceptuality slips between awareness and the unfolding moment, shielding us from life's ongoing storm of impermanence and contingency. Because it is an effective shield, intellectualization becomes a habit, strongly reinforced by our culture. The object of awareness is thought, but we become identified with this thought. That is, we are not aware that we are thinking; rather, we seem to become our thoughts. Our thoughts think us. In such a state we don't see that insight does not come with the pursuit of these thoughts. Insight comes by releasing conceptual thoughts or by dropping into a presently felt sense of the truth they point to.

Even in such a state, our emotions and hungers are still operating. The most defended cogitator has the same urges and fears as the pristine meditator—it is just that those urges are unseen. They dominate the moment, undetected. But if we simply bother to look, it becomes clear that ideas are functioning as a medium in which we act out the urges to have pleasure, be seen, or hide. "Listen to what a smart thing I'm saying. Respect me. Love me."

Intellect certainly has a place in Insight Dialogue meditation. Actually, it is unavoidable. Language is abstract, a conceptual representation of experience. To speak of an emotion or meditative insight is to express an idea of that emotion or insight. And the exchange of ideas can be wholesome, as we explore together the deeper nature and dynamics of lived experience. But do we know thought as it emerges, or do we get lost in it?

I was teaching a retreat at a spiritual community whose founder had been a revered mystical philosopher. The participants were deeply committed to their path, which had a strong intellectual element. I admired many things about this community, including a deeply felt sense of their role in healing a suffering society. Early in this retreat only a few participants had encountered a strong sense of the present moment. Many participants remained stuck in abstraction, trying to think their way to direct experience. Fortunately, the same energy that feeds thought can feed wakefulness, and the veil of conceptualization can quickly vaporize when recognized by mindfulness. Here is what Andreas had to say about it:

> It was a difficult start. The unfolding seemed intellectual. Gradually the silent experience came, the mystical point, and interaction and dialogue became fluid. With the sheath of resistance broken, there was clear, honest participation toward the end of day one.

When we recognize that our group has become lost in identification with thoughts, we need not despair. The shift into wakefulness can be simple and instantaneous. As with most diversions of practice, commitment to awakening is our starting point. Here are some ways we might interrupt the trance of the conceptualizing mind.

1. *Counter with grounding in the body.* Strengthen your sense of the body in this very moment and give voice to what you experience. Be detailed but not analytical as you experience and share your moment-to-moment sensations.

2. *Pause enough to slow down.* Recognize how thoughts fill the silent spaces. Notice how they proliferate within and between us, how they are constructed and empty.

3. *Listen carefully.* Note the tone of voice, facial expressions, and body movements of others. Listen for the human heart as it expresses itself in sound; feel the breath of your co-meditators and recognize that even ideas are an expression of a pulsating heart and vibrating awareness.

4. *Find humor in the absurdity of intellectual hubris.* Inquire into this; what do we really think we can know? How solid, stable, and meaningful are these ideas? Laugh your way out of arrogance.

5. *Contemplate death and disease.* What do all of these ideas mean in the eyes of eternity, of transience?

6. *Trust Emergence.* Actively contemplate change in everything, especially in the immediate experience of these people speaking and in your own reactions.

Groups lost in intellectual pursuit and identification with ideas are sitting on a gold mine of potential. The diversion into delusion can be turned if habit-mind can be exposed. Such groups have the basis for penetrating inquiry. Clarity is the sometimes hidden partner of the intellect. Just as energy gathers behind emotions, it also gathers behind ideas. A discussion group often has a commitment to practice that can be turned in its favor. In the group that has slipped into discussion mode, this commitment has become misplaced, and there is some lack of skillfulness in using the substantial power of the mind. With a slight shift in perspective, however, insights appear, like shiny pebbles in a stream.

Caught in the Teaching Stance

Sometimes the desire to help others leads people to give advice. With the best of intentions we may fall out of mindfulness and into the role of teacher. This distances us and puts others in the role of "one who needs to be taught." In this practice diversion, participants tell others about the Dhamma, analyze their emotions, tell others how to practice Insight Dialogue, and otherwise inhabit a knowing stance.

Getting stuck in teacher/student patterns is one way we identify with the fruits of the intellect. Being the "teacher," we make a place for ourselves where we are comfortable. We take a stance in the known, then discharge our knowing to the group, exhaust fumes from the furnace of the familiar. This flame may be further fed by our craving for respect. Fixing our attention on telling others what to do takes us out of our own center. It is just another way of missing the moment.

On the other side, having others tell us "how it is" makes us passive consumers of advice, waiting to be fed answers. A hierarchy is implied in this: the one who knows needs the subservience of the one who does not know. The one who does not know is assumed to lack valuable insight and so does not feel responsible for participating in the wisdom of the group. When a dyad or group system is locked in this pattern, there is little receptivity to the moment-to-moment mystery of experience.

A common type of teaching that takes place comes from a stance inside a philosophy or religion. At a Buddhist retreat this might look like a small Dhamma talk or advice couched in the teachings of the Buddha. Janet wanted nothing to do with it.

> I can usually Trust Emergence, but when it came to this specific situation—the tension between Eileen and Jim—I wanted to fix it. When I shared this with the group, Rob spoke up with a Dhamma teaching about the need to be present with and grow from what is difficult. I said nothing, but I wanted to say, "I've done that many times, but I'm giving an honest reaction in the present moment; not a Dhamma talk."

Janet was reeling, off balance, from diligently applying herself to meeting emotional tension with mindfulness. The insecurity of Trust Emergence was present for her, as was an experience of discomfort and a need for quiet. Rather than encountering human compassion, she found someone preaching to her about how to be. Rob was no doubt motivated in part by kindness, but the quality of his sharing was that of "talking at" Janet rather than joining her in human suffering.

Janet was repelled—but what of her would-be teacher? It is possible that as Rob shared this advice, he was disconnected from bodily experience, unaware of the arising of his thoughts and the urge to speak them. He may not have noticed the urge to be seen inherent in his delivery or the subtle disconnect from Janet. He may not have noticed the memories and feelings that arose as he prepared his advice. The substance of his sharing seems sound; we do benefit from being present with difficulties. But Rob's teaching stance, disconnected from his own and Janet's immediate experience, was distancing and not supportive of meditative depth. Rob's Dhamma teaching represents a common difficulty, one that paradoxically is more prevalent among meditators with significant background in formal Buddhist teachings.

Not surprisingly, I sometimes encounter this same knot in practice when meditation teachers or clergy attend Insight Dialogue retreats. Monks are far more comfortable offering little Dhamma talks than speaking the truth about personal experience. Therapists—or would-be therapists—also sometimes encounter special challenges in this practice. In a society steeped in pop psychology, and in a practice as psychologically sophisticated and alluring as Insight Dialogue, the therapist-teacher stance is all too common. Karen found herself on the horns of this dilemma—both as victim and as perpetrator.

> Too many people here seem to set themselves up as therapists. There are two things that I have feelings about right now: (1) I don't like being helped. I had the feeling of "don't try to fix my confusion/discomfort/aversion, just accept that it's there and offer me a sharing from your own heart—not necessarily in reaction to my sharing, just anything so we can meet, so I can feel your compassion." (2) Others are doing this wrong.

Karen didn't want to be fixed, and yet she found herself telling others how to practice—playing the "fixer" role!

Another meditator, Gordon, reflected on how responses from a teachy-preachy stance affected him:

> After many questions and doubts I finally got into sharing from the moment. I was doing it "right." Then somebody would react to my comments in that "helpful" way, and I would react, "You're not supposed to do that!" and I would back off.

Gordon was conscious of resisting these would-be helpers and teachers. He was able to observe how he distanced himself and dropped out of the flow of emergence. But a similar distancing happens even when we are not aware of it. And it happens whether we are the teacher or the one being "taught at." For all of us, the aliveness and unknowing of the moment disappear in the preaching dynamic.

It need not be this way. The desire to share what we know has wholesome roots in generosity. "Teachers" may want to be seen, yes, but they may also genuinely want to help. They are speaking out of compassion, hoping to lift the other person to a place of greater understanding. There is energy behind this sharing. Usually there is some grain of wisdom in what is shared, as there was in the advice given to Janet to stay with her pain. The problem arises when this wisdom is obscured by the preachy attitude, when the generosity is lost in the self-absorption of the giver. When we are the ones wanting to help or fix another, we can Pause and notice both the desire to relieve our own discomfort and the inherent generosity and compassion that go with it. As we accept ourselves, we may notice a newfound ability to join the other in this human experience.

It is not difficult to free up the practice group that is stuck in teachy dynamics. Harnessing the wisdom and generosity inherent in the "teacher" is straightforward when we take the time to enter the moment with honesty and humility. Here are a few things we can do:

1. *Relax.* Give some space, internally, to the urge to share. That is, do not give in to the habitual and impulsive energy to tell someone "how it is." Meet the tension you feel from the person's discomfort or unskillfulness with acceptance and ease.

2. *Inquire as to the substantiality of your own knowing.* Like other forms of identification with the intellect, the teacher stance dissolves in the solvent of humility. What do we know? Who knows? Consider all we do not know.

3. *Contemplate the shared human experience.* Rather than distance yourself by being a preacher or a passive member of the congregation, actively contemplate your commonality with your meditation partners. Join them on the equalizing path of compassion by being fully present to the hurt and brilliance of the human condition.

4. *Attend to balance.* If you are in a teacher role, focus on Listen Deeply. Listen for the wisdom in every word of your partners. If you find yourself in a passive student role, Speak Truth. Confidently speak out the wisdom of this moment of mindfulness.

When the members of a group free themselves from the diversion of telling and being told, they enter together into the astuteness of not knowing. Understanding that was formerly imposed by the would-be teacher is now available to the group as a whole for the use of all. Those whom we once attempted to teach now join us in sharing wisdom.

Silent Meditation
Retreating from the Interpersonal

Silence feels good, especially after we have dropped the loudest noises of the heart-mind and started to settle in. At the very least there is relief. There can be the physical delight of deep relaxation, akin to that pleasure some feel before falling asleep. We crave this ease, and when it arises, we hold to it. This is especially true, perhaps, of experienced meditators, who have come to want and even expect this silence as the reward for all their practice. "This is why I meditate" might be the felt response to quietude's calming visit. Resting peacefully alone, absorbed in internal experience, the meditator curls up like a child in a cozy bed. The mutuality element of practice droops. We snuggle into quiet's velvet nest.

Attachment to silence creates a kind of inertia, a slipping, loosening descent into individual silence, where the meditator wants to enjoy these fruits but not proceed to the next step of practice. In Insight Dialogue the step into engagement must be taken. Pause and Relax are followed by Open and Trust Emergence. We must wake the temporarily contented child; something awaits.

Even if we do not feel quiet and peaceful, we may believe that others are as peaceful as they appear to be, and we don't want to be cited for disturbing the peace. We may hold a stereotype that all good meditation practice is silent and so support a stuck silence for fear of being perceived as a bad meditator.

The slip into silence can also be a collapse into habit. Vic was a member of an interfaith community where I was invited to teach a weeklong retreat. He told me the practice had enlivened and deepened their communication, but after a while old patterns began to manifest.

Insight Dialogue has been a helpful challenge to our community. Sharing at more of an emotional and social level is very necessary for our harmony. We naturally fall into a silence mode, even in group settings, and we are satisfied with this time of silence or worship. With dialogue it seems we need to come to the session expecting to talk and not to sit in silence, negating thoughts as they arise or letting them go and return to the breath or the text we are contemplating. It was interesting to work with the dialogue process and the more worshipful practices. Some confusion arose because we naturally gravitate to this silence, and when we returned to dialogue we fell into long periods of silence with little sharing taking place. Thankfully some of us realized we were lost and called us back.

Why was Vic thankful that some members reminded the group to come back to the shared practice? Isn't it one of meditation's major benefits that it is calming, and when calm, we can more easily see things as they are? Unfortunately, the silence that would be revealing can also be concealing. We can hide in the quiet, protected from any discomfort that may arise from interpersonal contact. Silence can become a shelter, a barely fearful place tinged more by denial than by insight. Such practice is not based upon true and open tranquillity but upon self-absorption or torpor. One longtime practitioner put it bluntly:

> For people who have a hard time really locating other people, connecting with the outer world, this practice may feed an unhealthy tendency toward self-absorption.

In the wide view of the path that encompasses extraordinary interpersonal practice, personal silent meditation is honored, but engagement is essential if we want to gain the benefits of interactive meditation. We must realize that silence and engagement are not always mutually exclusive. As we begin practicing, tranquillity will naturally develop. We honor and appreciate that silence; it is good and necessary. But our silence must open, must become relational. So we attune to the silence, the clear awareness, that endures behind all words. If moved, we speak into and from this awareness.

Relational silence is found when we leave the attractive warmth of our first experience of silence and discover the hush that weaves itself in and around dynamic encounter with the world. In this way we come upon a peace that is flexible and alive, a peace that moves with experience. This peace is more robust than its sequestered cousin and is crucial to the continued evolution of understanding. For Jake this experience opened up all at once.

> Some people were expressing the intensity of their experience, and I realized that my torpor was insulating me from the experience. I had a sense of cracking open a shell around me, and awareness was clearer, more immediate.

The group that inclines toward individual silent practice has great potential. Such a group tends to value tranquillity, which is essential to interpersonal meditation. But quiet's velvet nest can exert a gravitational pull so strong that the light of interpersonal awareness cannot escape and be shared. The coexistence of helpful and unhelpful qualities makes this a difficult rut to recognize. It also makes it a recurring pattern as group practice matures.

There are several practice adjustments that can be helpful, but the first, Open, is by far the most important.

1. *Open.* Motivated by understanding and commitment to practice, arise from sunken personal practice into mutuality. Open your eyes. Feel your presence with others.

2. *Trust emergence.* Attune to the energy of impermanence. Even the deepest silence is alive with change. Let awareness be bright, not dull, as it reflects in itself the luminosity of emergence.

3. *Energize the body with physical movement.* Sit up straight and take a deep breath. It can be helpful for the group to take a break for walking, stretching, or simple formal practice like yoga or qigong.

4. *Find the humor in the human tendency to shrink.* Smile at the awkward predicament of not knowing what to say. Let the joy of our shared humanity lift you—everyone together—out of the quagmire of isolation.

5. *Contemplate something energetically alive.* One traditional object of contemplation that could be the focus of inquiry is the agitation that comes with worry and remorse. Another is energy as such—the vitality of the body, or the energy of nature, of awareness itself.

Shifting out of being stuck in silence, we often find that the gifts of silence remain with us. Alive, awake, speaking and listening with others, we remain attuned to the tranquillity that runs through wise engagement.

Trance, Gazing, and Greed for Experience

When we are still and awake, we encounter people in new ways: tender ways, attractive ways. It is not hard to become entranced, drawn to losing ourselves in each other. We gaze deeply into each other's eyes (if we are in pairs) or give ourselves over to collective trance. We are blind to the creeping greed for experience that arrives with its partner, oblivion.

Monique's story reveals both the challenge and the victory.

In the middle of a dialogue, as we were both gazing at each other, my partner said, "I am starting to feel we are one." This triggered some bodily felt experiences in me, familiar from other workshops, that would occur just before a breaking into reality. There was a deep, neutral pressure against my chest and a sense of sacredness, silence, and perhaps I noticed a little part of me felt gratified, like: "Oh, I am such a skillful seeker to get to this space!" I did not lose my consciousness of the body or the environment, so I felt I was following the guidelines of the Insight Dialogue pretty accurately. I heard or felt myself say, "Yep. It's the big one; yes, I recognize that feeling, that's the right one, great!"

And then the bell rang—mercifully. Time for a pause. Gregory, the teacher, having noticed our gazing and extreme slowness of words, made a thoughtful comment during that meditative pause about trance versus reality. He encouraged all of us to open our eyes next and look at each other with clarity. *Clarity* was a powerful word for me, like "we are one" was previously.

After I opened my eyes, I looked at my partner, and here it was, this pristine clarity, in my head, in my body. Even my partner's face looked clearer. We compared experiences and they matched—this is always such an exquisite moment in Insight Dialogue! But the most important for me is that after I experienced the clarity and then the shared love that flowed (with tears) between us, I realized that the previous experience, as profound as it might feel or sound, was very impersonal: not really connecting as the humans we are. It certainly was less satisfying and less real than the clarity and then clean love. That was where the real truth was!

There are many types of experience we could be greedy for, including merging with another, hypnotic trance, and collective intelligence. In such cases we are exhibiting a strong commitment to practice, tranquillity, and openness to others. It is only the greed that turns this into a problem. When greed infiltrates such an experience, we grasp onto it and become deluded, blind to its changing nature. We suffer when it passes and idealize it when looking back.

Just beginning to notice this greed for what it is can help. And if we can remember the purpose of our practice—releasing rather than feeding hungers—we can turn the challenge of this greed for experience into opportunity. Adjustments to practice might include the following:

1. *Ground awareness in the body.* Bring your attention to the real, felt sense of the body. You may notice energies rise and fall in the form of flowering sensations, but return to the earthiness of just sitting.

2. *Contemplate the body.* As a support for earthy engagement, practitioners might contemplate body parts in a way taught by the Buddha: we become aware of how we and others have head hair, body hair, nails, teeth, skin, muscles, sinews, bones, and so forth. Just review the body parts as you might review the contents of a bag from a recent trip to the store.

3. *Contemplate the wanting behind the desire for fancy experiences.* Take the larger context of greed, hatred, and delusion. How do these tendencies push us to unskillful actions? Do we want these forces to dominate our meditation practice also? Are they doing so now?

When the patina of trance is lifted and our motivation shifts from greed to the release of whatever obscures awakening, we can see things as they are, not as we want them to be. In place of grasping, the energy of interpersonal practice then yields interpersonal freedom.

In closing, all of these diversions in practice—the habits and identification, the grasping and retreating—can cut short our development or be a new starting point for awakening. Insight Dialogue should not be practiced only for the pleasures it offers. It is a practice undertaken with a sense of our potential for freedom and to help us act kindly and wisely as we touch the world.

Part Four

LIVING THE
TRADITION

20

TOUCHING
THE WORLD

Insight Dialogue is a meditation practice that touches our lives. It is based upon an interpersonal understanding of the Dhamma that transforms how we meet the world. The interpersonal path not only impacts our experience of the world as individuals, it sets deep roots in our relational and practical lives. This chapter offers an overview of how Insight Dialogue has begun to infuse people's lives at work, in their family relationships, and in society in general. Whether its impact takes the form of explicit application of the Insight Dialogue guidelines or of a practice of cross-cultural dialogue or therapeutic encounter, or if it simply affects an individual's way of relating to others, transformation manifests in its most visible way: in interaction with other people.

Work

Much of our lives are spent at work. For many, work environments are poor in values and rife with stress and idle chatter. It seems an insurmountable problem to bring to the workplace the essential qualities of the path of awakening. The apparent gap between this path and our lives at work can be bridged if we realize we are not trying to attain the elevated mind states of retreat. A retreatant named Elena described this dynamic: "Certainly the experience at my work is not the same as during the retreat, where my awareness was completely magnified and engulfing. Now back at work, in a busy office environment, I find I am more aware of what I'm thinking and feeling when I am with others—I used to check out into dreamland and stories."

Still, because Insight Dialogue is an interpersonal practice, and because much of our time at work finds us in contact with other people, the gap that many people feel between personal meditative practice and the work environment can be diminished. That's how it was for Kenneth: "I use the Pause all the time at work. It helps me get past my habitual response of 'I am right' and listen deeper. I've let others know that I pause sometimes to collect my thoughts. In the environment of overachievers, all trying to outperform each other, it doesn't always work. But people have begun to respect, even appreciate, my pauses. I even see them take a bit more time to think. In any event, I am more present with my own thoughts, and so more present with others."

Much of the stress at work—and much of the transformative potential—manifests in interpersonal contexts. Among coworkers we often see resentment, politicking, or simple personality conflicts. Meanwhile there are complex dynamics with customers, clients, vendors, or others outside the organization. In the helping professions, people are in close interpersonal contact most of every day, confronting the deepest stresses to the human heart. To address the wondrous question of awakening in such a complex environment in even a simple way, our aspirations should be straightforward: to be a bit kinder and clearer and not tie our knots tighter.

Our work lives often involve partnerships or collaborations in groups or teams. All collaborations, whatever their purpose, are first and foremost human relationships. They will be impeded by certain qualities and fortified by others. The practitioner of Insight Dialogue recognizes and begins to release in himself or herself those qualities that make collaborations unproductive or disagreeable. Insight Dialogue also nurtures those qualities that enable collaborations to reach their highest potential.

Mountains of literature have been produced, over many centuries, on the attributes that make for successful partnerships. I will note only briefly some qualities I have found to be essential for collaboration that are also positively impacted by Insight Dialogue. First and foremost is a willingness to engage. In Insight Dialogue, we practice with intense commitment to each other. This translates into commitment to our partnerships, energy to get work done, concentration, and a willingness to ride out interpersonal difficulties. Joining this willingness and ability to be present to others is the quality of compassion we gain from our insights into the shared human experience. Based upon compassion, we are more kind, and based upon kindness, we are more relaxed.

The tranquillity of engaged meditation also helps partners get through challenging passages, even to benefit from them. Commitment comes with mutual respect and joy, both intimate companions of good communication. Communication includes listening deeply and speaking truthfully on many levels simultaneously, essential qualities of partnership and leadership. Good communication both depends on safety and builds on that safety. Collaborators must know they will not be belittled or otherwise betrayed if they take risks or reveal their weaknesses. With safety, courage grows, and in collaborative efforts, interpersonal courage forms the foundation of intellectual, artistic, and political courage, among others. Knowing exactly what one is courageous about, what one stands for, is possible only with mental clarity, which is explicitly cultivated in Insight Dialogue when we Pause and Speak the Truth. With clear thinking, collaborators are sensitive to what matters, to what should be given attention in a sea of possibility.

Recognizing and connecting to this sea of possibility defines the generative partnership. To foster creativity and successfully tap new resources, collaborators must be willing to join each other in unknowing. That is, they must be willing to temporarily release clinging to assumptions, outcomes, and self-centered attachments and attend to the demands of the inquiry. Asking what is possible, they must trust that answers will emerge. This is a direct and practical application of Trust Emergence. Flexibility is crucial. Collaborators must be able to take a stance when appropriate and to release that stance easily when prompted by their partners or by the circumstances of the work. Flexibility includes knowing that it is possible to return to any position if it retains the ring of truth. Hence, the guidelines Trust Emergence and Speak the Truth segue from a meditative practice to a foundation for successful partnership. Collaboration requires patience with delayed outcomes, ideas that have not yet clarified, and partners who have taken a different tack; all of these are fostered by Pause-Relax. This points to a need for tolerance for ambiguity and a willingness to accept chaos and paradox, those inevitable visitors to any serious endeavor. Finally, when relationships are established, participants can bring to bear their competencies: in the subject field and with the milieu of collaboration itself. In Insight Dialogue one learns to establish and treasure excellence in relationship.

In addition to having the potential to broadly impact the quality of people's work lives and relationships, Insight Dialogue is specifically being applied in various fields where interpersonal encounter is at the heart of things. In some cases the practice is shared in its original form, as when I offer retreats for therapists that are very similar to other Insight Dialogue retreats. This functions as a kind of advanced professional training, based on and integrated with whatever personal benefits people enjoy. Sometimes the guidelines are combined with other forms of training, as when Insight Dialogue is integrated into a conflict-resolution or counseling program. In still other applications, the meditation guidelines, contemplations, or theory may be offered in a classroom setting or by health practitioners as part of a course in relationship. This is oriented toward improving the quality of life, including wakeful relationship, stress reduction, and enhanced communication. In all cases the motivation for moving this work from meditation to application centers around the power of its methodical approach to cultivate deep mindfulness, tranquillity, and clear understanding of the human experience.

Many qualities cultivated in Insight Dialogue meditation are applicable or even essential to all of these areas. In the book *Mindfulness and Psychotherapy*, in a chapter entitled "Mindfulness as Clinical Training," Paul Fulton describes in some detail the "therapist's cultivation of mental qualities, well described in the meditation literature, that relate to common factors underlying effective [psychotherapeutic] treatment."[1] These qualities include the capacity to pay wholehearted attention, increased affect tolerance, ever-deepening acceptance, greater empathy and compassion, insight into the constructed nature of our beliefs, an awareness of our own narcissistic needs, and equanimity along with an acceptance of the limits of our helpfulness. All of these qualities are cultivated in Insight Dialogue, in a fully interpersonal context.

Perhaps the practice guideline that has the most obvious relevance to helping professionals is Listen Deeply. In Insight Dialogue deep listening is not simply a set of skills to be applied but, rather, the natural result of a deeply attentive and awake mind state. Also, keen mindfulness is developed interpersonally and is explicitly applied both internally and externally, that is, to oneself and to others. Indeed, the ability to maintain an open awareness of self, other, and the topic at hand is one of the great gifts of practice. As one person noticed at a session with a client that followed her participation in an Insight Dialogue retreat: "I was less burdened by the thought of having to do something; I was in touch with the smallness of the content and the vastness of compassion that emerged from within me."

For people working in conflict resolution, relational tranquillity and nonjudgment are at the core of the connection between their work and Insight Dialogue. Sitting with disputants who may be embroiled in marital difficulties or the breakup of business relationships or who may even be trying to piece together ways to coexist following violent encounters, conflict-resolution professionals are called upon to bring peace into chaos, coolness into the fiercest heat we humans can create. While Insight Dialogue practice, particularly at retreats, tends to be relatively peaceful, the subjective experience of the practice is not necessarily serene. Rather, one continually brings refined mindfulness to the habitual turmoil of the mind and *invites* ever-deeper tranquillity. Entire armies of inner conflict are met and invited to tea. Practicing in this way, with commitment and courage, cultivates in one an intimate knowledge of and responsibility for one's own reactive mind. With this comes an appreciation of the need for relentless diligence if one is to meet the ever-present tendency to judgment and reaction. This courage and application, and the attendant tranquillity, are brought to the table with others engaged in conflict.

For those so inclined, the Insight Dialogue guidelines can be adapted to a specific therapeutic methodology, one based upon Buddhist insights. Several therapists have taught Pause-Relax-Open (P-R-O) to clients as a technique for managing difficult emotions. I have worked with a friend, the Korean Gestalt therapist Jungkyu Kim, to teach people with social anxiety disorders to use P-R-O, and the outcome of our pilot project was very promising.[2] Other therapists have found this meditation instruction to be a useful way of presenting the basics of mindfulness and concentration to clients with no prior meditation experience. They report that clients benefit from becoming more self-aware, less identified with reactive states, more accepting of their inner experiences, and more easily available to others in social situations.

The Insight Dialogue guidelines have been used by the Metta Foundation as the basis for the development of the Interpersonal Mindfulness program. In collaboration with a small group of Mindfulness-Based Stress Reduction instructors, trained in the work of Jon Kabat-Zinn, the basic Insight Dialogue teachings are offered in a course format, usually one evening per week for four to eight weeks, with one all-day retreat somewhere in the middle. Some combination of the six core guidelines is offered to students each week, together with a contemplation theme that can be taken into their daily lives via home practice. The intention is to bring some illumination to participants' lives about the sources of interpersonal stress and to share ways to cultivate interpersonal mindfulness and calm. Out of this we are seeing people's lives improve as they experience better communication at home and work, less stress and conflict, and greater understanding of themselves and of others in their lives.

Therapeutic interventions can be radically informed and transformed by the power of the interpersonal construal of the Buddha's teachings. Insight Dialogue is far more than a simple mindfulness practice. The full range of this meditation, together with its associated theory, offers a model of the human experience, and a way of working to improve that experience, that directly taps the power of the Dhamma. Binding and freedom, hungers, ignorance, and the subtle teachings on dependent origination all become available in a form that is both intuitively powerful and immediately applicable. For example, a thorough understanding of the hunger for non-being sheds light on the connections between addiction, self-loathing, and the urge to escape and points toward a way to work with this complex. Whether or not one explicitly uses the Insight Dialogue meditation instructions, the interpersonal Dhamma transforms the therapist and shifts the therapeutic process from an illness-based model to one rooted in letting go, a model of unhindered possibility.

Couples and Families

Insight Dialogue meditation can positively impact our most significant and intimate relationships, including the relationships within families or between couples. In these relationships habits, viewpoints, and images of self and other are built up over time, becoming very intricate. The special challenges of complex relationships mostly derive from the web of associations that have been constructed, which can dampen mindfulness. At the same time, tranquillity can be challenged by the tendency of the heart to be detonated into reaction at many trigger points. At the heart of it all is the basic dynamic that intimacy and reactivity are often paired; because of this, constructed intimate relationships provide some of our most powerful, charged, challenging, and potentially transformative encounters.

Interpersonal meditation can have a strong positive impact on intimate relations because it is a relational practice. Following an Insight Dialogue retreat, a participant named Richard shared: "I've noticed a lot of things since the postretreat buzz wore off. My sitting meditation is deeper, and I am much more mindful off the cushion, particularly with my family. I am less reactive with my children, which my wife has commented on several times. My sense of equanimity feels more solid across situations." Insight Dialogue practice can also help families meet life's inevitable difficulties. For Angela, a mother in Portland, Oregon, her experience with Insight

Dialogue groups came right into the crisis of her son's panic attacks: "Without even calling on the guidelines, I found myself able to apply them even as he sat curled up on the driveway and unable to move. I felt myself listening for signals from Kevin so that I could help him find his path." Richard and Angela both benefited from Insight Dialogue practice not because they practiced specifically with their families but because they had practiced with other people. The mindfulness and balance naturally migrated into their home lives.

When both partners in a long-term relationship are committed to relational meditation, Insight Dialogue can be a gateway through which our intimate relations and spiritual paths naturally intermingle. Because the practice is interpersonal, it does not need to be applied to relationships after the fact. Meditative awareness and compassion instantly become a real, accessible mode of relationship. A couple in San Francisco said that Insight Dialogue "had a big influence on our sense of hope and faith about what Dhamma practice is and what it could do for us as a couple." Having meditated in relationship, their relationship became more meditative, that is, more mindful, calm, and accepting. Meditation also contributes to our relationships by opening a kind of sacred space for partners, where kindness, generosity, and respect are the assumed norm. It often takes only a glimpse, a glancing expression of true care, to remind partners what glows at the heart of long-term commitment.

Moreover, our relationships can become more genuine and alive as mindfulness reveals where we are forming images of ourselves and relating more from persona than from honest experience. We also become aware of when we are forming images of our partners and taking those images as truth. It becomes possible to relate person-to-person rather than image-to-image. Relating only through these constructs is distancing and detrimental to the honesty, warmth, and vitality of relationships. As one practitioner put it, "In one way of being we show each other photographs of ourselves. In another we see the living glance in each other's eyes and feel the press of our hands in the impermanent moment."

It is good to remember that interpersonal meditation can also reveal that which is beyond or beneath the interpersonal. Renata, after practicing with her husband, shared: "Fear, suffering, and artifice fall aside when we practice. All that remains is love and trust. It is our intention to have nothing between us. Those commitments deepen this practice immeasurably for me and take it from helpful to almost divine." One could say that there is a transition from constructed to unconstructed intimacy. Here we see the contribution that personal commitment to an intimate relationship can make toward the unfolding of insight. We come full circle and see the reciprocity between our emotional and spiritual lives: each can support the other. Intimate relations can be playgrounds where the constructed and unconstructed commingle, where the mundane and the sacred play and the full and the empty are both honored.

Society

Interpersonal meditation yields a refined awareness that can bring us beneath the constructions that define the personal and social self. These constructs are often based upon physical differences such as race, sex, age, and physical ability. Just as often they are based entirely on socially derived forms such as gender, ethnicity, religion, nationality, sexual orientation, and wealth. In all cases the basic formula could be schematically stated like this: contact and perception (we see, hear, or otherwise encounter the other) produce conception and memory (we form mental-emotional images of the other), which produce recirculation and proliferation (the images arise and rearise, recursively gathering nuance and power according to new data and circumstances). We take these habitually regenerated images as truths ("People of lower castes are dirty") and act according to these formations.

Might it be possible that the extraordinary interpersonal path reduces our clinging to and belief in the hard reality of these differences? Or, more directly, can we be more free than we currently are of the corrosive effects of perceived or conceived differences? The first step in such a process is to become aware of our participation in fabricating barriers. Historically, or at any particular moment, we may be the perpetrator or victim of othering, but in both perpetrator and victim we see the mind's tendency to concoct and cling to notions of difference. Interpersonal meditation can reveal this movement of the mind in the moment it happens and reveal wholesome alternatives.

Transcending roles is not always so easy. A significant barrier to truly multiethnic concourse is the prior hurt that has been stored as a knot in the heart of those who have been marginalized. If we frame this in terms of our underlying hungers, the question arises, "Do we have to be fed before we can release hunger?" More specifically, do we have to be seen before we can release the urge to be seen? Do we have to feel safe—that is, not singled out for abuse—before we can release the vigilance born of the urge to escape? The urge to not be seen is a natural result when visibility equates with vulnerability and hurt. But to be invisible in a society is to have the basic longing for acknowledgment unmet. So in addition to the fundamental biopsychological longing to be seen that issues from having a body, being born into a family, and so on, there may be an explicit and sometimes extreme social layer of invisibility. Such layers are laid bare for the courageous practitioner of Insight Dialogue. Does the female, the Hispanic, the poor person, long to be seen? Does the gay or disabled person long to hide? How does one distinguish among the functionally essential need for acknowledgment, the wise decision to remain low-profile, and unnecessary and painful layers of hunger? Likewise, will mindfulness at the moment of interpersonal contact reveal the hungers for pleasure and visibility among members of the majority or dominant culture? Can such hungers ever be satisfied? Can one be truly free when one's privileges are contingent upon the exploitation of others?

Interpersonal meditation will not eliminate the human tendency to identify and classify what is perceived. This is innate and important to our physical survival as a species. What interpersonal meditation will do, however, is allow us to discard habitual categorizations when they are unhelpful or even harmful, which is often the case concerning interpersonal relationships. Likewise, meditation by an individual or small groups will not immediately eradicate long-established social structures that hold hierarchies and privileges in place. Even in more or less homogeneous groups, differences can arise in the form of spontaneous hierarchies: in-groups and out-groups, subtle power differentials, and so on. But for those who actually participate in deep or sustained regular practice, habitual interpersonal behavior is seen for what it is. We can then cease our participation in, and change our reactions to, the many unjust or unkind social structures. I have seen how wholesome this process can be when it unfolds in intentional communities. We can also fundamentally transform our views of other people and cultures by way of multicultural dialogue that, powered by meditative awareness and concentration, slices through the fog of social assumptions. Such individual transformation will have an impact on social structures over time. As we evolve, so does our society and so does our world—gradually.

This approach to social transformation is substantive and lasting because it springs from fundamental transformation of those who make up that community or society. In interpersonal meditation we see the poisonous habit of constructing otherness in ourselves on a moment-to-moment basis. We see the pain it causes ourselves and others and naturally let it go, just as one would reject any poison. Our relationships become different, guided by perceptions untainted by fear and longing. We do not leave our rational minds behind. We unleash them to function fearlessly, lovingly, and with natural, unfabricated compassion. As Buddhist scholar Peter Hershock notes, "Ch'an [Buddhist] enlightenment should not be seen as private and experiential in nature, but as irreducibly and intimately social."[3]

Social change does not come easily or quickly. The world is in a sorry state. As the fourteenth Dalai Lama has noted, it took many years for humans to get into this place of hurt, and it will take many years for us to get out of it. Social change begins with individual change. Insight Dialogue offers a clear path for the migration of individual transformation into interpersonal and societal transformation. It is a path that is good in the beginning, good in the middle, and good at the end. When we meditate together, the values revealed by the shared human experience become the basis of our life's path. We are informed and nourished in this supreme and necessary challenge: the opportunity to meet the world, meet each other, in peace.

~ 21 ~

INSIGHT DIALOGUE
AND TRADITIONAL
BUDDHIST TEACHINGS

EVEN THOUGH Insight Dialogue is an example of an interpersonal practice and is part of a path that is broadly human rather than religiously sectarian, it has its roots in the central teachings of the Buddha. This chapter surveys how Insight Dialogue is situated in traditional teachings, so that readers with a background in Buddhist meditation or study, or who are curious about those teachings, can have a starting point to explore this formal association. This is not a detailed exposition, however: the connections are wider and more detailed than I offer here.

The Guidelines and Contemplations

As we have seen, the six meditation instructions and the use of contemplations all have their origins in traditional practices. I will state these links in the simplest terms.

The Pause is essentially mindfulness (*sati* in Pali) and the onset of nonclinging, as found in vipassana meditation; it is nonclinging and an instantaneous stepping out of ignorance, as commonly seen in radical Zen or Ch'an practice. Relax is rooted in tranquillity and concentration practices (*samadhi*); there is a host of such practices that range from calming the breath and relaxing the body to stabilizing the mind. Relax is also the practice that stabilizes nonclinging. Open is associated with the spacious practices of lovingkindness (*metta*) and compassion, nonduality of subject and object, and the spacious stability of *dzogchen* (turning toward innate awareness) and the cultivation of *bodhicitta* (the heart awakened in compassion).

Trust Emergence is a living contemplation of impermanence and emptiness: the absence in all things, especially our thoughts and emotions, of a substantial core. Listen Deeply has roots not only in the permeability of the spaciousness practices but also in the sensory awareness of vipassana and even tantric practice. There are also explicit listening practices in many Buddhist traditions. Speak the Truth is Right Speech, but it is also mindfulness in action. The contemplations are, themselves, essential consideration of the Buddha's observations of the human condition. Contemplation topics cover the elemental teachings of impermanence-suffering-impersonality, greed-hatred-delusion as roots of thought; love-compassion-joy-equanimity; and so forth. They share characteristics with Tibetan analytical meditation. The contemplations are also opportunities to contemplate the nature of mind directly; that is, the contemplations are a practice of inquiry.

The Path and Teachings in General

During the practice of Insight Dialogue, the techniques and dynamics of traditional meditation often become clearer. We can see the dynamics of the heart-mind unfold in interaction, outside the almost imperceptible recesses of our minds. We see truth not just in ourselves but as it manifests for others and as it manifests between us. Interest in traditional knowledge of the path can also arise as a result of Insight Dialogue practice because we have seen new things and want to understand the human condition more accurately. If we are well versed in the Buddha's teachings, we may be challenged to expand or abandon old understandings of the Dhamma as a nonrelational teaching. For example, we may hold philosophically subtle ideas about emptiness—but if these ideas do not encompass a lived experience of the emptiness of the social forms we continually create, these ideas must grow or be abandoned.

Integration from the Bottom Up

Many people find that the wakefulness, ease, and even love they feel while in formal meditation do not integrate well into their lives. These formal practices can be quite pristine and therefore distinct from our very busy everyday lives. There is no clear path for blending formal practice with everyday living, and for many, the act of integrating the benefits of meditation is sort of pasted on after the fact. That is, we meditate alone and in silence, then try to map the same mindfulness and nonclinging to speaking with others. There is a gap. In Insight Dialogue the integration happens from the bottom up. That is, the heart of the practice is relational, so that the mindfulness and compassion that we cultivate on retreat do not need to be artificially appended to relatedness.

Integration following Insight Dialogue retreats and groups is still necessary, because these are "extraordinary" practices. That is, they take place outside the norms of our lives; this is one reason such deep transformation is possible. Because the practice is interpersonal, however, bottom-up integration is possible. There is not such a big gap to be bridged, and the integration process tends to flow naturally: more smoothly, more deeply felt, and more robust.

Research on neuroplasticity provides another way to think about the process of integration. Neurological function and even structure can be changed by long-term meditative practice, as has been established in a number of recent studies.[1] These changes are measurable physical aspects of the changed patterns of thought and emotion that result from the integration of insight into our habitual ways of living. Deep and extended Insight Dialogue practice offers deep meditative experience and simultaneously provides a series of opportunities to apply insight immediately in the usually disruptive realm of human relationships. Changes in perspective and behavior can become integrated very quickly when both these opportunities are present. These changes would almost certainly be reflected in changes to the brain structures involved in interpersonal functioning, such as the limbic system, and perhaps also the prefrontal areas known to change as the result of compassion meditation practice.

Mutual Benefits of Personal and Interpersonal Meditation

As we've explored elsewhere, personal (more precisely, intrapersonal) and interpersonal meditation support each other. Or rather, both support the maturation of the practitioner. Bonnie saw this clearly.

I appreciate and am inspired by this practice because it bridges my personal meditation practice with my interpersonal practice, recognizing and validating what arises in the interpersonal domain as not a secondary practice to formal sitting but as vitally necessary for growth, healing, and awakening.

Insight Dialogue Compared to Traditional Retreat

There are surprising similarities between intrapersonal and interpersonal meditation retreats. In both, silence is a cathedral. One meditator wrote:

> I am so very glad that you insisted on silence except when we were in dialogue. It caused me to really slow down and was the only way I could have been truly mindful throughout.

Likewise, both retreat forms can engender deep concentration. Diane had trained in Zen for several years before taking residence at a Zen monastery. After two years at the monastery, this was her self-assessment after only one weekend of Insight Dialogue practice:

> I am very appreciative of my Zen practice going into the Insight Dialogue retreat because the sitting we did was long and intense—very comparable to a week-long *sesshin* [retreat] to me. After your retreat I had very similar reactions (headache, dreaminess, deep calm, alignment, and so on) as I do after *sesshin*. This tells me the practice was deep.

Diane's experience is in alignment with that of a longtime vipassana meditator who attended a retreat in Europe and was surprised at the depth of her concentration during that retreat. She told the group that during the silent sessions between dialogues, she had settled attention on that point between the in-breath and the out-breath, and it expanded infinitely. It surprised her that such a refined state should arise during a retreat that involved so much talking and forced her to reexamine the nature of concentration. Another meditator, a former monk with decades of practice and long retreat experience, said his experience of deep concentration on Insight Dialogue retreat was essentially the same as in his *jhana* (absorption) practice, only wider and more flexible. He said it also yielded similarly deep insights.

Not all meditators experience such deep concentration, of course. Practice can also be gentle. Indeed, interpersonal meditation can help free us from the tension and agenda we may bring to traditional practice. Sylvia had wondered if she could even make it through a retreat.

I've been meditating for many years. Over the last few years my health has deteriorated, and I've been experiencing extreme fatigue and headaches. This and hormonal changes have made meditation difficult for me. My practice has suffered; I wasn't sure if I would be able to come to this retreat, but while here I felt peace and ease in just being. I found that it is possible to touch freedom even in this state. Meditating with others, I came to see how, when we come from a place of compassion and "no agenda," the act of giving is so much more beautiful than when we do it to feed a disguised hunger.

From Sylvia's story we can see that, as in traditional retreat, many flavors of experience can arise in Insight Dialogue. Had she been forced to sit still for several days, alone in her physical pain, Sylvia might not have been able to make it through to "compassion" and "no agenda," to a place where she could see and release her hungers. Sylvia may not have experienced the deep concentration that Diane enjoyed, but she gained other benefits from her practice.

The Noble Eightfold Path Becomes Real

Following a weeklong retreat in western Massachusetts, Debra was delighted that her personal path and formal path had merged.

The Eightfold Path became very much alive in the light of all the very real work that we had done through the week. I was able to see much more clearly how it all works in my real life. So I was able to take the instruction directly into my experience with the van driver and with security people at the airport. There was more spaciousness, more clarity about Right Effort, and, especially, an ability not to take my mental constructs so seriously.

The Noble Eightfold Path is a broad schema for understanding how we can live in wise and wholesome ways. As Debra left retreat, she saw this path as something eminently livable; she was living it then and there, with no effort. This clarity may have faded as she got farther from retreat, but we have remained in touch, and I know that the experience and vision of what is possible remains with her.

The formal path is associated with this practice by virtue of the explicit teachings regarding Right View, Right Effort, and Right Mindfulness. These are defining elements of the extraordinary path. They underpin all of the meditation instructions as well as the attitude of commitment that one brings to retreat and to one's everyday life. Right View, or Wise Understanding, is practiced most directly in the contemplations and directly experienced in the insights that emerge during Insight Dialogue practice. Right Mindfulness is most clearly represented by the guideline Pause; it is also inferred by Speak the Truth.

The role of Right Effort is represented in the way Insight Dialogue helps one "abandon the unwholesome" and "cultivate the wholesome." To focus on Pause means both abandoning attachment to our thoughts and reactions and cultivating mindfulness in the moment. Relax means releasing tension and cultivating ease. Open means letting go of the encapsulated sense of self and nurturing an extended and inclusive awareness. Trust Emergence means abandoning the illusion of control or hope for a certain outcome and cultivating flexibility and the appreciation of impermanence. Listen Deeply means letting go of self-absorption and cultivating a receptive awareness of what others are saying. Speak the Truth means abandoning a preoccupied and deluded mind state and cultivating sensitivity to what has a rightness to be said, and the courage to say it. Each of these abandoning-cultivating pairs is an explicit invitation to practice, not a theoretical formula. Inherent in each is the invitation to bring forth energy and commitment to the engaged path, to let go here and now, to recognize wisdom here and now.

Foundations of Mindfulness

The discourse on the four foundations of mindfulness, the *Satipatthana Sutta,* is the central teaching of Insight meditation, vipassana.[2] In this discourse the Buddha offers specific practices for cultivating mindfulness, calling this teaching "the direct path for the purification of beings, for the overcoming of sorrow and lamentation, for the disappearance of pain and distress, for the attainment of the right method, and for the realization of Unbinding [*nibanna*/nirvana]." These four foundations are also foundations for Insight Dialogue practice: the body, feelings, mental states, and phenomena.

The body is the most fundamental and reliable home base for insight practice. Under the teachings on mindfulness of the body, instructions are offered for cultivating "clear awareness." The Buddha advises meditators to be clearly aware while standing, sitting, stretching, looking forward and away, defecating, and other everyday actions. Notable here is that he includes in this list clear awareness while "speaking and remaining silent." The more explicit instructions in this discourse on body awareness play an important role in defining Insight Dialogue. During retreats meditators are regularly invited to recenter in the body. During the Pause they can always come home to the moment by recognizing and clarifying their awareness of the simple form of the sitting body. Most important, awareness of our body posture provides a reference point amid the turbulence of interpersonal engagement. Thoughts and emotions move quickly; the body can be more readily known.

In addition to bringing stability to the practice, we find that the body reveals what is going on in our hearts and minds. As this happens, body awareness leads us to the foundations of pleasant, unpleasant, and neutral feelings, and states of the mind—such as expanded or contracted mind, agitated or tranquil mind—and emotions such as happiness, sadness, and fear. Garth shared the following:

> Several times I experienced a feeling of inferiority in regard to other people. I observed my body, feeling fear coming up from my stomach. But I didn't pull myself back this time, and stayed with the process.

As practice deepens, meditators become more able to remain present with the subtler foundations of mental and emotional states and with the more refined observations of phenomena, including their own doubts, rapture, or equanimity. Also, following this discourse, the body, feelings, and other objects of mindfulness are observed "internally, externally, and both"—as they are in the guideline Open—and in their "arising and vanishing factors," as practiced in the guideline Trust Emergence.

Such practice is possible only when we do not identify with, or inhabit, these qualities of mind. For example, if we identify with doubt, we "become" doubtful and are thrown off course. Having a map of human experience, such as the Buddha's teachings on cultivating mindfulness, is valuable for both personal and interpersonal meditation.

Dependent Origination

The Buddha's teaching on dependent origination is one of the most profound psychological teachings to be found anywhere.[3] It is also a mystical teaching. Anyone who contemplates it must confront the unknowable behind and within each moment of experience.

This teaching is fabulously subtle; dependent origination is both a sequential and simultaneous set of relationships. I often take the basic framework of dependent origination as a template for individual Insight Dialogue retreats and a beacon for the evolution of the practice. In general, we begin by noticing how the immediate experience of interpersonal contact generates pleasant or unpleasant feelings, how these are the foundation for hungers—we want these feelings to endure or to go away—and the hunger yields grasping, so we suffer. As the meditators become more settled, skillful, and alert, I point them toward the root source of this unfolding. We come closer to apprehending how the mind is blinded by ignorance and moved to activate the constructions established by past thoughts and actions—patterns of the personality. We see how consciousness takes root in these patterns and proliferates into a "self" that would grasp at experience.

From any point on this continuum—and I am leaving out several steps of the formal dependent origination teachings—we can see interpersonal grasping and the suffering it creates. Seeing clearly in this way, we are often able to release old patterns. The mystery in this teaching is in dependent origination's simultaneous and sequential manifestation, its subtlety, its time scale across lives, and its capacity to reveal the fabricated nature of everything we take as "real." In this light, behind the ignorance is the ultimate paradox of emptiness—an emptiness that is formless yet populated with form, radiant with awareness that is without a self center, and at once substanceless, enduring, and timeless.

These are some of the touch points linking Insight Dialogue with traditional Buddhist philosophy and practice. The ultimate connecting point is experience, however. And with experience we are, once again, simply human.

22

SIMPLY HUMAN

THERE COMES a time to leave systems and teachings, to set aside dualities. The personal and the interpersonal, the ordinary and the extraordinary, compassion and wisdom—these dualities can be helpful, but now it is time to let them go. There is just this life, and we do the best we can.

The personal path and the interpersonal path are not two. The personal self, the self in relationship, and the social self are not separate constructions. They are interwoven: I am alone; I am alone with you; I am alone in this society, in this world. These different I's make use of overlapping synaptic connections and bind us terribly.

In the same way, the personal and interpersonal paths to unbinding are fully interwoven. They are ultimately one. It doesn't matter whether our pain is triggered by a diagnosis of cancer, by an angry interaction, or by social injustice; the mechanisms of binding and unbinding are the same. The release of clinging is also one. The path to unbinding is just a path. We walk alone at one moment and with others the next. These are simply our way of tilting toward release. Sometimes human warmth is most helpful; sometimes we walk in the cool solitude of release. The clear acknowledgment of the interpersonal path, in its integrity and beauty, brings renewed balance and wholeness.

Now we see that compassion and wisdom are also not two paths, despite a thousand-year-old debate that might confuse us. The personal and interpersonal, ordinary and extraordinary, all contribute to both. To awaken in wisdom is to understand how things actually are. True awakening has no boundaries, so the bright mind is unarmored; the free heart is touched by the world. Suffering is a compelling actuality of being human—indeed, of being sentient. To awaken in wisdom is to awaken in compassion, and to awaken in compassion is to awaken in wisdom.

The ordinary and extraordinary are also not two paths. Distinguishing the ordinary from the extraordinary is realistic and helpful. In doing so we acknowledge the value of special practices to diminish the unwholesome and to cultivate and maintain what is good in us. Acknowledging that value, we undertake extraordinary things. But now we can set aside this concept. In any moment there is only experience. There is no practice, ordinary or extraordinary. The mind knows sitting, walking, standing, and lying down. It knows seeing, hearing, tasting, smelling, touching, and thinking. Whether one sits cross-legged and silent on a cushion or lounges in a chair while conversing with a friend, there is only the one changing moment. All distinctions are fabricated. What matters is how the heart-mind manifests from one instant to the next. Does the heart cling? Does the mind judge? Does life slip by unnoticed, hidden by self-obsession? Or are we sometimes awake?

We now see that mystery saturates the obvious. Extraordinary mind states, once thought unusual, are recognized as they rise and fall in the flux of daily life. With minds transformed, ordinary thoughts and actions spring from the same purpose as the extraordinary. All that remains is innate intelligence and care.

When all is said and done, we come back to our basic humanity. The ordinary and the extraordinary are in the service of decency as well as insight. We wake up and go to sleep in our skin: the same skin that feels the caress of our lover, the skin that is abraded raw when we tip our bicycle, the skin that ages during our thirty thousand days of sun and hail. Can we meet the caresses of love and abrasions of the earth with acceptance? Can we, between birth and death, offer our best?

This—this offering our best—is what we all do. It is all that we can do. Truth is revealed at the kitchen table and in the meditation hall. Special practices, clear awareness, careful attention: these all contribute to our capacity to do our best. So does sharing a meal, asking our children how their day was, and listening to their answers with a heart that knows the world is harrowed with pain and aware that this moment of their reply is nevertheless unique.

Born into this world, with its disease, injustice, and wars, where food costs too much and medical care is a privilege, we are called to the quietness of tolerance—and, at times, to the clamor of the prophetic, where dishonesty is not an option and honesty is not possible without a courage beyond all rationality. Still in the same skin we entered as infants, though now stretched to fit our grown hearts, we do our best. We meet the disruptions of life with flexibility; the highs and the lows are accepted, valued, and released. Compassion is ready to be active yet accepts being still. We are patient. In the sea of hurt—out there, in here; there is no difference—we do our best: we care.

Ultimately, diligence is all we can offer. Perhaps, in moments, we pause. Perhaps this prevents us from following through with a hurtful comment or a harmful action. Perhaps we remember, just then, to treat others with kindness. Perhaps, in that pause, the moment comes alive: we are awake and one conditioned thread is cut.

Perhaps a moment of serenity offers itself. Just in that moment, our aching muscles relax, our heart rate slows, and the chemistry of urgency abates. A moment, a blessed moment, of unfettered acceptance arises, and we receive this instant's best effort with gratitude. All is received, and, just then, love is simple. It has no practice or brilliance, only the gentle luster of an unassuming awareness.

Just this pond of awareness—with unseen life darting below its rippled surface, floating leaves, and sodden moss—is what we call choicelessness. The humble best, our own and others', is greeted, welcomed, and known. "I have nothing to offer but what you see—my sadness, my confusion, and occasionally my exuberance—but I am open. Let's be open together." In this way, from time to time, there is meeting. This is how we gather: in simplicity.

It can be no other way. Life is too full of unknowns to anticipate or control. The roar of the rapids grows louder, then surrounds us. We are forced to surrender, to the emergence and to the dissolution. But we don't surrender alone. In crisis, time freezes, and we see that everyone is being carried on the same emergence. In this shared tumult, we trust. We recognize the bobbing heads of our friends and see in the eyes of our adversaries and of our teachers the same fear that coils around our own heart.

At last we can listen to their fear. Whether or not they can hear us over the stony thunder, we can hear them, and we can listen to their hurt. We give ear to our aging father; it is the best we have to offer. We listen to the hurting Earth and the crying children, to abandoned animals and soldiers in battle, and our hearts vibrate with care for them and for the mothers bringing another generation that they will care for into this carnivorous world because that is what mothers do. We listen to the astonishing songs of the artist and the healer, to the talk of the banker and baker, and we receive, with our best appreciation, every facet of a goodly and confused humanity.

With every instant of listening, we speak. With every glimpse inside ourselves, and every glance given to others, we say who we are. Every act, done and undone, is the truth we offer in response to the world. This is our best. Each word spoken is an invitation to awakening. This is the care we offer. This is the care we receive. This is our whole humanity: the wail of the holding heart, the sigh of release. Our diligence has come to this: we let go as we go. It is modest, but it is all we have to offer, this truth of our shared humanity.

> We share
> pain,
> desire,
> each moment's potential for release,
> and a way of unbinding.

Acknowledgments

T HE THOUSANDS of people who have attended Insight Dialogue retreats and groups, and integrated this practice into their lives, have made it possible for these teachings to evolve. I offer them my gratitude: thank you for trusting the Dhamma and for trusting me. I offer my apologies: I am sorry for anything unskillful I may have done or not done during my learning process. I rejoice in our camaraderie and solidarity: we have always been together in this human experience.

Insight Dialogue first took form in a collaboration between myself and Terri O'Fallon. I am thankful to Terri for her graceful support as I have carried this work forward. David Selwyn read the earliest drafts of this book, Gary Steinberg provided careful reading and feedback, and Lori Ebert generously helped edit and restructure important chapters. The penultimate draft was also carefully read by Anne Michel, Sharon Beckman-Brindley, Phyllis Hicks, and Joyce Kornblatt. All of these people helped refine this work and provided warmth and encouragement. My appreciation goes also to the team associated with Shambhala: senior editor Dave O'Neal and Shambhala's skillful team of book crafters.

The editorial work of Martha Turner has been indispensable to the development of this book; much of the credit for its readability is due to her. She worked with me to reshape an unruly manuscript—unfinished at four hundred pages—into the present work. She asked difficult yet practically focused questions and helped me find structural solutions to present the work clearly. I am still amazed at her ability to maintain my voice and intentions throughout our extensive editorial process. She brought insight and keen intelligence to the work, as well as editorial skill. I offer her my gratitude.

I offer my gratitude to Mu Soeng, Andrew Olendski, Joseph Goldstein, and Ajahn Passano. They have been supportive of this work from its inception. It has been a gift to speak with them about how the heart of the Buddha's teachings manifest in this time and place. I am also grateful for the commitment and enthusiasm of the small group of people I am training to teach this practice; we are learning together where Insight Dialogue is headed. It is good to have all these friends in the Dhamma.

It is also good to have support in day-to-day life; for this I offer my gratitude to my wife Martha, our three sons Zed, Jared, and Max, my sister Jacqueline, and my father Irving, who died just as this book went to press. This book took years—too long—to complete, and my family remained patient and supportive throughout.

Finally, although it may sound odd, I am moved to thank the Buddha. Of course, he is no longer alive, and would not have cared much about my thanks one way or the other. But as I have developed this practice and worked on this book, and have immersed myself in his teachings, I have come to see him as a profoundly human figure, even a friend. His wisdom and compassion humble me, and I make no claim to meet him as an equal in those qualities. But we are both human, and this has been, and continues to be, a profound inspiration for me.

Notes

Abbreviations

AN = Anguttara Nikaya. Except where noted otherwise, references are to *The Numerical Discourses of the Buddha: An Anthology of Suttas from the "Anguttara Nikaya,"* trans. Nyanaponika Thera, ed. Bhikkhu Bodhi (Lanham, Md.: AltaMira Press, 2000).

DN = Digha Nikaya. References are to *The Long Discourses of the Buddha: A Translation of the "Digha Nikaya,"* trans. Maurice Walshe (Boston: Wisdom Publications, 1995).

MN = Majjhima Nikaya. Except where noted otherwise, all references are from *The Middle Length Discourses of the Buddha: A Translation of the "Majjhima Nikaya,"* trans. Bhikkhu Nanamoli and Bhikkhu Bodhi (Boston: Wisdom Publications, 1995).

SN = Samyutta Nikaya. Except where noted, references are to *The Connected Discourses of the Buddha: A Translation of the "Samyutta Nikaya,"* trans. Bhikkhu Bodhi (Boston: Wisdom Publications, 2000).

Chapter 2

1. David Bohm, *On Dialogue* (London: Routledge, 1996).

Chapter 3

1. Stephen Batchelor, *Buddhism without Beliefs* (New York: Riverhead Books, 1997), pp. 4–5.
2. *DN* 16.25.

Chapter 4

1. *SN* 56.11, trans. Nanamoli Thera, http://accesstoinsight.org/tipitaka/sn/sn 56/sn56.011.nymo.html.
2. *MN* 141.17.
3. *DN* 22.18.

4. *AN* 6.63, trans. Thanissaro Bhikkhu, http://accesstoinsight.org/tipitaka/an/an06/an06.063.than.html.

Chapter 5

1. With Nanamoli and Bodhi, I translate *bhava* as "being"; it is also translated as "becoming" (Thanissaro) and "existence" (Piyadassi). (Thanissaro, an American-born Buddhist translator and commentator, is a monk in the Thai forest tradition. Piyadassi Mahatherea was a wandering Sri Lankan monk and missionary.) The use of *being* does not imply the existence of an enduring being but rather the hunger for such being (or nonbeing). I use "hunger" to translate the Pali word *tanha*. *Tanha* translates literally as "thirst"; the most common translation in the context of the Dhamma is "craving."
2. *MN* 141.21. I have taken the liberty of using Bhikkhu Nanamoli's and Bhikkhu Bodhi's translations, substituting the word *hunger* for their word *craving*. The Pali word is *tanha*, literally "thirst."
3. Daniel Siegel, *The Developing Mind* (New York: Guilford Press, 1999).
4. Aldous Huxley, *Doors of Perception* (New York: Harper and Row, 1954).
5. Tara Brach, chapter 1, *Radical Acceptance* (New York: Bantam, 2004).
6. *AN* 3.65, trans. Thanissaro Bhikkhu, http://accesstoinsight.org/tipitaka/an/an03/an03.065.than.html

Chapter 6

1. *MN* 141.22. Again, *hunger* is substituted for *craving*. (See chap. 5, note 2 above.)
2. *MN* 9.12.
3. *Visuddhi Magga* 17.275, trans. Bhadantacariya Buddhagosa and Bhikkhu Nanamoli (Kandy, Sri Lanka: Buddhist Publication Society, 1979).
4. *MN* 22.20.
5. *MN* 140.30–31.
6. *MN* 11.17.
7. *The Itiuuttaka: The Buddha's Sayings*, chap. 44, trans. John D. Ireland (Kandy, Sri Lanka: Buddhist Publication Society, 1997).
8. *MN* 64.9.

Chapter 7

1. *MN* 141.23.
2. *SN* 45.2.
3. *MN* 43.13.

4. *MN* 117.59.

5. *AN* 2.19, trans. Thanissaro Bhikkhu, http://accesstoinsight.org/tipitaka/an/an02/an02.019.than.html.

6. *William Wordsworth: The Major Works,* ed. Stephen Gill (New York: Oxford University Press, 2000), p. 132.

7. *SN* 45.6.

Chapter 8

1. *MN* 44.11.

2. *SN* 45.149.

3. *MN* 102.17.

4. *AN* 10.2.

5. *AN* 5.25, trans. Thanissaro Bhikkhu, http://accesstoinsight.org/tipitaka/an/an05/an05.025.than.html.

6. *MN* 61.9.

7. *MN* 48.8.

8. Daniel Goleman, *Social Intelligence: The New Science of Human Relationships* (New York: Bantam, 2006).

Chapter 12

1. *MN* 10.5.

2. Joseph Goldstein, *One Dharma* (San Francisco: HarperSanFrancisco, 2002), pp. 186–87.

3. Douglas Steere, *On Being Present Where You Are* (Wallingford, Pa.: Pendle Hill Press, 1967), p. 9.

Chapter 13

1. I am here using this word in the sense recognized by the authors collected in *Emergence: Contemporary Readings in Philosophy and Science,* ed. M. Bedau and P. Humphries (Cambridge, Mass.: MIT Press, 2007).

2. Alan Watts, *The Wisdom of Insecurity* (New York: Pantheon Books, 1951).

3. Shunryu Suzuki, *Zen Mind, Beginner's Mind* (Trumble, Conn.: Weatherhill, 1973).

4. *MN* 10.5.

5. Lao Tzu, "Tao Te Ching," in *A Source Book in Chinese Philosophy,* trans. and comp. Wing-Tsit Chan (Princeton, N.J.: Princeton University Press, 1969).

Chapter 14

1. Douglas Steere, *Where Words Come From* (London: Friends Home Service, 1955), p. 14.

Chapter 15

1. *AN* 5.198, trans. Thanissaro Bhikkhu, http://accesstoinsight.org/tipitaka/an/an05/an05.198.than.html.
2. George Loewenstein and Jennifer S. Lerner, "The Role of Affect in Decision Making," in *Handbook of Affective Sciences,* ed. R. J. Davidson et al. (New York: Oxford University Press, 2003), pp. 619–42.
3. Eugene Gendlin, *Focusing-Oriented Psychotherapy: A Manual of the Experiential Method* (New York: Guilford Press, 1998).
4. George Lakoff and Mark Johnson, *Philosophy in the Flesh: The Embodied Mind and Its Challenge to Western Thought* (New York: Basic Books, 1999).
5. Marshall Rosenberg, *Nonviolent Communication: A Language of Compassion* (Encinitas, Calif.: Puddledancer Press, 2003).
6. *MN.*122.12, trans. Thanissaro Bhikkhu, http://accesstoinsight.org/tipitaka/mn/mn122.than.html.
7. *Khuddaka Nikaya* 3.3, trans. Thanissaro Bhikkhu, http://accesstoinsight.org/tipitaka/kn/snp/snp.303.than.html.
8. *MN* 122.12.

Chapter 17

1. Edward Conze, trans., *The Diamond Sutra and the Heart Sutra* (New York: Harper & Row, 1958), p. 81.
2. *AN* 11.12.

Chapter 18

1. *MN* 10.3.
2. Gregory Kramer and Terri O'Fallon, "Insight Dialogue and Insight Dialogic Inquiry" (PhD dissertation, California Institute of Integral Studies, 1997).
3. *MN* 141.29.
4. *SN* 15.140.

Chapter 20

1. Paul Fulton, "Mindfulness in Clinical Training," in *Mindfulness and Psychotherapy,* ed. Christopher Germer, Ronald Siegel, and Paul Fulton (New York: Guilford Press, 2005), p. 58.

2. Jungkyu Kim and Gregory Kramer, "Insight Dialogue Meditation with Anxiety Problems," *Gestalt!* 6 (2002); available at http://www.g-gej.org/6-1/insightdialogue.html.

3. Peter Hershock, *Liberating Intimacy* (Albany: State University of New York Press, 1996), p. x.

Chapter 21

1. See Sharon Begley, *Train Your Mind, Change Your Brain* (New York: Ballantine, 2007) for an easy and accessible source for this research. See also Antoine Lutz, John D. Dunne, and Richard J. Davidson, "Meditation and the Neuroscience of Consciousness" in P. Zelazo, M. Moscovitch, and E. Thompson, eds., *Cambridge Handbook of Consciousness* (Cambridge, U.K.: Cambridge University Press, forthcoming).

2. *MN* 10, *DN* 22.

3. See, for example, the *Nidana-samyutta, SN* 12.

Index

Buddha (cont.)
  on Right View and Intention, 102
  on *samadhi*, 101
  on sensation and perception, 25
  on suffering, 24, 26, 33–34, 55, 71
  on support of spiritual friends and
      community, 104
  teachings, 8, 12, 14, 41, 86, 191, 202
      (*see also* Four Noble Truths)
    relational elements, 26
  on three tendencies, 50
  on truth, 176
Buddhadasa, 79
Buddhism. *See also specific topics*
  traditions of, 16–17
Buddhist teachings, traditional. *See
    also specific topics*
  Insight Dialogue and, 263–71

Calm Concentration, 125. *See also*
    Right Calm Concentration;
    samadhi
calmness, 101. *See also* tranquillity
caring, 72–75
certainty, 148
cessation, 55–56, 65, 66
  fear of, 66–67
  gradual, 54–56
  and happiness of the unintoxicated
      life, 70–75
change, 145–47, 209. *See also* imper-
    manence; transformation
chaos, 236
chat rooms (Internet), 216–18
clinging, 32–33, 68, 112
communication. *See* Listen Deeply;
    Speak the Truth
compassion, 70–75, 105, 197–98
concentration, 199. *See also* Right
    Calm Concentration

conflict resolution, 214, 256–57
contemplation(s), 12, 69, 103, 200,
    263–64
  examples, 190, 194–99
  in Insight Dialogue, 186–94
  tailored, 189–90
  traditional vs. contemporary, 189, 190
coolness, 68, 69
couples, 258–60

dana. See generosity
death
  contemplating, 241
  fear of, 41
  delusion (*moha*)
  diminishing, 60, 62–64
  energy that drives, 50, 52–53
dependent origination, 270–71
Dhamma (Dharma), 8, 9, 11, 12, 209,
    222, 242, 258
Dhammadina, Anagarika, 8, 9, 94
dialogue, meditative, 10
difference. *See also* separation/
    separateness
  sense of, 36, 37
diligence, 228–29, 274, 275
discernment, 174–77
discussion group, diversion into a,
    237–41
"don't know mind," 178
dosa. See hatred

effort. *See* Right Effort
Eightfold Path. *See* Noble Eightfold
    Path
embodied knowing, 167
emergence, 139, 140. *See also* Trust
    Emergence
  evolutionary basis for wisdom of,
      141–42

emotions. *See also* attachments;
    thought
  contemplating the impersonal
    nature of, 235
  identifying with, 232–35
empathy, 151–52
emptiness, 41, 74, 161
  fear of, 58
ethics. *See* morality
exercise, physical, 237
existential crisis, 49
existential emptiness, 41
explorative listening, 153
extraordinary practices, 14–15, 87,
    99
  elements, 99–101
  vs. ordinary practices, 84–93,
    272–73
  transformation and integration,
    89–90
eye contact. *See* gazing

families, 258–60
fear(s). *See also* stress; *specific fears*
  hunger and, 57
  interpersonal longings and, 15–16
"focusing" (Gendlin), 167
Four Noble Truths, 21, 24, 70. *See also*
  Noble Eightfold Path
freedom, 29, 187. *See also* Noble
  Eightfold Path
  Buddha on, 70, 76–77
Freud, Sigmund, 71
friends, 274
  importance of, 80, 104
Fulton, Paul, 256

gazing, diversion into, 247–48
generosity, 60–61, 75. *See also* caring;
  greed

golden rule, 172
Goldstein, Joseph, 134
grandiosity, 42
grasping, 32–33
greed
  diminishing, 60–61, 64
  energy that drives, 50–51
  for experience, 248, 249
grief, 65–66
groups, weekly. *See* Insight Dialogue
  groups

habit, interrupting automatic, 109–10,
  225
happiness, 55, 68, 101. *See also* joy;
  pleasure
  of the unintoxicated life, 70–75
hatred (*dosa*). *See also* aversion and
  aversive thoughts
  diminishing, 60–62
  energy that drives, 50–52
Hershock, Peter, 262
honesty. *See* Speak the Truth
humanity, 273–75
humor, 240, 247
hunger(s), 249
  behavior produced from, 169
  behind tensions, 121
  cessation of (*see* cessation)
  clinging to, as causing suffering,
    31–34
  greed, hatred, delusion, and, 50–53
  social identities and, 67
  three basic, 33–34 (*see also specific*
    hungers)
    fading of, 56–60, 70 (*see also* ces-
      sation)
    intermingled, 48–49
hypersweet group, diversion into a,
    235–37

Lao Tsu, 148

liberation, 187. *See also* freedom

life. *See also* Right Living
as process of being who one is, 219

Listen Deeply, 102, 107, 150–62, 181, 183, 184, 216, 223
explorative and receptive qualities, 153, 159–61
helping professionals and, 256

Listen Deeply—Speak the Truth, 12, 104, 165, 180, 182

listening, 104–5, 240
focused vs. wide, 157

lobha. See greed

loneliness, 28–29, 39

loss, 65–66

love, 62
hunger and, 72, 73

lovingkindness, 62, 105, 126–28. *See also* kindness

lust. *See* greed

meditating. *See also specific topics*
alone/individually, 3–4 (*see also* silent meditation)
intention in, 219

meditative intimacy, 136

metta. See lovingkindness

Metta Foundation, 257, 284

mind state, 84, 85, 87

mindfulness, 5–7, 10–12, 29, 170, 198–99, 236–37. *See also* Right Mindfulness
of body and feelings, 166–67
certainty and, 148
foundations, 269–70
of internal and external, 129–35, 158
Pause and, 110–14, 125, 127
Speak the Truth and, 164
while speaking, 165–67

"Mindfulness in Clinical Training" (Fulton), 256

moha. See delusion

morality, 99–100, 104, 164. *See also under* Noble Eightfold Path; Right Action; Right View

mourning, 65–66

music, 146

mutual practice, 113–14

mutuality, 82–83, 99, 104

Namto, Achan Sobin, 9

neurobiology, 265
interpersonal, 35

neurosis, 71

nirvana, 68–70

Noble Eightfold Path, 99, 100, 104, 189, 267–68
as full-spectrum path, 91–95
moral factors, 77, 92–94, 99–100
nature of, 76–78
ordinary and extraordinary manifestations, 83–88
as personal and interpersonal, 78–83
transformation and integration, 88–89

nonaversion (*adosa*), 61. *See also* hatred

nonbeing. *See also* being
fear of, 41–45
hunger for, 34 (*see also* being, hunger to avoid; hunger)

nondelusion (*amoha*), 62–64. *See also* delusion

nonverbal communication, 155–56

Nonviolent Communication (NVC), 169

O'Fallon, Terri, 10, 81

oneness, 161–62

in our functional lives, 195
in our relational lives, 195–96
transcending, 260–61

About the Metta
Foundation

THE TRANSFORMATION of human consciousness toward personal freedom, interpersonal compassion, and social wholeness is at the heart of the Metta Foundation's vision. Metta offers nonsectarian teachings, publications, and service programs, based upon original Buddhist principles and trainings, that integrate new approaches to human development, learning modalities, and technology. Wisdom and compassion are nurtured by a wide path that includes individual and interpersonal practices, undertaken on retreat and in everyday life.

The Metta Foundation has fostered the new but traditionally grounded practices of Insight Dialogue and Dharma Contemplation, and offers them through retreats, practice groups, and the Web. Metta's programs are intended to convey wisdom in new and compelling forms that augment traditional approaches, particularly by including interpersonal practices. Metta.org provides opportunities to engage in online meditation and contemplation with members of a worldwide practice community. Visitors to the online community will also find information on current programs and retreats. Information and links to the international Insight Dialogue practice community can be found at www.insightdialogue.org.